The Kid Glove Pilot

A personal account of flying Sunderlands in World War Two

Alan W Deller

**To Margaret, my late wife,
whose loving care and support
saw me through the aftermath of war
to a happy and fulfilled life.**

**To those many good friends
who did not come back.**

6 5 4 3 2 1

Designed by Colourpoint Books,
Newtownards
Printed by W&G Baird Limited

ISBN 1 904242 20 0

Colourpoint Books
Colourpoint House
Jubilee Business Park
21 Jubilee Road
NEWTOWNARDS
County Down
Northern Ireland
BT23 4YH
Tel: 028 9182 0505
Fax: 028 9182 1900
E-mail: info@colourpoint.co.uk
Web-site: www.colourpoint.co.uk

About the Author

Alan Deller was born in London in 1915, the son of a City banker. He was educated at the City of London School and, after winning a travelling scholarship from the Worshipful Company of Cutlers of the City of London, continued his studies in Paris, Hamburg and Madrid.

In the Second World War he took part in two abortive Secret Service sabotage initiatives before joining the RAF, where he was able to satisfy his ambition to fly the magnificent Sunderland flying boat. He habitually wore kid gloves while flying and this led to his nickname 'The Kid Glove Pilot'. He was awarded the Distinguished Flying Cross, for leading the Chindwin Operation in 1945, adding this to his 1939-45 Star, Atlantic Star, Africa Star, Burma Star and Defence Medal. During his time in the Far East he met his late wife, Margaret, who was serving in the WRNS.

Alan is a Freeman of the City of London and a Fellow of the Institute of Energy and of the Royal Society of Arts.

Cover Pictures:

Front: Mk I Sunderland and a Walrus on Atlantic convoy duty in 1941.

from a painting by RB Way

Rear: The last convoy escort of the Second World War was flown by a Mk V Sunderland of No 201 Squadron, RAF, on 15 June 1945. These escorts were continued after the formal end of the war on 8 May 1945 to guard against possible attacks by U-boat commanders refusing to accept defeat.

Imperial War Museum, London (CH 15303)

Contents

Foreword

In writing these reminiscences I had in mind primarily the interest of my family – "What did you do in the war, Daddy?" – and the sources were my spasmodically-kept diaries, my flying log book and my own memory, this last proving surprisingly fecund.

Sixty or more years on some of the attitudes, emotions and even language may appear somewhat alien to the readers of 2004 but I can assure them that all is faithfully reproduced as it was; indeed I was very surprised, as I wrote, at the intensity of the feelings as I found myself back in the atmosphere of those times at least some of which I hope I have succeeded in conveying to the reader, even if only in a small way.

In relation to the early part of this story, it is right to remember that, in 1939, Britain and the Empire were relatively unprepared for war and when Winston Churchill ordered the Secret Service to "set Europe ablaze" (and other parts of the world also) people familiar with clandestine operations were few in number; it was hardly possible to advertise for recruits so, in the early months particularly, word of mouth – "I know a good chap I was at school with . . ." or " . . . in my sports club" – and similar avenues had to be used. Numbers of brave, patriotic men and women volunteered, all more or less unfamiliar with the requirements of a demanding activity but keen to do their best in the service of their country in its hour of acute need. At all levels, there were inevitably some who, while having the very best of intentions, were simply unsuited to the task. When looking at that which went wrong it is only fair to remember the difficulties and to salute both the heroic successes and, no less, the brave failures.

I am enormously indebted to Mrs Rosanne Sansom, my quite superb personal assistant in Shell of almost forty years ago, who nobly undertook the work of typing what turned out to be more of a book than a simple memoir, succeeding in producing an elegant typescript from my often barely-decipherable pencil scribbles.

London
April 2004

First Movement

". . . and consequently this country is at war with Germany"

Those portentous words, spoken by Neville Chamberlain, the Prime Minister at 11 o'clock on Sunday morning 3 September 1939 set the seal on the opening of a chapter in my life and that of millions of fellow countrymen and women that, in varying degrees, brought changes that had been unimaginable in that glorious holiday month of August when we hung onto the sights and sounds and feelings of peace while the physical and psychological preparations for war rumbled ominously in the background all round us.

I was working in the Shell international headquarters, one part of which was in The Hague and the other in St Helen's Court in the City. I was due, in fact, to go on a three-year oil industry training course in the USA in November. But with war threatening this was unfortunately cancelled. As part of the company's preparations for war all staff were divided into three categories: 'A' – those who were vital for the wartime running of the industry; 'B' – those whom it would be important to hold on to if at all possible; and 'C' – those who would be released immediately on the outbreak of war for other forms of service. The St Helen's Court offices were to move immediately to the company's Lensbury residential sports club at Teddington where many of us had had to give up our bedrooms some weeks before to enable them to be prepared for conversion to offices.

Friday 1 September was one of those days in the office rather like Christmas Eve when thoughts of work are overlaid by anticipation of closing down – it does not seem worth starting anything and that which is under way loses its urgency. It was a day of rumours, with the German armies in position on the Polish frontier and last-minute diplomacy desperately confronting the inevitable.

In the St Helen's Court office blocks there were internal wells, lined with white tiles to give some daylight to the inner offices. One or two people on that Friday had brought radios with them and these they perched on window-ledges so that they could be heard far and wide. About midday we all heard the announcement that German troops had crossed the Polish frontier and the German Air Force, the Luftwaffe, was bombing Warsaw and many other cities. None of us doubted in that moment that we and the French would be at war within days at the most and our feeling, like that of the nation as a whole, was a mixture of relief that the months of brooding uncertainty were clearly over, together with a sober realisation that a most severe trial lay ahead of us, the outcome of which, in the defeat of the monstrous horror of Nazism, none really had any doubt. Very many of us also felt a tinge of satisfaction that we were now about to expiate the shame of Munich, while for me it was the final justification of the increasingly confident view I had maintained since my sojourns in

Germany in the early and middle 1930s that Germany would eventually be at war with us.

So on that fateful Friday afternoon we all knew that we were spending our last moments in St Helen's Court and people were saying goodbye all round, we 'C' men in particular wondering when, if ever, we should see each other again. Many in the Territorials and the Royal Naval and Royal Air Force Volunteer Reserves had already received their papers and the rest of us in category C were preparing to enlist – Douglas Bader and I, together in Shell's international aviation department, determined to see who could get into the RAF first, he, of course, having the advantage of Cranwell and several years' commissioned RAF service as a pilot – but now he had two tin legs while I had aspirations and some technical knowledge but nothing else. We did both eventually make it but not quite as straightforwardly as I had imagined, at least as far as I was concerned. Meanwhile it appeared to be goodbye to Shell for the duration.

Phoney War

A pub called the 'Yorkshire Grey' in Streatham had been designated as a recruiting station for Royal Air Force air-crew. Early on Monday morning, 4th September, I joined a crowd of eager young men and was somewhat chastened to hear, on submitting my application form for pilot training, that there was such a backlog that I would have to wait at least several weeks although if I would like to be an air-gunner they could take me there and then! I settled for waiting several weeks and, to fill in the time usefully, decided to take up the offer of unpaid work on a cousin's farm in Shropshire.

The weather was beautiful and I thoroughly enjoyed the long sunny days driving a Fordson tractor. I became quite skilled at cultivating huge fields with harrow and Cambridge roller and the time passed very pleasantly for over a month until there arrived out of the blue a summons from Shell to report to the wartime headquarters at Lensbury Club, Teddington for air-raid precautions duties pending my call-up by the RAF.

There were eight or nine of us at various times, two or three older men and the rest of us youngsters, awaiting the call to one sort of service or another. We were to be firemen as well as wardens and were kitted out with blue overalls, Wellingtons, a fireman's belt, complete with axe and a steel helmet. We wore a red armband with the letters F and W embroidered in white – the more skittish among the numerous and desirable secretarial staff interpreted this as 'Free and Willing'. It was a curious experience to be in those surroundings so full of memories of sports, dances and many other convivial activities, now converted to a humming centre of deadly serious business, supporting our country about to fight for its very life.

As wardens we were responsible for the blackout throughout the club building, maintaining communication with the local Air Raid Precautions organisation and, in the event of a raid, ensuring orderly evacuation of everybody to the air-raid shelters in the club grounds. As firemen we were expected to do no more than hold the line, with the aid of a trailer pump housed in a sandbag shelter by the river, until the fire service arrived. Working 12 hour shifts and night duty, with the concomitant difficulty of daytime sleeping, was a new experience that prepared at least some of us for similar but rather more rigorous regimes later on. At night people played chess, read or pursued various hobbies – one newly-joined young company trainee made model aeroplanes and played some beautiful records of Chopin's 'Les Sylphides' ballet music that gave us great pleasure – he was Clive Davies, whom I was to meet again by an extraordinary coincidence two and a half years later, only a few days before he was killed.

That winter of 1939–40 was exceptionally cold. The Thames was frozen solid for weeks all the way from Kingston Bridge to Teddington Lock, by the club. Largely as a consequence of the cold quite large numbers of the office staff gathered in the big lounge each evening to drink and talk and listen to gramophone concerts. As time went on one after another of the younger members of staff would leave to join up and some of them would return shortly after, with modest pride, in uniform – Bobby Colt, captured with the 51st Highland Division in June 1940 at St Valéry-en-Caux, escaped and later was killed in Italy, John Ramsden the archetypal tough infantry private, Peter Attwood who was believed to have died after hitting a concrete post as he jumped from a train taking him and other prisoners of war to a German prison camp – and so they went, already so different from the gay, carefree chums we had known. But for me there was just the constant refrain "Oh yes, I applied on the first Monday of the war for pilot training but I'm still waiting – can't be long now."

Second Movement

Off to war – at last

Then, in the middle of March came the long-awaited Air Ministry telegram "Report to Uxbridge for interview and medical" – this was *it* after all those months! My mind filled with imagination of what this exciting new future might hold, I was at last able to tell people that I was on my way.

Not for the first or the last time I discovered that very morning that just when things seem firmly settled there is about to occur a total upset and change. Only an hour or so after the arrival of the beautiful telegram I was summoned, discreetly, to the presence of a very senior man in the company, Sir Peter Norton-Griffiths. After warning me to observe total secrecy, he explained that it was planned to send a small team to Romania, ostensibly as refinery trainees but in reality to prepare to sabotage the Shell refinery at Ploeşti, then the biggest in Europe, in the event of the Germans appearing likely to invade the country. An experienced refinery man would lead the team but the rest would be young, recently-joined trainees and it was felt that there should be a slightly more mature member to act as number two – 'platoon sergeant' as he described it – preferably with some foreign language abilities. Would I be prepared to take on that job? After a metaphorical sharp intake of breath my first reaction, instantly, was that here was another adventure, something a little out of the ordinary – I was single, my mother and sister were not dependent on me – there could be no question of turning it down and when Sir Peter asked whether I would like ten minutes to think it over I said straight away that I would go. He said that arrangements would be made for my RAF call-up to be cancelled and that I should be in Romania as soon as possible and not later than the end of March.

This was in fact something of a coincidence; earlier in the year I had been at a luncheon hosted by the Institution of Petroleum Technologists (as the Institute of Petroleum was then known) at which a small, stocky man called Sir Julian Cahn had made a speech highlighting the danger that oil-starved Germany, almost entirely dependent on synthetic oil produced from coal, would at some stage make a drive to seize the Romanian oilfields at Câmpina and the refineries at Ploeşti of which the biggest and most efficient was owned by Shell; he urged the Government to overcome its complacent reliance on Romanian neutrality and take steps to ensure that these prizes could be denied to the Germans – now I was to have some part in that endeavour.

Interpolation

(see Appendix 1)

My reaction as 'another adventure' derived from, and was made easier by, an experience I had in Spain in April 1934. In February of that year I had been a student in Paris, aged 18, at a time of great political turmoil there and on the 6th very widespread rioting occurred in many parts of the city. Out of curiosity I had spent the evening in the Place de la Concorde; for a youthful visitor from England, such a quiet and law-abiding country in those days, there was an enjoyable excitement in dodging waves of baton-wielding police.

Two months later I was studying in Madrid. Spain, in the third year of its short-lived republic, was also beset by unrest. On Sunday 24 April there was to be a general strike with the possibility of some trouble in the streets so I went into the centre of the city in the afternoon to see how they did these things in Madrid compared with Paris. Tension was in the air and everywhere there were large numbers of police – not the Guardia Civil – all with rifles. At one point a man with a motorcycle and sidecar turned out of a side street too fast and overturned; several people rushed to help him and his passengers. At that moment one of the open-sided police buses happened to pass and all the police inside jumped out and started hitting out at the little crowd with rifle butts, without waiting to find out what had happened. It was clear that things were getting rather more serious than I had expected but I went on to the central square, the Puerta del Sol, where, at around six in the evening, the crowds were taking their customary Sunday evening *paseo*, apparently undisturbed by the dozens of well-armed police mingling with them.

All of a sudden, on the far side of the *plaza*, a youth in a brown leather jacket started to run, pursued by two policemen; they were losing him so they stopped and opened fire on him with their rifles. At that, firing broke out everywhere and the crowds rushed for shelter in the shops, doorways, wherever they could get. I was out in the middle and, feeling rather vulnerable, ran as hard as I could to shelter against a wall. As I ran I felt a pat on my left cheek which I scarcely noticed and flung myself on the pavement hard up against the wall of an office building. Instantly blood started gushing on the pavement. As a boy I had read a great deal about the First World War and the terrible wounds men suffered and, realising what had happened to me, I let out a sort of moan and said to myself "Oh! I've been shot!" and it sounded so wimpish that I instantly told myself "You bloody fool, get up and do something!" and I got to my feet. As I turned round two policemen about 20 yards away pointed their rifles at me; I put up my hands and pointed to the mess on the left side of my face, so they motioned me to get into a shop by where they were standing. It happened to be a chemist's and was packed with people; as I went in all the women started wailing and shouting "¡Ay, pobrecito!" "¡Ay, qué horror, qué lástima!" I asked the chemist to give me a dressing but he said he was not allowed by regulation to treat wounded. However I eventually persuaded him to give me a big wad of cotton wool which I was able to hold against my left jaw to contain the blood flow. All this time the firing was continuing outside and it was about 20 minutes before it stopped and an ambulance could get through to take me to the police surgery nearby. I felt quite calm and collected; I had no pain and my overriding feeling was that this was an experience, something that did not happen to everyone, to be savoured to the full in every respect. Two newspaper photographers took pictures of me sitting on the rear step of the ambulance with a broad smile and my big wad of cotton wool and blood-soaked shirt and jacket and my tie neatly cut in half by the bullet. It had been fired from a rooftop, entering beside my mouth and passing through the jaw and out through the top of my shoulder, missing the carotid artery by the thickness of the wall of the artery itself. I was taken from the police surgery to the excellent Anglo-American Nursing Home where I was greeted by a shocked matron and staff and put to bed. It was about eight o'clock in the evening, some two hours later, and in those two hours I grew up.

By ten o'clock the Press Association had telephoned the news to my family. In those days Spain was relatively little known to the average person in Britain and few people visited there; consequently it was a somewhat romantic story for the home press – even *The Times* printed a note on my progress every day for the first week or so, recording the daily visit by the British Ambassador, Sir George Grahame, a Scot with a delightful old-world charm.

After about three weeks I was able to walk out in the street with my head bandaged rather like the Invisible Man in the film of HG Wells's story. One after another people in the street would come up to me and say "¿Es usted el herido de la Puerta de Sol?" ("Are you the one who was wounded in the Puerta de Sol?") and try to peer inside the bandages – "autres pays, autres moeurs!" The brief experience of fame was quite amusing; and a piece on the incident in the City of London School magazine ended with the rhetorical question "Where will Alan Deller go next?" Answer, six years later . . . Romania.

Romania

While getting ready to leave for Romania I was interviewed by two of the top people from the early days of the Shell Group, Mr (later Lord) Godber and Sir George Legh-Jones, who kindly wished me luck. I was briefed at the Ministry of Mines and finally had all papers and books I was taking with me examined by the censors to ensure that nothing could compromise my, or the nation's, security.

I was due to travel out to Bucharest with another member of our team, Ronnie Robb, a young Scottish chemical engineering graduate who also had a useful command of the mouth organ. Unfortunately I was delayed because shortly before departure date I developed a bad dose of 'flu, so I was on my own when, one mid-April night I left eerie blacked-out Waterloo station for Portsmouth, Le Havre, Paris and a future which was highly uncertain but promised to be interesting.

It was still the period that became known as the 'Phoney War' when nothing much happened apart from small patrol actions on the Western Front and flights over Germany by the RAF dropping leaflets warning the enemy of the wrath to come – nothing much, that is, except for the U-boat war at sea which was a terrible reality from Day One. I spent the day renewing my acquaintance with Paris and in the evening made my way to the Gare de Lyon to join the Simplon-Orient Express for Bucharest. The blacked-out station was as eerie as Waterloo had been the previous night and the thought of my mission added powerfully to the sense of drama. Passing down the dark blue Wagon-Lits sleeping cars I read the destination boards – Zürich, Milan, Venice, Trieste, Zagreb, Bucharest, Sofia, Istanbul – names that in other times would have brought visions of romantic travel but which now strongly reinforced the peculiar feeling of circling through a darkened world round the edge of a huge portion of Europe in which the sinister forces of the Nazi Reich were lying in wait. I settled down immediately in my cabin, conscious of the need to avoid contact with any of the other passengers but at the same time not to make myself in any way conspicuous.

The next morning saw us already through the Simplon tunnel and pulling into Domodossola, the Italian customs post. Italy was still officially neutral, Mussolini waiting for Hitler to deliver what he hoped would be the deathblow to Britain and France before he leapt boldly into the fray. All day the train made its slow way across northern Italy until in the evening we approached Venice and a most beautiful sight that I remember quite clearly even today; about three miles away there was that lovely city spread out beyond an expanse of sparkling blue water, serene in the evening sunshine – it was truly breathtaking.

The train had already been dropping off one or two sleeping cars and the restaurant car was becoming progressively emptier; it became easier to keep an eye on anyone who might appear to be taking more than a passing interest in me. By nightfall we were in Trieste and at breakfast-time the following morning we were in Yugoslavia and a total change. The train was reduced to a baggage car, one sleeping car and the restaurant car in which I sat down to breakfast, the only other people being Sir Reginald Hoare, the British Minister in Bucharest, and Lady Hoare together with EA (later Sir Eric) Berthoud, the Petroleum Attaché at the legation. To preserve my anonymity in public I studiously avoided eye contact or any other contact with the legation party, although of course they knew perfectly well who I was.

The scenery also had changed completely. It was largely open agricultural country, devoid of hedges, no roads that we saw, only muddy tracks churned up by cart wheels, few habitations and – most striking of all to me – women in headscarves dragging ploughs in the fields. The train meandered slowly on throughout the day, mostly on a single track, and stopped every now and again for the driver to get down to switch the points – an astonishing contrast to the smart speedy express the train had been three days earlier.

Towards the end of the day we reached the Romanian frontier and I had momentary thoughts of being grilled by suspicious immigration officials trying to discover my nefarious mission – it was almost a disappointment to be greeted with total indifference. For a time early in the night we were climbing through the Carpathian mountains. I could hear the thunderous exhaust of the big diesel locomotive echoing back from the surrounding mountainsides and, looking out into the black moonless night, I had a feeling of being about to jump into a big lake and wondering whether and, if so, through what sort of experiences, I should reach the other side. It was an intriguing prospect.

Beginning of the real thing

I arrived in Bucharest at 1.35am on Friday 19 April, 1940, just over three days after leaving London. I spent two days in Bucharest making my number with the Shell head office (the company was actually a Romanian company called Astra Română), being introduced briefly to Otto Stern, the General Manager, and then moving on to the usual formalities in a new post, interviews with RG Searight, the General Manager's deputy, and Alexander Miller, the Finance Manager who also oversaw personnel matters – he had been many years in the country and spoke perfect Romanian, a language that is mostly spoken at speed and with rapid changes up and down the scale so that conversation tends to sound like an exceedingly animated argument. Romania was originally a Roman penal colony and the language has remained much closer to Latin than have Italian, French and Spanish; there is a very considerable admixture of Slav words also.

On the Sunday I was taken to the company's residential and sports club at Snagov on the shores of a large lake about half-an-hour's drive north of Bucharest on the way to Ploeşti (pronounced Plo-ee-esht). It was a beautiful place, very well equipped in the Shell tradition, and was to play no small part in our lives in the near future.

The following day I finally arrived at Ploeşti, a busy small town with several smaller refineries as well as the big Shell one and there joined up with the rest of the team, except the leader, TC Henderson, who was to arrive shortly after. Ronnie Robb, Geoffrey Stanger, Tom Tigg and Ralph van den Bosch were all trainee chemical engineers; apart from myself there was an older man, Stanley Riley, who had been an operator on the Dubbs cracking unit in the Shell refinery at Suez and possessed a wonderfully wry sense of humour.

Soon after my arrival we were summoned to Bucharest and there, in great secrecy, in a hotel bedroom, Searight administered the oath of loyalty to the King and commissioned each of us as Second Lieutenant, Royal Engineers in the Army Emergency Reserve. We were then told to go round to the British Legation and report to Major Green, an Assistant Military Attaché. The Legation was a rather pleasant white stone building with a large courtyard in front, entered through big wrought-iron ornamental gates. The Military Attaché's office was a small separate building at the far end of the courtyard. As our little party entered there was a man just outside the gates, a couple of yards or so away, who took photographs of us as we went through the gates into the courtyard and then strode, all too openly, across to the Military Attaché's office.

Major Green was very welcoming and proceeded to tell us the detail of the job we had come to do. It was, not unnaturally, of great interest to us, particularly when he told us that the amount of explosive available was only five pounds, so we would have to devise additional techniques of destruction. A little later another Assistant Military Attaché, Major Davidson-Houston, gave us more detailed information on using explosives, including the intriguing 'pencils'; these looked very like pencils but were fitted on to detonators to allow a time-delay to be set before the main explosive charge went up: inside the 'pencil' was a spring-loaded striker held back by a wire; when the top end of the 'pencil' was crushed a precise amount of acid was released to eat away at the wire holding the striker until it broke, releasing the striker which then hit and set off the detonator which in turn set off the main explosive charge. The amount of acid and the strength of the wire controlled the length of the delay; the 'pencils' were coloured according to their delay time.

Having been introduced to the job we were then shown our uniforms which were hidden in the Legation building – khaki battle dress with Second Lieutenant's single 'pip' on each shoulder, steel helmet and a holster with a small automatic pistol. The idea was that when the moment came we would put on our uniforms and sally forth in the hope that if we were eventually captured we would be treated as prisoners or war and not as saboteurs – this seemed a somewhat unconvincing scenario.

Back in Ploeşti a day or two later we were having tea in the refinery hostel called Casinou (the 'u' being the definite article). The door opened and Tommy Henderson appeared. He was a Glaswegian and, as a sergeant in the Highland Light Infantry in the First World War had been wounded fifteen times – I once saw him in the shower and could believe it. He was an engineer with long years of experience in the Mexican and Venezuelan oil refineries. One of his wounds had caused one side of his forehead to drop somewhat and this, added to his evident feeling of uncertainty in meeting a bunch of youngsters, gave him a demeanour that can only be described as formidable. He looked every bit as tough as he was but we quickly settled down together and we had tremendous confidence in him. He had a half-cynical sense of humour and a wealth of experience of life which was an eye-opener to us youngsters. He also had a set of poker dice and a repertoire of games such as Chingona which, together with Ronnie Robb's mouth organ, lightened our hearts in several mildly unpromising situations. Chatting with him one day I asked, as his number two, what were the arrangements for our get-away from Ploeşti after the job and he gave a little laugh and said "Don't worry, we shan't even get there" and, knowing something of the actual situation in Ploeşti – more than the Military Attachés knew – I saw his point. One of these young officers later admitted to me at a party in the Legation that none of them had ever been to Ploeşti to assess the situation that we would face – the delights of Bucharest were indeed seductive.

We started to get settled into our various jobs in the refinery, the others on different processing units and I, as a sort of generalist, with a roving commission. On the whole people were quite friendly but there was an undercurrent of suspicion – in fact one man did say to me that it was a bit odd suddenly to have seven visiting staff whereas hitherto the most they had had was two; my explanation was that in normal times many trainees were sent to the Far East as well as to Europe but that in wartime it was judged necessary to keep people nearer to home. It was a bit thin and was not helped by two of the others having innocently let slip that they had been pulled off a ship at Port Said that was taking them to the Dutch East Indies and told to get smartly off to Romania – and nothing else!

It was among the supervisory grades in the refinery staff that we felt least welcome; they were mostly from ex-Hungarian Transylvania, generally of a higher level of intelligence and strongly pro-Nazi. From various straws in the wind we gathered that many, if not all, were armed and indeed we learned a little later on that a number of unidentified men had been surprised by the police in one of the smaller refineries unloading a variety of light arms from empty tank cars returned from Germany, presumably not the first or the last of such occasions. A large proportion of Romania's oil was transported to Germany in long trains of tank cars and specially designed flat-bottomed barges on the Danube.

While we worked hard at our jobs in the refinery we also managed to have a lot of fun, not only at the Snagov club on some weekends but also in Ploeşti itself. Our favourite coffee shop was called Berbec and the little Romanian waitresses were amused and slightly puzzled at our two words of Romanian and constant uproarious laughter. There was a rather seedy night-spot called Doina, all red décor and subdued lights, which produced an even seedier stage show at which we were audibly amused – not, however, to the extent portrayed luridly in the nationally-circulated German daily newspaper, the *Berliner Illustrierte Zeitung*, later in the year and of which I obtained a copy through friends. The hostel, Casinou, had good tennis courts and we invited one or two local Romanian girls to join us; in fact the above-mentioned newspaper included a photograph of Tom Tigg and a Dutch trainee with one of them – poor girl, I have often wondered, in the light of subsequent events, what happened to her.

One day I heard a lot of chattering in the street outside and as I looked out a column of soldiers was approaching, led by an officer dressed in a handsome uniform with brilliantly polished Wellington boots and a flowing cape, lined with red silk; he wore his cap at a rakish angle and he twirled his swagger-stick as he minced along flashing smiles at all the girls – he could have stepped straight out of a Ruritanian operetta. Behind him slouched his troops dressed in khaki uniforms the tunics of which consisted of thin material with no form of lining and frequently without even proper hems, the roughly-cut edge of the material just hanging down. The majority had boots, very many of them without soles, while not a few had no boots at all, only socks or even bare feet. The enormous contrast between these two forms of human being seemed to represent this peasant country in which a small middle class lived comfortably while an even smaller aristocracy and high society pursued an international lifestyle with high fashion, theatre, opera and music in Bucharest, dubbed with some justification 'Paris in the East'. The only first-class road led northwards from Bucharest via Ploeşti to the King's summer palace at Sinaia; otherwise there were two or three modest roads such as those to Giurgiu on the Danube and the Black Sea port of Constanţa (Constanza), but the rest were rutted cart-tracks which spread widely in places where each vehicle had tried to avoid the worst of the winter mud churned up by the last one to pass that way.

In many of our leisure-time activities we were accompanied by a young Dutchman, a self-confident young man whose job we never precisely pinned down but who tacked himself on to us quite uninvited. He affected a very British style of youthful jollity and was fluent in the appropriate light-hearted English, though when things went wrong he used to exclaim "Oh, Helly Bell!" At the time when he appeared it was still the 'Phoney War' and Holland had not been invaded – in any case, in Royal Dutch-Shell we were used to friendly neutral Dutchmen. We were at times surprised that the authorities seemed to know our every move in advance and I have since wondered whether we were rather naïve and our friend was perhaps not so friendly.

While pursuing our studies in the refinery we were busy working out a plan for sabotage. The refinery covered a very large area and was a maze of pipelines, many kinds of processing unit with large columns, heat exchange vessels and pump houses, and 52 storage tanks in compounds surrounded by bund walls, earth and rock banks some five feet high to contain the tank contents in the event of an accident. Our limited amount of explosive meant that only a few strategic targets could be blown up so we devised some other approaches to the rest of our task. Two of the team, who worked on the thermal cracking unit (which operated at very high pressure and high temperature), found that they should have just enough time to screw down the safety valve on the top of the reactor column and run down to shelter behind the armoured wall that protected the instruments and controls and turn the pumps to maximum before the whole thing went up. I had memorised the contents of every one of the 52 storage tanks, the idea being that, where there were several different products as well as crude in a particular compound, the lightest products such as gasoline and kerosene (petrol and paraffin) would be allowed to run out and be set on fire which would then ignite the heavier products in neighbouring tanks. These and other such plans were obviously a fairly desperate alternative.

The company decided that we should have tuition in the language by a little Romanian man who lived in a flat in Bucharest. On our first visit he started with verbs, using the verb cântare – to sing; when he pronounced the words for 'I sing' it sounded exactly like a very rude English epithet. We all seven collapsed into helpless laughter and staggered forth from the flat, never to return.

As far as I was concerned, based on a fluent knowledge of French and Spanish, I had begun to acquire a modest knowledge of Romanian which, as already mentioned, is a relatively undeveloped Romance language with Slav additions. This proved quite helpful when we found ourselves in various police stations where we had to report each time we left one place and arrived at another. Often we had to wait a considerable time for clearance and we used to amuse ourselves with raucous games of one or other of Tommy Henderson's numerous variations of poker dice; there were always a number of rather glum locals also waiting and they clearly thought we were mad.

At times when we were in Bucharest we went for a pre-lunch drink to the 'Ritz' of Bucharest, the Athénée Palace Hotel, and as we walked through the spacious hall to the bar, we invariably saw three shaven-headed Germans, smoking big cigars, who stared at us as we passed – they were the Gestapo. After the invasion of France and the Low Countries German influence became more and more marked, particularly in Bucharest itself. Cinemas showed German newsreels devoted almost entirely to brilliant pictures of the war in Poland and later on in the west as well, numerous cars with German numberplates appeared in the streets and in cafés and restaurants the Germans would turn to stare at us and then talk among themselves in a way that made us feel very far from secret.

One result – as we assumed it to be – of the increasing German influence was a summons on the morning of 5 June to report to the Ploeşti police station where we were told that we must be out of the 'oil zone' (which encompassed the oil fields as well as the Ploeşti refineries) by 3 o'clock that afternoon. We were taken in company cars to Bucharest while the German radio gleefully announced our expulsion, complete with all our names – via our Dutch friend perhaps? Who knows? However, by then we had gathered all the information we needed and it appeared that it would be only a little less convenient if we had to travel from Bucharest or, more probably, from Snagov (which was fortunately outside the oil zone) when the time came to carry out the job we had come to do. Meanwhile, as a non-technical person I would be able to be fitted into a job in the Bucharest head office while the others for whom no suitable activity was available would stay at Snagov. On our departure from Ploeşti we had been escorted to Snagov by plainclothes police who carefully checked everything as we got out of the cars in front of the club. Geoff Stanger was a keen golfer and he had a big leather golf bag with a leather hood covering the clubs. As the police saw him getting this out of the car they made a rush at him and seized the golf bag – which they obviously thought concealed a lethal weapon – while we all roared with laughter, upsetting the police considerably.

I was able to join the others at Snagov from time to time and one Monday morning in the middle of June Tommy Henderson and I were returning to Bucharest; we travelled in two separate company cars for security. He was some distance ahead of me and at a road junction at a small place called Ţigâneşti, not far from Snagov, police stopped the car, made me get out and took me under arrest to the local police station where I was interrogated for an hour and a half by a lugubrious police chief; fortunately my efforts of the past weeks to acquire passable Romanian paid off and I was able to keep things under control although I was given no inkling of the reason for my arrest. Meanwhile Tommy Henderson, just ahead, had seen what happened and drove straight off to Bucharest where he raised the alarm at the office. The company lawyer swiftly made the necessary contacts and after the hour and a half my interrogator had a telephone call ordering me to be released. Later in the day the German radio broadcast a story that Tommy and I had taken a boat on the previous Saturday night and rowed silently across the lake to a point near the house of a Major Louba of the Romanian General Staff where we had supposedly fired shots into his bed while the gentleman was providentially in his bath. This story also featured in the article in the *Berliner Illustrierte Zeitung* mentioned earlier on page 15. The whole thing was of course pure fabrication but was part of an increasing build up of hostile propaganda against the British in Romania.

At this time we were becoming concerned, with the lessons of Holland and Belgium fresh in the mind, that the possible seizure of the country by the Germans might be very close. But the Minister, Sir Reginald Hoare, would not countenance any moves until the fairly numerous British citizens, largely upcountry and long-established, could be persuaded to heed his warnings and prepare to leave the country – caution which later events would show to have been soundly based. Typically, the British were determined to stay until thrown out. We could do no more than possess our souls in patience.

As Astra Română, the Shell company, was a Romanian company and Romania was still neutral, Astra was also neutral. Consequently it maintained normal relations with businesses and diplomats of many countries established in Romania, including those of Germany; entertainment was, naturally, a part of these relationships. One Saturday, 22 June, the company put on a big party at the Snagov club for a mixed crowd of people including many French and Germans. For us, newly out from a Britain now heavily engaged in war – no longer 'phoney' following the rape of Holland and Belgium on 10 May – it seemed a little strange to be talking in a polite way, as hosts, to a number of the enemy. A little after 10 o'clock we were quietly summoned to the club secretary's office by Alex Miller who told us that France had just surrendered to the Germans and it was therefore vital, in order to avoid any awkward incident, that we should get the French and Germans, in particular, off the premises before the news leaked out. Any diplomats would have applauded the way, with our hearts in our mouths, we quietly but just sufficiently firmly shepherded all our guests out into the night in the most cordial atmosphere imaginable.

By now our own position was becoming palpably more uncertain, but our talent for enjoyment was undiminished and a party, with quite a number of men and girls from the Bucharest head office, was organised to celebrate my birthday on 26 June at Snagov. It was a hilarious event helped considerably by a gift from the girls of six bottles of three-year-old tuică, the Romanian prune brandy not unlike Yugoslav slivovitz. Tuică is commonly drunk young when it is pale yellow in colour; after three years these bottles contained a beautiful pink liquid, mellow and exceedingly potent. The party went with a swing; there was dancing and we sang to Ronnie Robb's ever-popular mouth organ, the Assistant Chief Accountant fell down 18 concrete steps from the bar into the cellar, severely cutting his head, and I woke up next morning on my bed wearing nothing but a very large straw hat.

It so happened, however, that on that same day, 26 June, Romania had been forced to cede the long-disputed territory of Bessarabia to Russia. The unfortunate Romanians' sense of national humiliation was naturally overwhelming and the Germans capitalised on this immediately in order to blacken the British and particularly our team; their radio claimed that we had been at our 'luxurious country club' celebrating Romania's tragedy in wine and song. The details in the broadcast of numbers of guests at the party, with some of our names and what we did, were so accurate that it finally brought home to us that a spy was very close to us, though even then it did not occur to us to suspect our affable Dutch friend. To cap it all the Romanians next day circulated a grubby roneoed leaflet in the streets of Bucharest carrying much the same message; I saw a copy myself and was even then surprised at the scurrilous nature of it. We really did then feel very much in the firing line.

The other members of the team were now brought in to join me in Bucharest and at the beginning of July we were told we were to leave the country within twenty-four hours. All the other British citizens were also given the same notice and it was a disastrous shock for very many of them who were upcountry and in most cases had been established in Romania for a considerable number of years. We and a number of other Shell people went with the company's lawyer to the Siguranţã (the security services' headquarters) to negotiate for an extension of time and the Legation was obviously taking similar steps on behalf of the rest. An extension to forty-eight hours was in fact granted and the next day we took a last look round Bucharest before attending an absolutely superb lunch, given by His Excellency for all the fifty-or-so 'expellees', at Cina, the most beautiful open-air restaurant in Bucharest – an action that many people afterwards criticised as being needlessly provocative whereas with hindsight it can perhaps be seen as intended to show that we still had our tails up.

Whatever the intended effect may have been, as we all returned to our hotels everyone was met by a tough-looking plain clothes policeman and escorted to their rooms where they were made to pack. It was quite a new experience to be packing one's things while a policeman with gun in hand stood over one. We were then taken to the Siguranţã and put into a moderate-sized office, watched by several uniformed police. It was about four o'clock in the afternoon; our little team was among the first to arrive and, as usual, we set about improving the shining hour with noisy poker dice games. As more and more of the men-folk arrived, many understandably looking exceedingly glum, we raised a great cheer at each arrival and this not only puzzled the many policemen but did a little to lighten the mood of so many of those whose whole life was being so brutally disrupted. We kept loudly demanding supplies of beer to be sent in; this provoked agitated discussion among the officials each time but failed to produce anything but a pile of cigarettes.

Eventually, at about eight o'clock in the evening, it was suddenly announced that we must all take the midnight train to Constanţa and board ship from there. This provoked furious protests, especially from those, unlike ourselves, who had to collect as many of their personal possessions as they could, as well as their families. Finally, after much discussion it was agreed that we should leave the next day and we departed much relieved and cheerily shaking all the officials by the hand as we did so – they were totally nonplussed and a little embarrassed too.

Early the next morning the Shell party, about 20 in all, decided not to travel under the wing of the legation, which had arranged for train travel to Constanţa and then a voyage by coastal steamer down the Black Sea to Istanbul. Instead, the company organised a fleet of luxurious limousines which took us, two to a car, to Giurgiu on the Danube where we were to cross over to Bulgaria and go on by train to Istanbul. The experience of all of us who have travelled with the company is that there is invariably a little man at every port, customs point or whatever who sees to all formalities, irons out all problems and sends the traveller happily on his way – we were blessed with one such in Bucharest. On the journey to Giurgiu we were held up twice at barriers where our papers were checked – miraculously there was our little man at each one, ready to help us through as he did, finally, in the customs at Giurgiu where he nearly wept as he said goodbye and continued to wave with both hands until the ferry reached the other side.

In the customs we learned that the authorities in Bucharest, doubtless inspired by the Germans, had reported that we might be carrying certain plans among our documents. Nearly all of the party had their luggage rigorously scrutinised and two or three of our team had treasured technical notes, the result of their work in the refinery, confiscated. I adopted a ruse I had learned during much continental travel: I kept my luggage back until I spotted one customs man who was less rigorous than the others and pushed my things in front of him – as a result I did not have a single thing disturbed.

On reaching Rusçuk on the Bulgarian side of the Danube we were met by yet another of Shell's little men who shepherded us through friendly customs and on to the Istanbul-bound Simplon-Orient express which had been held for us. As soon as the train started Ronnie Robb brought out his mouth organ and we gave a hilarious impromptu concert which amused even the stuffiest of the 'top people' who must, in fact, have had heavy hearts at that moment, leaving a country where some had spent as many as twenty years. That evening one of the senior men told me quietly that they had not wanted tell us before but that they had not expected that our team would get out alive – I told him, quietly, that we had known that all along.

We were in fact fortunate to get away unscathed. Two or three British men had been allowed to stay behind temporarily to clear up businesses. One was Alex Miller, the company's Finance Director; he was obviously well known to have been associated with our team and some while after we had left he was taken by the Romanian fascists, the Iron Guard, and tortured. Another businessman from upcountry, entirely innocent of any connection with us, was even more severely handled. I saw him later at the Gezira Club in Cairo just after he had come out, a pathetic figure huddled in a corner with his face puffy from beatings and his arms crossed to keep his hands protected under his armpits, all his fingernails having been pulled out. Saddest of all, we heard later that the beautiful Romanian secretary of the company's Managing Director, who would have been assumed also to know of our mission, had died under torture.

A little while after we had all left, the German daily newspaper *Berliner Illustrierte Zeitung*, as already mentioned, published its double-page spread headed "Secret orders – destroy the oil wells – English conspirators on the Black Sea" (Geheimauftrag – Zerstört die Ölquellen! – Englische Verschwörer am Schwarzen Meer) (see Appendix 2). The whole feature was a highly-coloured farrago; a section headed "Pencils from the Nile" ("Bleistifte vom Nil") purported to deal with our activities including our supposed assassination attempt on Major Louba of the Romanian General Staff (see page 17). All our names were mentioned and I have often wondered how many of our prewar German friends read the story or heard the 'birthday' radio broadcasts (see page 18); indeed after the war my sister actually visited one strongly pro-Nazi family in Mainz who had heard the radio story and displayed an understandably equivocal reaction.

To return to our journey: our train arrived early the following morning in Sofia where it halted for some three hours. We were met by some local Shell people and others from the British Consulate who had organised a splendid breakfast for us on the station platform followed by a whirlwind tour of the city for our team, the senior folk having opted to stay longer and take the faster, first-class express. From what we saw it was a rather intriguing and beautiful city and as it was Sunday we were fortunate in hearing part of a service in the magnificent Orthodox cathedral where we were deeply impressed by a glorious unaccompanied Russian choir – in a small way a cleansing experience after our last few weeks.

Soon after ten o'clock the train set off on a rather slow but fascinating journey through the Bulgarian countryside. The heat was intense in the train and we interspersed our song sessions with frequent visits to the dining car for beer. We began to notice that a man in a grey suit, who had earlier joined our sleeping car at Rusçuk, seemed to be taking a special interest in us; each time we went to the dining car he followed shortly after and sat at a neighbouring table listening to our conversation which we started to lard with remarks about the unpleasantness of being followed around by certain types of creep – he certainly understood but, in spite of obvious embarrassment, stood his ground. Very shortly we took to waiting until he had just started his drink and then downing ours and rushing back to our sleeper – he had to follow us immediately, leaving his drink behind.

The train stopped quite frequently, even at quite small stations, and often waited for twenty minutes or more. It appeared to be the custom in Bulgaria, at least at weekends (this was Sunday) for large numbers of local people to wander up and down the platform chattering and gazing at the intrepid travellers within. At nearly every stop there was someone, not always a policeman, who made a point of engaging us – and only us – in conversation (mostly with me as they nearly all spoke German), quite clearly trying to find out what we were doing and where we were going. I just joked with them and they quickly gave up, like the policeman at one station, with a big German machine pistol hanging from his belt, who asked who we were; I said we were Indians and when he said "Warum sind Sie nicht braun wie die meisten Neger?" (Why aren't you brown like most niggers?) I told him it had come out in the wash in Romania. He looked hard at me for a moment and then just shrugged his shoulders and raised his eyes heavenwards. The others meanwhile carried on ridiculous conversations in broken English – the people thought we were mad, which seemed the best way of attempting to disarm suspicion. This part of the drill had invariably been preceded by a dash to the station buffet as soon as the train stopped; within a few minutes our man in the grey suit would come in and order a drink and as soon as he had started it we left and climbed back on to the train where, of course, he followed us straight away, leaving behind yet another of a succession of abandoned drinks all the way across Bulgaria.

We crossed the Turkish frontier at one in the morning, met by very friendly customs men and shortly before nine o'clock caught our first glimpse, across an expanse of shining blue water, of the city of Istanbul spread out in the morning sun and dominated by numerous white mosques with their slender minarets. Shortly after, the train rolled slowly in through the massive old city walls and we arrived, to be greeted by the manager of Shell Turkey and by Otto Stern, the General Manager of Astra Română, who had got out very secretly just before us. Several members of the British Consulate staff were also there to organise us into a fleet of taxis which took us to our hotels. It was an amazing feeling to be at last in Istanbul and able to breathe freely without the weight of concern and extreme caution that had burdened us for so many weeks past. Even now, however, we were warned to be on our guard as there were people who were trying to find out when, where and how we were going to move on.

In spite of that inconvenience – it was, after all, wartime – we made the most of the opportunity to see the many aspects of the fascinating mixture of east and west that is Istanbul. Most impressive were, naturally, the beautiful mosques, but the bazaars as well as the excellent restaurants and, above all, the cabarets were a wonderful relaxation for us. It was all new, noisy and colourful – except for the taxis whose drivers invariably overcharged quite shamelessly and furthermore used the infuriating fuel-saving technique of working up to a reasonable speed then shifting into neutral, stopping the engine and letting the thing glide on, getting slower and slower until, oblivious of the preceding cascade of apoplectic urgings, would restart the engine and go on to repeat the whole procedure until eventual arrival at destination, invariably by a roundabout route.

The older married members of our Shell party were booked to travel to Egypt by train through Turkey, Syria and Palestine. Our team and two or three other younger Shell men were told to stand by for instructions; we assumed that Egypt would be our destination also. One afternoon Tommy Henderson took me down to the great Galata Bridge that crosses the Golden Horn. While we leant nonchalantly on the parapet he murmured to me to look down quickly at a small tramp steamer just below the bridge – she was flying the Red Ensign and bore the name *Sardinian Prince* on her stern.

Third Movement

Into Egypt

At lunch time on Tuesday 16 July, we were quietly told to pack and be at the quayside at 3pm to embark. Fleets of taxis brought us and another 60 men from hotels all over Istanbul to board the *Sardinian Prince* of 1870 tons – 72 passengers in a ship whose normal accommodation was for 12. Three of our team won a ballot to share cabins with others but they were very hot and the rest of us fared a little better, equipped with hard mattresses on boards covering the forward main hold and protected by a huge canvas sheet slung across two derrick arms, making a vast tent. The rest of the passengers were a mixture of all sorts of people in addition to the 'oil exiles', various commercial folk and many refugees from Poland and Czechoslovakia who had escaped into Romania and thence down to Turkey. As soon as all were on board we were told that the ship was indeed bound for Egypt.

Within an hour or two life on board started to settle down and everyone took a share in stewarding, peeling potatoes and so forth; once we sailed our team and a number of Czech pilots stood regular anti-submarine and anti-aircraft watches round the clock. We also struck up a splendid relationship with the ship's personnel – the officers, in particular, were all young and exceedingly cheerful, so we anticipated a good deal of amusement as well as whatever else the voyage might produce. We had taken the precaution of buying several five litre carboys of raki, the Turkish aniseed drink similar to absinthe or ouzo, and as long as it lasted – which was not long – we organised hilarious parties in one of the cabins with two or three of the brightest among the other passengers, among them a very senior banker who had a rich repertoire of songs none of us had ever heard before and who later became aide-de-camp to General Wavell in Cairo; there was also an Australian aircraft engineer who contributed a rich Sydney accent which stunned us when we first heard it.

At two o'clock the following morning we sailed and after a sunlit passage through the Sea of Marmora we dropped anchor in the Dardanelles, at Chanak of infamous memory from the Gallipoli disaster. We waited there for nine days, part of the time accompanied by a small Greek ship which left a day or two before us; it became clear later that during this time the Navy had been assembling several other vessels that, together with the *Sardinian Prince*, were to form the first convoy they were to push through the Aegean Sea to Egypt past the islands many of which, such as Cos and Rhodes, were held by the newly-hostile Italians.

On Friday 26 July, we eventually weighed anchor at Chanak and sailed unescorted out through the first of the islands. As armament our ship had only a useful-looking anti-submarine gun mounted aft and five ancient rifles that ships customarily carry to repel pirates and cope with mutiny – but no anti-aircraft weapons. The day after we left Chanak we were all idling about on deck when one of the Czech pilots spotted an aircraft approaching; the ship's air-raid siren immediately sounded – a horrible "Oo-oo-oop" starting low and rising rapidly, almost as frightening as the bombs. We watched as the little single-engined biplane with floats circled the ship flying very low; we saw no markings and we wondered what it was up to. All of a sudden, as it was flying past alongside us, someone spotted Italian markings on its top wing and in the same moment that he let out a warning shout we saw a few small bombs start to fall; we threw ourselves flat and there was a loud explosion and a rush of hot air, but the bombs fell 20 yards or more off our port side and did no damage. It did, however, suddenly bring it home to us that war for us was no longer just newspaper headlines and radio broadcasts. And we felt very lonely, ploughing along at some 12 knots on an empty sea, well aware that our recent visitor was at that moment making his reconnaissance report – doubtless claiming, in spirited Italian prose, to have severely damaged a large merchant vessel, while his bigger brethren prepared to get airborne to finish the job.

Sure enough, just after lunch the siren sounded again. Big bombers were coming up astern and then down came a salvo of eight bombs, well behind the ship. At that very moment one of the lookouts shouted that a warship was approaching from southward. We rushed out from our woefully inadequate shelter in the saloon and sundry passageways and there, clearly visible coming over the horizon at full speed, was a British destroyer which opened fire at extreme range on the Italian bombers, causing them to depart for home.

All this happened within not more than two or three minutes from the sounding of the ship's siren – it was in truth extremely dramatic. Then, very shortly the beautiful, sleek-looking destroyer approached in a spectacular sweeping curve to finish close alongside us. An officer on the bridge told us that they would be escorting us until we joined a convoy in some hours time. It was all very relaxed and efficient and made a big impression, particularly on many of the east Europeans who, as they told us, had until then only read stories of Britain's navy.

Next morning we awoke to find ourselves the largest ship in a convoy with the small Greek ship from Chanak and two other even smaller merchant ships, together with two long low vessels that we later learned were Danube oil barges which their crews had sailed secretly all the way from Romania, determined that they should not fall into the hands of the Germans. They were flat-bottomed, shallow-draught vessels and must have been a nightmare to handle in a seaway. Little did I know that this would not be last that I should see of one of them, *Princess Elizabeth*, or of one of their skippers.

Our escort was impressive. The Senior Officer of the Escort was in HMS *Gloucester*, one of the handsome six-inch gun 'Southampton class' cruisers of 6000 tons; HMS *Cairo*, a specialised anti-aircraft cruiser of 4190 tons and four destroyers completed the close escort while the aircraft carrier HMS *Eagle* was cruising over the horizon. All this to shepherd just six very small civilian ships in what was clearly a challenge to the Italians, aimed at establishing the feasibility of what could prove an important line of communication to the Russians.

The following day we sailed on in the sunshine while we watched the ships of the escort busying themselves around the convoy. At one point *Gloucester*, which had been quietly zig-zagging across the rear of the convoy, presumably picked up a suspicious Asdic contact and suddenly went full ahead – that great ship put her stern down and raised her bows like a speedboat getting under way while a huge white plume of propeller-wash shot out astern and in seconds she must have been making 28-30 knots – a wonderful sight.

Next day we were all just getting up when the ship's air-raid siren sounded at the same time as the destroyers careered round with their urgent-sounding "Whoo-ip, whoo-ip" sirens reinforcing the message. Everybody grabbed their emergency packs of personal belongings and their life belts and rushed for shelter and barely twenty seconds later the rushing-wind sound of the bombs came, followed by heavy thudding explosions that shook the ship; they appeared to have been aimed at our ship, as the largest in the convoy, but fortunately all missed. At this time we were only some 60 miles to the west of Rhodes – a short trip for the bombers – and they started coming over with increasing frequency. On one occasion a very heavy bomb was aimed at us; it sounded just like an Underground train in a tunnel as it came down and we all felt this was it – it landed in the water about five yards off our port side amidships (the intrepid Third Mate photographed the splash from the bridge) and failed to explode. The warships were of course also heavily attacked – often the 20-30 foot high splashes from the salvoes completely hid them until they emerged, seemingly by a miracle, unscathed. The only hit was by a 1000 pound bomb on *Gloucester* which failed to explode but penetrated two decks and killed an unfortunate stoker, as we learned later.

The raids, mostly by three-engined Savoia-Marchetti bombers, continued every fifteen minutes or so. They reached a climax at lunchtime; we had to get down on the floor four times and I nearly spilt my soup. Soon afterwards they started to become less frequent and finally ceased when an aircraft from *Eagle* succeeded in shooting down one of the bombers – we saw the welcome plume of black smoke on the horizon. The raids had lasted just seven hours and it was estimated that 250 bombs had been dropped on the convoy alone and many more on the warships; at the end the only damage done was the single hit on *Gloucester*. For most of us it had been a new experience and when it was all over we just fell asleep where we were sitting.

That day was the Italians all-out effort to prevent the convoy getting through intact and two days later on 31 July, we sailed into Port Said without further incident. As our naval escort left us they passed close by and all those of their crews on deck returned our heartfelt cheers of thanks. Our ship was quickly surrounded by a swarm of small boats jockeying for position to be able to shout their varied and more or less desirable wares, some even offering their daughters for gainful employment. We collected our luggage, said goodbye to the splendid ship's officers and our other friends and, under the envious gaze of our fellow passengers, were whisked ashore in a smart launch with the Shell house-flag fluttering at the stern.

It took a few days to settle back into normal life again after the moderately colourful existence of the past four months. We were relieved to have been able to get out of Romania safely but, while there was some sense of anticlimax after our high expectations, it was clear to us all that, in practice, there had been no possibility of our doing a job in which, had we had a chance of succeeding, there was the potential of a worthwhile contribution to the overall war effort. Later, on the night of 11/12 June 1942 the US Air Force, operating from the Middle East, sent a force of heavy bombers to raid Ploeşti; on the way in, the lead navigator's aircraft was shot down and several aircraft failed to find the target, while anti-aircraft fire on the long journey out and back inflicted heavy losses and four aircraft landed in neutral Turkey. It is believed that only insignificant damage was done.

So in the end the Germans, as they say, got the lot – in spite of Sir Julian Cahn's urging at the beginning of 1940. Later events as described, and others, showed that Sir Reginald Hoare's concern that action by our team would invite reprisals on the other British people working in Romania was justified. And when those British people did finally leave, any possibility of carrying out a denying action was ruled out, ipso facto, by our expulsion along with them.

The Company dispersed the rest of our team to new posts; some of them went to the Dutch East Indies (Indonesia) where, eighteen months later, they did heroic work in destroying the oil fields and refineries, often almost only yards ahead of the Japanese invasion forces. I went immediately to the RAF to apply a second time for pilot training, getting the same warning as before to prepare for a long wait. To fill in the time I was given a job in the Cairo office, in the Aviation Department.

From land to sea

One day early in September, after some two months civilian life the telegram arrived – "Report to RAF Station Heliopolis for interview and medical". Now at last, another chance to fly! And, true to form, that very afternoon the telephone rang. It was RG Searight who, it may be remembered, was the senior Shell manager in Bucharest responsible for our team; he asked what I was doing and said he thought he had something that would interest me – would I come to the offices of the Economic Advisory Committee - Middle East, near the Abbas Bridge, to discuss it? I said I would and promptly took a taxi to the building which, according to Artemis Cooper in her book *Cairo in the War 1939-1945*, later became known to every taxi driver as Secret House.

I was introduced to the head of the organisation, Colonel Pollock, who explained, after suitable security precautions, that they were not very economic and did no advising; they were in fact part of a Secret Service organisation responsible for sabotage and subversion. As I found out much later it was the Middle East branch of Section D of the Secret Intelligence Service which was subsequently known as SOE, the Special Operations Executive. I was told that they had acquired a small sailing vessel, of the caïque type, with an auxiliary diesel engine, and which they had equipped with a gun. The purpose of this craft was to enable a small crew of five to commit sabotage and other offensive actions on the Italian-held Aegean islands – would I be prepared to be one of the five? Yet again the attraction of an unusual experience proved even stronger than the desire to fly and I said yes. As a result I was given a special commission as a Sub Lieutenant in the Royal Naval Volunteer Reserve and a code identification; once again a minimal uniform (in this case short-sleeved white shirt with epaulettes, white shorts, stockings and shoes and a service cap) was provided, partly for one or two official contacts but mainly to be concealed on board and changed into – rapidly – if we looked like being captured, in the far-fetched hope that we should be treated as prisoners of war instead of as saboteurs (shades of Romania!). The ship would carry no identification and wear no flag, although a White Ensign would be carried, to be hoisted in the event of action; our dress on board would be that of rough seamen. It sounded intriguing.

My application to join the Royal Air Force having been officially cancelled for the second time, I set about learning what I could about my new environment. The area of operations seemed to be fairly broad: odd-looking people from the Balkans moved in and as quickly disappeared, I was asked to draw a sketch map of part of northern Persia (as it was then) for an elderly gentleman who was apparently an eminent traveller in the region associated with the likes of Gertrude Stein, and Peter Fleming floated in from time to time, clad in absolutely immaculate army uniform, to the delight of the office girls. I learned that our ship was to operate under the aegis of the Navy but under the operational control of Section D in Cairo; she was called HMS *Dolphin*, a name which was used in all our official dealings, appeared on all our ship's stores and ammunition and was accepted when we were challenged at sea – this despite the fact that HMS *Dolphin* was, and still is, the name of another 'ship', the Submarine Service's headquarters at Gosport.

Within a few days I met the second member of our crew, an entertaining character called Clement Shread who sold big accounting machines, played top-class golf and sailed a sporty dinghy on the Nile. We got on well on the whole and during the odd times we spent in Cairo in the next few weeks I gained a good deal of useful experience crewing for him in his dinghy. One day, soon after we had joined, the office manager handed each of us an envelope; his bore the typed legend DH/4 and mine the legend DH/5 and when we expressed mystification as to what we were to do with these envelopes we were told that they contained our salary and the legend was our code designation – it all seemed a trifle light-hearted.

Shortly afterwards we met the Captain and the Radio Officer. The former was a confident young man who had been an apprentice aboard BP tankers before the war; he was very keen and gave an impression of some toughness of attitude – a good man to have with one in a tight spot; he was a collector of handguns. He also affected the merchant seamen's mild contempt for the Navy which they considered performed all that they did with half the efficiency and twice the 'bull' – an attitude that had consequences later on. He had the rank of Lieutenant, RNVR and was called Westall; I discovered later that, by coincidence, his father, who was a badly-injured ex-racing driver, had sold my father our beautiful 2-litre Lagonda touring car back in 1936.

The Radio Officer, named Bustin, was a rather uneasy companion whose background Shread and I were never able to discover – whether colourful or not it could not have compared with that of the fifth crew member. He was an Engineer Lieutenant Commander in the Royal Naval Reserve and had, in fact, skippered the *Princess Elizabeth*, one of the two Danube barges in our convoy back in July. He was Charles Blackley, a big, bluff Scot who, aiming to escape unemployment in Glasgow in the early 1930s and, as he told me once, discovering that the most passionate women in Europe were in Romania, went there and bought himself an oil well. When the war came he stayed on and developed a ploy to hinder the rail shipments of oil to Germany: at night he would get into the marshalling yard where the trains of tank cars were assembled, wearing an overcoat in a pocket of which he concealed a small bottle of strong sulphuric acid; at each third or fourth tank car he would open the lid of an axle-box and pour in a carefully-judged amount of acid such that the oil in the axle-box would be gradually destroyed, causing the axle to seize up and catch fire, thus causing the whole train-load of oil to go up in flames – over the border in Yugoslavia so as to make detection of the cause difficult.

Charles Blackley was also involved in an interesting scheme to blow up dynamite-filled Danube barges at the Iron Gates, a point where the river had cut a deep gully through a line of hills, so that the rock sides of the gully would collapse into the river, thus blocking it to the oil barges going upstream to Germany. The prime mover of the scheme was called Captain Despard, a wonderfully appropriate name for such an enterprise. Unfortunately, a number of British merchant seamen had been recruited to work the barges, rather too early as it proved; they were kitted out with very British sports jackets and grey flannels and were stationed in the port of Constanţa, with adequate living allowances, and it was not long before the tedium of waiting led to the inevitable leakages of information and they were invited to leave the country. Charles Blackley followed them, complete with one Danube barge, the *Princess Elizabeth* aforementioned.

As it was anticipated that we should in some circumstances need to sail our ship, the four deck members of the crew – Captain Westall, Bustin, Shread and I – were sent to Alexandria for instruction in sailing, using a splendid schooner lent to us by one of the local cotton magnates. We learned a great deal about handling sail and helmsmanship while sailing about in the huge Alexandria harbour and later outside in the open sea.

One hot afternoon, after lunch, I was walking down the road towards the harbour when I heard a magnificent sound like a rich diapason organ note. I thought it could only be a flotilla of motor torpedo-boats on the move but, as I watched, there rose slowly above the tangle of ships masts a stately Sunderland flying boat on its way out to sea. It was a wonderful sight and made a profound impression on me.

We returned to Cairo to start collecting the gear for fitting out our ship. I was to pick up some stores from a naval depot and for the first and last-but-one time,

I put on my uniform. While I managed to get myself photographed in it for the benefit of posterity, the main business was to deliver the load to the ship as she lay in Thomas Cook's shipbuilding yard where she had been converted from her original rôle as a Red Sea fish-carrier. The first sight of HMS *Dolphin* was a mild shock as she was smaller than I had expected, though very solid and tough-looking. She was 50 feet long, 43 tons, and had a mainmast and a mizzenmast, the latter stepped aft of the wheelhouse. The three-cylinder 85 horsepower Deutz diesel engine was below the wheelhouse from which it was reached by a small companionway. Amidships was the cabin in which we also cooked; on each side was a bunk/seat with lockers underneath while above and set further into each side of the ship was another bunk that was so close to the deck-head that it took an athletic movement to get into it and one could almost feel the wind as the cockroaches skittered across the deck-head inches from one's face. Leading on from the cabin, on the starboard side, was an alley-way going right for'ard to the bow with, to port, the radio cabin followed by stowage space, then right in the 'eyes' of the ship, the 'heads', a small yacht-type lavatory, and finally the chain locker holding the anchor chain.

There was a small dinghy/lifeboat with outboard motor slung from davits on the port side aft. Between it and the wheelhouse was the mizzenmast which was the original mainmast; it had apparently been planned at first that the ship would be used in the Red Sea in support of the campaign in Italian-held east Africa and, to cope with the lighter winds in that area, a huge substitute mainmast was stepped in order to support a 42 foot gaff mainsail. The ship had a rounded bottom with a fairly small keel with the result that she rolled very easily, a characteristic that was naturally exacerbated by the pendulum effect of the tall, heavy mainmast. She also had a pronounced Maier-form bow – sloping round quite sharply down towards the keel – and the stern was similar; as a result the keel was relatively short and the ship was comparatively unstable directionally, necessitating very hard work on the wheel even in quite light seas. Fortunately Shread and I, having no such experience, had been given a short 'blooding' by being taken out to sea from Alexandria in one of the two Danube barges which, as described earlier, were flat-bottomed and thus extremely difficult to steer on a straight course; the wheel was very large, some four and a half or five feet in diameter, and the sheer physical effort of keeping the compass reading anywhere near the correct course was exhausting for us tyros.

HMS *Dolphin* carried in the bows a Hotchkiss three-pounder quick-firing gun (ie the round and the charge were all contained in the one case) and we also had two Lewis guns for anti-aircraft use, to be supported on Thomas Cook's spindly notion of a gun-mounting. Shread and I, again unlike the others, having had no experience of the Lewis gun, were sent on a short course at the barracks in Alexandria. Our instructor was a diminutive corporal of the Royal Welch Fusiliers who introduced himself and then said "I can see you're gentlemen and I won't chase you around like the other instrooctors. It's a shame", he said, "they shout and bawl at these poor little sods 'til they don't know whether they're in for a shit, shave or 'aircoot!"

Our final preparation, for all of us except our engineer Charles Blackley, who obviously knew it all, was a day spent in the Western Desert with a supply of gelignite, detonators and various 'pencils' (see page 14) learning how to blow up some of the plentiful pieces of scrap metal that told of earlier battles. We also learned that we would carry another type of 'pencil'; instead of the wire holding back the striker being broken by corrosion through acid it was released from retention by a carefully-calculated amount of sugar that was slowly melted by the action of sea-water. These 'pencils' were for use with limpet-mines, steel hemispheres packed with explosive and fitted on the flat side with powerful magnets that enabled them to be attached to a ship's side or bottom. The 'pencil pocket' in the mine should face forward so that the ship's motion would force sea-water into the 'pencil', dissolving the sugar after a predetermined time (as indicated by the colour of the 'pencil') and thereby initiating a very large bang which caused considerable damage to the ship.

To sea

Our ship had been sailed round from Cairo to Ismailia on the Great Bitter Lake from where we were to sail to Athens to receive our operation orders. Shread and I joined her there late one evening in time to take part in the transfer from some naval lorries of ammunition for the ship's armament, victuals and some five to six tons of nitroglycerine, limpet-mines, 'pencils', hand grenades and 3000 fulminate of mercury detonators; the function of these last was to initiate the explosion in those various munitions. The detonators were small copper cylinders, about the size of a cigarette, and were liable to explode if they were dropped on the ground or otherwise roughly handled.

Once at sea we took comfort from the knowledge that, with such a cargo, if we were hit or even suffered only a near-miss we would not be around to see the big bang, being part of it.

In his book *Baker Street Irregular*, Bickham Sweet-Escott told of his anger at this dispersal of the relatively small stock of explosives and explosive devices that, working from the SOE headquarters in London at 64 Baker Street, he had struggled with great difficulty to accumulate in Cairo for use by that branch of the organisation.

The captain was anxious, very rightly, to clear Port Said and be in the open sea before daylight. Consequently we loaded everything on board as quickly as possible, leaving it all to be stowed once we were at sea. We cast off from Ismailia a little before midnight and proceeded northwards up the Suez Canal to Port Said. It was a dark night and it was a slightly eerie feeling gliding along that great ribbon of water, faintly gleaming, with the desert silence on either hand broken only by the steady "te-trumm, te-trumm, te-trumm" of our diesel engine – what were we launching ourselves into? Any feelings of apprehension there might have been were swamped by the business of getting to know our new 'home' and settling in; I unloaded my kit into one of the lockers which I then locked, only to be told smartly by the captain that you never locked your gear aboard ship – lesson number one in the seafaring life, to be followed by many, many more in days to come.

Once clear of the mainland we set about stowing our stores (the Navy had generously provided us with submarine rations – real quality stuff), cargo and ammunition. Packing cases in all shapes and sizes had to be manoeuvred down the companionway into the cabin to end up under the cabin floorboards or lashed firmly in the stowage area for'ard – all this with the ship producing her soon-to-be-familiar rolling motion. The fulminate of mercury detonators were stowed well for'ard, right beneath the gun which, understandably, was not practice-fired! Hand grenades and Lewis guns were positioned accessibly as were the boxes of shells for the three-pounder-high explosive, 'common shot' (solid) and tracer; a box of each, as ready-use ammunition, was lashed firmly on deck to starboard, close to the gun. Round the gun itself we put a few odd boxes and covered these and the gun with a tarpaulin, hoping to make it look like a pile of fish cases. We grabbed a bite of food now and then but otherwise worked continuously throughout the first day and on until early the following morning.

Twenty hours out from Port Said, just as we were preparing to settle down for some rest, the engine stopped. Charles immediately went below into the engine room and tried to restart the diesel. The method of starting was by blowing compressed air from a big high-pressure air bottle into the cylinders through an array of pipes. As we were all by now suffering from extreme fatigue I went below to help as an oil-man knowing a good deal about engines; Charles and I examined everything that in our bleary-eyed state we could think of; time and again we tried the start-up procedure with absolutely no faint response. Then the compressed air ran out. There was a large iron bar that fitted into slots round the periphery of the flywheel to enable it to be moved round while the fuel injector and valve clearances were being adjusted; we both hung on this bar and tried time and again to pull it down fast enough to swing the engine but the compression was much too high and we were much too exhausted. As we sat getting our breath back I belatedly applied my mechanical first-aid reasoning and said "Let's look at the fuel filter"; we went over to the tank, removed the filter and instantly cursed ourselves for our dimwittedness – the filter was completely clogged with wood chippings, bits of dried paint, etc., all the debris that would fall into a tank with the top left open while the local workmen finished their various jobs, the tank then being filled and closed without further inspection!

Without the engine there was only one thing for it – hoist sail and continue the voyage to Athens. By this time our radio had broken down and our radio operator proved unable to get it working again so there was, in any case, not even the remote hope that some swift naval vessel might bring us life-giving compressed air from Alex. We spent two hours or more getting out the heavy sails, securing them and organising all the attendant rope-work, finally securing the windward backstay and hoisting foresail, main and mizzen. All the ropes were new coir – none of your soft, smooth manila hemp – and tore our hands to pieces while we heaved at them and tried to get them to flex sufficiently to belay.

At sea the deck crew stood alternating six hour watches of two men each, one at the wheel and the other as lookout for'ard, changing over from time to time.

After our deck watch our watch below was fully occupied with cooking, eating, washing, various jobs about the ship and sleeping before our next six hour stint. The ship had been quite a handful to keep on course under engine; under sail there was the additional task of keeping an eye on the sails – not easy at night. If the wind changed the man on lookout needed to reset the sails and, in heavy weather, it was sometimes necessary to call up the watch below to help, which was not popular. The wind was mainly from the northeast so we were mostly sailing close-hauled to make our northwest by north course, slackening sail a little in stronger winds. At the same time the ship was permanently rolling; in heavy weather she would roll over well past 30 degrees and hang there for perhaps ten or twelve seconds before rolling over in the same way the other side; one very rough night I was at the wheel and she rolled to starboard farther than I had ever experienced before and everything that was stowed on the port side of the wheelhouse came down on me in a shower – charts, parallel rules, compasses, coastal pilots, signal flags and a mug of very hot cocoa. The angry grey waters of the eastern Mediterranean and cloud-hung islands of the Aegean in winter presented a very different picture from the sun-drenched blue of the travel brochures.

One particularly stormy night Shread and I were asleep on our watch below when we were hauled out of our bunks and told to get on deck 'double quick' – trousers and shoes slipped on in a hurry and we were out in the howling night to join the other three with the ship rolling and pitching and solid seas breaking across the ship every ten or fifteen seconds. The big semi-circular steel jaws, called the 'throat', that held the inner end of the gaff to the mast and allowed it to rotate round the mast when the sail shifted, had broken in half; the gaff, a heavy 12 foot spar, with the 42 foot mainsail attached, had been lowered close to the deck where it was suspended by its halyard which was attached some two-thirds of the way towards the tip; in the violent wind the whole thing, gaff and mainsail, was thrashing around in the midst of the continual crashing seas. In pitch blackness and blinded by sea water all five of us struggled to control the beast, while holding on for dear life with one hand, so as to secure the broken throat to the mast in order that the mainsail could be furled and secured, with the gaff, to the boom. I have no idea how long it took us to complete the job but we were fortunate that no one was lost overboard and none suffered more than cuts and bruises – it was also very cold and wet. All we could do was keep the ship head-to-sea with the foresail and mizzen and wait for daylight to enable the broken throat to be jury-rigged so that we could hoist the mainsail again.

We had taken stores only for the voyage to Piræus, normally a fairly short one, and our food stocks were rapidly dwindling. Partly because of this and partly to give ourselves a change from tinned food we decided to dynamite some fish. We brought up from below a box of hand grenades and the captain took one and pulled the pin; counting the regulation five seconds he hurled it overboard while we crouched down in case the thing exploded above the water. Silence – not a bang, not a dead fish. We checked and found that the grenades had no detonators in them so they were useless for fishing or for defence in the event of attack by an enemy vessel. They were returned, detonator-less below, to join the Lewis guns from which we never fired a single round.

All the time since the engine failed we had kept a sharp lookout for a ship that might help us or even a friendly aircraft that would take a message back to Alexandria – our radio being useless they could at least report our situation. Early on one of the big four-engined Sunderland flying boats had come very low and circled us while we signalled with the Aldis lamp, but as our captain had not bothered with such naval details as recognition codes the pilot made no reply and flew off on his lawful occasions. Some days later a fast troop convoy – two big liners escorted by two destroyers – passed about a mile away; we signalled the leading destroyer "Have you any compressed air?"; back came the reply "Yes" and the ships continued at high speed straight ahead. They were bound for Greece where the Greeks were putting up heroic resistance to the invading Italians.

After these disappointments we became rather desperate and when, two or three days later, another Sunderland passed near, flying northwards at about 1500 feet, we let fly with everything – we waved, we set off a red 'Very' light, we flashed furiously on the Aldis lamp, all to no avail. Some weeks later, back in Cairo, I was reading a despatch in the *Egyptian Mail* by the famous war correspondent Alan Moorehead; he had recently flown from Egypt to Greece in a Sunderland, with General Sir Archibald Wavell, Commander-in-Chief, Middle East and his staff and described how, on the way, they had seen ". . . a small grey ship with a number of ragged seamen gesticulating wildly" – at least we made the local newspaper!

Finally, one lovely quiet evening we came up with a convoy of several ships escorted by an armed merchant cruiser (AMC) to which we repeated our despairing signal "Have you any compressed air?", with our hearts in our mouths. The reply was "Yes, but only at a thousand pounds per square inch." Charles Blackley reckoned we could cope by opening the valve very slowly so we signalled back that we would take it and the cruiser signalled "Please come alongside." The big ship, about 16,000 tons, was stopped and we let out sail so as to approach. We were hailed from the bridge "What ship?" and our captain replied, "HMS *Dolphin*", then from the bridge, "Captain's name?" and our captain shouted "Lieutenant Westall" after which from the bridge "Come alongside." To my astonishment our captain took the ship up to the weather side of the AMC, a prewar ocean liner and, although the sea was no more than light, the waves, being driven against the towering 45 or 50 foot side of the ship, swept a long way up the side; one wave caught us and lifted the ship a good 20 feet up against the side of the AMC – she, as was normal in wartime, had her lifeboats swung outboard and mercifully our huge mast passed between one of them and her hull without doing any damage. The AMC's master, in a split second, ordered "Full ahead" and this great ship literally leapt ahead, clear of us, and stopped a quarter of a mile away. Thinking about the incident later, it occurred to me that, had we instead tried to approach the lee side of the ship, her huge bulk would have taken our wind so that we lost way and thus would have become out of control.

A boat was lowered with the Second Officer and Chief Engineer in it, and the precious cylinder: this was about six feet long and about a foot and a half in diameter and was very heavy. After a considerable struggle we got it aboard and down into the engine room. We offered our saviours a tot of rum down below in the cabin where they told us that the convoy had been heavily bombed half an hour earlier. They said they had heard there was a secret service ship somewhere around but we were very cautious; after we had chatted for about five or six minutes I happened to go on deck in time to see the AMC flash "Boat to return immediately" and our guests made full speed to what was no doubt a warm reception, the convoy by then being well on the way to the rapidly darkening horizon. Then Charles and I went down into the engine room and managed to rig up a connection between the compressed air cylinder and the engine. We checked everything carefully to make sure the engine was completely ready to start and then cautiously opened the valve; there was a faint hiss and a sort of sigh – the cylinder was empty.

Earlier in the day, at noon, our captain had taken his usual sun-sight; the position he worked out showed that, beating more or less against the wind as we were, in the last twenty-four hours we had made three nautical miles headway towards Greece and 63 miles leeway (ie virtually sideways) towards the enemy-occupied coast of Libya some 200 miles away. It was all too clear that without the engine we had no hope of making Athens; the unhappy decision was therefore taken to go about and sail before the wind to Alexandria.

Once we had started the return voyage the weather had improved and the tension of the past weeks had gone out of all the crew. Sailing before the wind the ship was much easier to handle and for the first time I experienced the joy of being in charge of a ship moving briskly over the water with no sound save the rushing bow-wave and the creaking rigging. At night the magic was even more intense; one was alone at the wheel, watching the huge mast and mainsail swinging gently to and fro against a dark blue-black star-filled sky, alone on an empty sea, in closest touch with the very elements, alive to and overwhelmed by the vastness and wonder of creation – and in those moments truly very near the Creator.

We reached Alexandria in under three days, creeping into the harbour with our nautical tail between our legs after two fruitless weeks at sea. In the harbour we were directed to moor at a wharf immediately astern of the depot ship HMS *Resource* so that our fuel system and radio could be worked on. We also took on board badly-needed supplies of food as well as 'Nelson's blood', the thick, dark Navy rum which, mixed with hot water and the rich dark-green Navy lime juice, made a wonderful drink to fortify one before going on a cold six hour night watch. Once safely moored we were able to observe the mass of warships in the harbour; they were of every size from motor torpedo boats to the three great battleships *Warspite*, *Valiant* and *Queen Elizabeth*. Although we did not know it at the time the latter two battleships were in fact sitting on the bottom having been holed just before our arrival by Italian two-man torpedoes, known as 'chariots', piloted in by extremely brave men who had been launched from a submarine offshore – they survived and were taken prisoner.

On our second night the Italians came over to bomb the harbour and every ship opened up with anti-aircraft fire. Actually we had already seen the fleet barrage by day; as we were entering port the day before an Italian 'shufti-kite' (reconnaissance aircraft) flew over very low, presumably to check the handywork of the 'charioteers' – not easy to do as the big ships, although sitting on the bottom, were upright and looking perfectly normal. However when, on this night, the barrage started again the captain and I, who were alone on board, thought we would take a look at what promised to be a brilliant display. I went first and had just got halfway up the companionway, with my head and shoulders emerging from the cabin entrance hatch, when my face was banged heavily down on the deck – as already mentioned, we were moored right astern of the depot ship HMS *Resource* and she had a 5.9 inch anti-aircraft gun on her stern about 25 feet above us and firing straight over us. The muzzle-blast was so powerful that it not only flattened me but pushed the ship about nine inches down into the water each time the gun was fired. It may be remembered that we still had our cargo of some six tons of high-explosive on board together with those 3000 very sensitive fulminate of mercury detonators; it was a curious feeling for the two of us just sitting below in the cabin chatting and wondering, in a strangely detached way, whether the next blast would send the whole lot up. In the event HMS *Resource* and HMS *Dolphin* were still there next morning. I did not go ashore as I had already settled completely into the feeling that the ship was my home.

"Once more unto the breach . . ."

Two days later, the captain having collected his sailing directions and codes from the naval headquarters at Ras-el-Tin on the other side of the harbour, we started our engine and sallied forth once more to Athens and our real job. The first two days out the weather was fine and the sea fairly calm; the rhythmic "te-trumm, te-trumm, te-trumm" of the engine was comforting as we rolled gently over the empty sea at eight and a half knots, seeing absolutely nothing except one Sunderland flying boat that circled us very low and then flew off. Then suddenly the whole scene changed – black skies with low cloud scudding over angry seas and the wind howling in the rigging. As on the previous voyage, the wind was from a point nearly dead ahead of us; this meant that we were continuously ploughing into a head sea which often broke over the bows, some of the water getting into the chain locker through the hawsehole, (the opening through which the chain passed from the chain locker) and thence into the bilges. The bilge pump was mounted on the engine right aft and the bilges should have drained aft to be pumped overboard; it became increasingly evident that this was not happening for some reason, and as the days passed the ship became progressively heavier by the head so that, when any wave bigger than about six feet approached, the bows would plunge into the trough and then rise slowly to about halfway up the wave, the top part of which would then sweep in a flood from end to end of the ship, the force being only partially broken by the gun and its wrapping in the bows. It was a particularly impressive sight at night in a heavy sea with eight and ten foot waves, the ship ploughing straight into each dark grey and white wall of water with no sign of the bows lifting anywhere near the crest.

Before long we were among the many small islands of the southern Cyclades, at this time – in mid-winter – just low-lying dark grey and black shapes set in a heaving grey-black sea and partially hidden by the overhanging pall of dark, angry cloud, very unfriendly. Then we reached the wide Gulf of Athens and the captain shaped a course to take us straight through the middle of the Gulf to Piræus, the port of Athens, to the north. The sea was moderately calm after the conditions we had met among the islands and we were making good headway when, about halfway across the Gulf, we noticed anti-aircraft guns firing on the cliffs to the north. I was at the wheel and Shread was on lookout; it seemed as though we might be about to suffer attack from the air and as we were quite alone in the middle of the Gulf (for good reason as we soon learned) we felt exceedingly vulnerable. However, nothing else happened and in the afternoon we entered Piræus harbour, to be told amid huge excitement that the Greek army had achieved a great victory over the invading Italians the day before. Looking over the waters of the harbour it was evident that the Greeks had last night celebrated their victory in a magnificently passionate fashion, leaving a water-borne carpet of little white mementoes.

For us, however, there was no such joyous reception. Our captain, self-confident and contemptuous of naval procedures, had ignored the sailing directions he had been given in Alexandria and sailed up the Gulf straight through the huge Greek minefield that covered the entire area, except for a swept passage close to the northern shore. The Greeks had fired anti-aircraft guns in a vain attempt to warn us off. The only reason we escaped was our very small draught of a mere 3'6"; even at that, if the sea had been rougher we might well have hit a mine in a trough between waves. The Greek authorities were furious and our own naval representatives joined in heaping their quota of opprobrium on the captain's head. The atmosphere surrounding HMS *Dolphin* at that point was further soured by our radio operator going ashore in full uniform as an army captain, wearing what the Navy call 'a full set', ie full beard and moustache such as three of us had grown while at sea. In the Navy it has to be a full set or nothing, whereas in the army only a trimmed moustache is allowed, never ever a beard. In any case, given the secret nature of our mission, we were not to wear uniform at all, so Bustin also was wheeled in for his share of the action.

The next thing was for our rather crestfallen little unit to report to the organisation's office in Athens to get our operation orders; up to this point we had no idea of what our activities were to be beyond a general notion of sailing into and out of many islands doing damage. We rang the bell and the door was opened by a small man with curly blond hair wearing a snappy suit who introduced himself as Ian Pirie and who proved to be, indeed, DH/A, the head of the Athens Office. He asked how he could help us and when we said we had come for our operation orders he appeared nonplussed and said "I'm not well up in these things – you see, I'm only a film director". We all felt a sudden hollow feeling – it seemed unbelievable that all of such training as we had had and our keenness to do a worthwhile job should lead to a fiasco of this magnitude. In the end we just reported that we had a problem with a piece of equipment on board that required engineering attention and it was decided that we should see whether Shell could help.

We went along to the Shell office where I introduced myself to AM Churchman, the genial General Manager, who was most anxious to help and took us to see the Operations Manager, a merry soul called Southam. It was explained that a rather tricky repair was needed on our 'strum', a special kind of filter protecting the bilge pump; the word 'strum' struck him, and us, as just so slightly vulgar that we all burst into uproarious laughter, the work was swiftly put in hand – as part of Shell's war effort – and we all had a splendid drink at his house in the evening.

The next job, while some sort of operation was sorted out for us, was to clear what we estimated was a good three tons of sea water that, as mentioned earlier, had got into the for'ard bilges and been unable to drain away aft to where the engine-driven bilge pump would pick it up and discharge it overboard. The other three of the crew had pressing business of some kind ashore so, as happened not infrequently, the dirty job was left to Shread and me. When we lifted the boards we peered down into a sort of medium grey soup that filled the whole for'ard part of the hull below the lower deck and smelt positively lavatorial, so before we could think of starting we threw down a bottleful of Jeyes Fluid. We rigged up the emergency semi-rotary pump we had on board and then discovered that its discharge hose was not long enough to reach all the way aft through the cabin and over the side. The thought of attempting to get a Greek storeman to search for and produce a long hose that would fit exactly on our pump did not appeal so we set about scooping up the water in a saucepan each and pouring it into a bucket which was then carried carefully through the cabin and up on to the deck to be emptied into the harbour. Three tons of water by the bucketful adds up to a lot of labour and several hours spent inhaling the nauseous vapours that were only slightly disguised by bottle after bottle of Jeyes' Fluid. As the water level dropped we had to lean further and further down into the revolting void to reach it until finally the transverse frames of the hull were exposed; these were only some nine inches apart so the saucepans were too big to fit the space and we had to resort to Players' cigarette tins to get out the last 15 or 20 gallons. It was then that we discovered why the water had not drained aft as it should have done: all the ship's frames should have had holes drilled in them down by the keel to enable the water to pass through but, as the frames were extremely hard eucalyptus wood the Arab boat builders had evidently had one go and thought better of it, so a transverse bulkhead and the solid frames formed an impenetrable barrier keeping the water in the fore-part of the ship, the weight of it preventing the bows from rising fully to the waves.

Shread and I then had forty-eight hours ashore while the others came back on board to guard the ship. We took rooms in the Hotel Grande Bretagne on the central Omonia Square and became temporary tourists, visiting the Acropolis and a few of the other sites. The hotel was full of a typical wartime medley of people: there were war correspondents, including Richard Dimbleby, most of the members of the Yugoslav royal family who, with their numerous entourage, had just escaped from the German occupation of their country and were to be flown to Egypt by Sunderland flying boat, and a number of RAF pilots and navigators who were flying Wellingtons and Blenheims to bomb the Italians in the wild mountains in the north where their casualties were very heavy. Many civilians, including some assorted British, were evidently engaged mainly in having a good time in a city which provided many diversions even with the nation fighting for its life.

We off-loaded some of our munitions and then set sail for Suda Bay in Crete on a mission whose nature our captain did not disclose to us. The Bay is a huge inlet forming a natural harbour five miles long, guarded originally by a Venetian castle, now a ruin, at its mouth; Suda village and its quay are situated at the far end. We came alongside with some difficulty because the arrangement of levers that Cook's had invented as a means of controlling the engine directly from the wheelhouse proved useless and the captain had to shout his orders down to Blackley in the engine room, who then operated the engine controls to give Ahead, Slow Astern and so on – all this while the ship was tending to behave with a mind of its own. Once in position it was essential to moor up quickly in the offshore wind and Shread and I leapt ashore to secure head and stern ropes to the bollards on the quay, watched by a solitary sentry huddled in his greatcoat and steel helmet. At the very moment when we were both busy with the mooring ropes an Italian reconnaissance aircraft shot across the bay very low and a ring of anti-aircraft guns all round the harbour let fly with everything they had; what goes up must come down and the two of us, with no time to grab steel helmets, were surrounded by a hail of shrapnel bouncing off the quay and raising tiny fountains in the water just like a very heavy rainstorm. It only lasted for about a couple of minutes and being busy helped us to take our minds off the metallic precipitation. The Italians were evidently wanting to confirm the sinking the day before of the six-inch gun cruiser HMS *York* which now lay beneath the waters of the harbour.

Charles Blackley discovered that Captain Nichol RN, the Naval Officer-in-Charge (NOIC) Suda Bay was an old shipmate so that evening he went ashore to celebrate. Bustin also departed to seek out the nearest army Officers Mess and the captain disappeared on an errand of his own. Shread and I were left to look after the ship. We had both turned in, balancing in our minute upper bunks, when towards midnight we heard Blackley stumbling aboard, he having evidently enjoyed a good deal of the extremely fierce Cretan wine. He started shouting "That bugger Deller's talking French down there – if he comes up on deck I'll knock his ******* block off!" In a rather foolish fit of bravado I called back "OK, Charles, I'm coming up." Just as I got my head out of the cabin entrance he swung his fist straight into my face and knocked me down into the cabin below. Silence in such circumstances – with a much heftier, raging drunk Scot – being the wisest course, I left him to cool off on deck, from whence he staggered below before long and sat quietly on his bunk.

Not long afterwards Bustin arrived on board, in a similar state, and sat down on the opposite bunk. After some minutes they started mumbling insults at each other and when the temperature had risen considerably they both got out their commando knives; we had all been issued with these – big brass knuckle-dusters with a very sharp ripping-knife attached to one end – and the two drunks started waving these around while Shread and I, only inches away from our nearer protagonist on each side of the cabin, waited somewhat apprehensively for the next bit of action. Suddenly Blackley was overwhelmed by a call of nature and staggered through the radio cabin and the stowage area to the bows and our small yacht-type lavatory. Bustin promptly went to sleep and after a short while I went to see how Blackley was getting on – he was lying on the deck fast asleep with a blissful smile on his face and his right arm lovingly round the lavatory pan in which position he slumbered happily till morning.

Next day I went with Shread to look at the small sea port of Khania just across the hills from Suda. It was a fascinating place, full of picturesque old buildings, cafés where old men sat gossiping and smoking their hookahs and bustling crowds of people in colourful clothes; most of the men wore small round caps on their heads, baggy trousers bound at the knee rather like plus-fours and loose blouses with large sashes from which protruded impressive ivory-handled daggers in elaborate silver scabbards adorned with little silver chains carrying small old silver coins. The men were dark-complexioned, often with big black moustaches, and the overall picture was somewhat fierce as, indeed, they proved to be in the resistance movement after the German airborne invasion of the island in the following year.

We returned to Athens to find ourselves recalled to Egypt, calling at Suda Bay on the way. Shortly after we sailed I became ill with what later proved to be jaundice, apparently caused by inhalation of nitroglycerine fumes from our cargo. It was a thoroughly unpleasant trip as I had to stand my watches and could keep nothing down but a few slices of orange and some water, so became rather weak – in particular the smell of cigarette smoke took on an almost intolerable quality. On arrival in Alexandria on Christmas Day I was immediately taken off the ship and sent to the 2/5 General Hospital, in a naval ward, where I met several of the pilots and navigators who had been wounded in the astonishing night raid on the Italian fleet in Taranto harbour by a force of 21 old-fashioned Swordfish biplane torpedo-carriers and bombers the previous November. They sank or damaged so many capital ships and lesser vessels that the fleet was effectively crippled. We had regular visits from kind elderly ladies of the British community whose notions of life, poor dears, were light years away from those of young active servicemen. I did not see either HMS *Dolphin*, Westall, our captain, Bustin or Charles Blackley again.

When fit enough I was given convalescent leave with one of the many wealthy families of local British business people who were most generous to countless service personnel throughout the war. One afternoon I was invited to tea by a Flight Lieutenant Mike Bentley, who was the adjutant of No 230 Squadron of the Royal Air Force, one of the two squadrons of Sunderland flying boats operating out of Alexandria which a short while later performed miracles of heroic airmanship in the evacuation from Greece and Crete.

The other officer present at tea was Wing Commander Geoffrey Francis, the Commanding Officer of 230 Squadron; we had much talk of Sunderland flying boats to which I was feeling increasingly drawn. We were to meet again towards the end of the war.

We were removed as a crew from HMS *Dolphin* and, back in the Cairo office following such an ignominious end to our equally fruitless voyaging in the eastern Mediterranean, Shread and I decided that we would each write a report to the boss on the highly unsatisfactory way in which the ship had been run. We were both very frank and our views were backed up by the findings of an examination of the ship herself – even the gun, which we had never fired or even uncovered, was found to have the breechblock rusted completely solid, sails were ruined having been stowed away damp and so on. Searight once remarked to me that they had thought our captain had "an unusually old head on young shoulders" and the others of us had initially had great confidence also. The whole episode had turned out to be a sad waste of resources and enthusiasm.

Apart from one or two minor secret missions I had very little to do in the office and, traditionally, a junior officer who has criticised his captain – and in writing – is in a fairly dubious situation as regards a new appointment. Furthermore my feeling of disillusionment arose in no small measure from the organisation itself and I felt increasingly that the war was going on without me. I told Pollock and Searight how I felt and they agreed that I could go ahead and apply – yet again! – for RAF pilot training and that I would cease to belong to SOE and would resign my RNVR commission on joining the RAF. Without delay I filled in the requisite papers, passed the aircrew medical tests at RAF Heliopolis with an AIB category (fully operational, home and overseas) and was told to wait for a week or two for instructions to report for joining. I was able to face that small delay with a light heart – I was really on my way to learning to fly!

Meanwhile, as related by Artemis Cooper in her book (see page 26), there had been for some time a good deal of concern in senior military quarters over the operation of our Cairo-based organisation. It had too few results to show for it and the office appeared over-full of young men and women who enjoyed a fast lifestyle while dropping not very heavily-veiled hints that they were engaged in secret work. One of these appeared to be Lady Ranfurly whose husband, the Earl of Ranfurly, had been taken prisoner in the Western Desert – seeing her around the office I thought "Typical!" However, this was far from the truth: she was in fact responsible for the clerical element of the office administration and quickly became disturbed by some of what she saw going on. Her concern was such that she eventually managed to speak to Anthony Eden, the Foreign Secretary, as he was passing through Cairo on his way to talk to the Greek government. As a result there was eventually a wholesale change of personnel in August 1941 from George Pollock down. Meanwhile, a few days before I left I had glimpsed the first of what were to be many 'new brooms' – Commander Mike Cumberlege RNR, who was to take over as captain of *Dolphin*; he and his cousin and two others subsequently had a very active career during the battle for Crete and in various escapades thereafter until he was captured in a raid on the Corinth Canal in late 1942, and was taken with his gunner to Flossenburg concentration camp; after who knows what experiences they were taken out and shot two days before the German surrender in May 1945, doubtless to hide from the civilised world what had been done to them.

Before leaving to join the RAF I thought I would enjoy a last taste of hedonism by taking a trip to Luxor and Aswan, benefiting from services' cheap travel rates. For the second and last time I put on my naval uniform and caught the night train to Luxor being slightly embarrassed by having only a short-sleeved shirt and shorts whereas regulations required long sleeves and trousers at night. I felt even more uncomfortable at dinner when I was joined at table by an RAMC Lieutenant Colonel who in fact turned out to be an exceedingly amiable and entertaining companion throughout much of the trip and was quite unperturbed by my improper dress – after dark only, of course – or the large difference in rank. He was Lieutenant Colonel Alexander Simpson-Smith who became a legend as a brilliant surgeon in the Western Desert and, like so many others of the medics, worked night and day under extreme difficulties – he died of exhaustion sometime in, I think, 1944. On our arrival at Luxor we spotted a rather lonely-looking army nurse who was also making the trip so we took her under our wing.

In Luxor we were guided by a voluble dragoman through the immensely impressive temples in which we were completely dwarfed physically and mentally by the colossal figures and by the thought of the almost unimaginable effort that must have gone into such stunning works of man. As well as witnessing the ritual demonstrations of snake-charming and other unlikely tricks we had the good fortune to be invited to tea by the head man of a neighbouring village; taking my cue from my eminent medical companion I embarked confidently on a somewhat strange, slightly tea-like beverage and munched little sweet cakes while we exercised our few words of Arabic, sitting on rickety chairs in a semicircle of local dignitaries who, with exquisite courtesy, made the same efforts to appear to understand our speech as we did to understand theirs.

The following day we crossed over the Nile to the Valley of Kings where we were all three instantly overwhelmed by the most extraordinary feeling of being no longer in the twentieth century but, rather, in the ghostly company of those monarchs of five, six, seven thousand years ago. We were, of course, fortunate in being able to experience all this more or less undisturbed because apart from one or two other service people there were no tourists at all in wartime. Even more remarkable as an experience was visiting the tomb of one of the pharaohs whose name escapes me: we walked down and down a low narrow passage whose walls were covered with fascinating drawings of people and animals engaged in all sorts of everyday life – the figures were perfectly executed in black outline filled in with colours that were as bright as on the day they were painted. This freshness of the drawings added powerfully to the extraordinary feeling of being a contemporary spectator, a feeling that became even more striking when we neared the tomb itself as, first, some of the figures were only partly coloured, then appeared in black outline only and, finally, even the outlines were in decreasing stages of completion so that one had an almost totally convincing feeling that the artists were just away for lunch and would shortly return to carry on their work.

The colonel and the nurse had to return north and I went on to Aswan where I fell in with three young army subalterns who were having a brief rest from recovering damaged tanks in the Western Desert battles. We spent a day sailing in a felucca on the Nile and the great lake that had been created by flooding a once-inhabited valley; in several places just some two or three feet of the tops of temples and pylons (triumphal arches) rose above the water and it felt odd to be standing on them, rather as it might feel if it were possible to stand on the top of the tower of some church in a flooded valley, thinking of the life that had gone on in those places now deep beneath the water under one's feet.

Back in Cairo I set about clearing up my affairs and saying goodbye to a number of good friends. I spent most of my remaining pennies having a last dinner on the lovely roof-garden of the Continental Hotel where I had spent many evenings with a drink watching the cabaret; there was a spectacular belly-dancer called Hekmat Fahmy, reputed to be a mistress of King Farouk, as well as a Hungarian dance troupe of three girls with one of whom I fell distantly in love. The other attraction was the parties presided over by the genial and enormously tall British ambassador, Sir Miles Lampson, with his beautiful Italian wife; there were always a number of young officers from great regiments like the 11th Hussars, 'The Cherry-pickers', in their cerise-coloured trousers – seeing them there in their immaculate uniforms in cheerful, civilised conversation it was hard to realise that shortly – in many cases only hours – before they had been in the heat of battle in the Western Desert.

Thus I spent my last days as an officer in the Royal Navy.

Fourth Movement

(i) Training

In the air

On Monday 6 April 1941 a telegram arrived from Headquarters Royal Air Force Middle East instructing me to report on Thursday 9 April to RAF Station Heliopolis to join up as an Aircraftman Second Class – the lowest form of animal life, but nevertheless at least in the General Duties branch as 'pilot under training'. (For the reason why I could not transfer my officer's commission to the RAF see page 44.)

On 10 April, I was received into my third Service, the Royal Air Force, together with another 'u/t pilot', Bill Ruck-Keene, formerly a minor racing driver. We were to go to Bulawayo in Southern Rhodesia (now Zimbabwe) to begin our Initial Training Wing (ITW) ground training. Somewhat to our amazement we were to fly from Cairo to Kisumu by one of BOAC's Empire flying boats and on 15 April in the early morning we sped across the still waters of the Nile in a smart motor launch to board the huge silver four-engined aircraft of the type from which the military Sunderland had been derived – an omen perhaps? On board everything was spacious and luxuriously comfortable and when we had been settled in our seats by the stewards we experienced that unique thrill of a flying boat takeoff – the slight shuddering of the aircraft as the engines were opened up to full power, the rush of sparkling water past the portholes until the aircraft came up on to the step of the hull, skimming across the water with increasing speed until it rose smoothly into the air and we watched the Nile, the feluccas and the square white blocks of flats and humbler houses drop rapidly away below us.

The only other passengers besides us two 'lowest of the low' were a Dutch general and his ADC and the Governor-General of Tanganyika, General Sir Philip Mitchell, with an impressive entourage of senior officers. Bill and I were hardly noticed but we had the same superb service and delicious food and drink as the 'high heed-yins'. We dropped in to Wadi Halfa to refuel and I was very interested to watch the aircraft being refuelled by one of the 25 or so handsome fuelling tank launches that Shell had stationed all along the Empire routes to South Africa and Australia: when I first joined the Aviation Department in 1935 I did a few menial jobs for FM Ventris who was organising the preparation and positioning of these launches.

The overnight stop was at Khartoum where we stayed at the Grand Hotel in superb comfort. Next morning we were called very early for a takeoff before the day's real heat developed. On the way via Malakal and Juba the pilot flew very low over the bush in many places to that we could see the giraffes, elephants, antelopes and numerous other wildlife, a really fascinating experience.

At Kisumu Bill and I left the flying boat and the next day were flown in a German-made Junkers JU52 to Nairobi. Here we descended with a bump into our humble station in Royal Air Force life, being accommodated in a barrack hut with the cooks and butchers who were just about the roughest, coarsest lot that could be imagined. Three days later we finally arrived at RAF Station Kumalo at Bulawayo.

The principle of the Royal Air Force flying training at that time was that every pupil pilot should start off in the ranks, a sound idea because in due course we should become the 'kings' – after all the Service exists for and by flying – and it was important that we should have experienced the life of the ground crews to be able to respect them and their abilities on which we would, eventually, entirely depend.

At the start of our ITW course we were promoted to Leading Aircraftman (LAC) and attended our first pay parade. We were all lined up opposite the paying officer at his table and when the sergeant called out, for example, "LAC Deller" I had to shout "Sir, 178", advance to the table, salute, grab my money and return to the line. 178 was the last three figures of my service number (791178) and I soon learned that 'your last three' was – and doubtless still is – the common form of identification in the 'Other Ranks'; the greeting "Wot's yer name an' last three" was the usual form of address by the seemingly innumerable personages of superior status to one's own.

Shortly after our arrival we were interviewed and asked what sort of aircraft we wished to fly if we qualified eventually as pilots. When I was preparing to go to sea the previous year I was totally baffled, being the world's non-mathematician, by the complications of marine navigation so it was clear to me that I would only be able to cope in fighters where ground controllers would tell me which way to go. In consequence that was the choice I stated at the interview and which was noted in my records.

When we started lectures it was immediately obvious to me that, at the age of 27, I was going to have to work hard to compete with the others on the course, the majority of whom were youngsters not all that long out of school and thus accustomed to learning. Over seven weeks we studied such things as airmanship, theory of flight, meteorology, mathematics, engines and airframes (ie the structure of the aeroplane itself) and navigation and we learned to signal in Morse code. We also had periods of drill, learning to march smartly and salute correctly ("longest way up, shortest way down"). At that time the RAF wore pith helmets in hot climates and, all equipment being currently in short supply, the only pith helmet for my 6⅝ head was something about 9 – the only way I could peep out from under it was by pulling very tight on the string round the top of the leather headband as a result of which the thing sat on top of my head – every time I did a smart about-turn the helmet rotated on my head and remained pointing firmly in the original direction, causing much hilarity.

Scurrying from lecture to lecture and marching up and down the parade ground to the accompanying noise of twin-engined Oxford training aircraft taking off and flying round we all felt terribly earth-bound. All the pilots who were doing flying training at this same station wore a white armband and I remember sitting in the station cinema looking at the front rows of seats where the staff sat and, immediately behind them, the pilots with their armbands – they seemed like minor gods to me!

At this time I was beginning to discover that the RAF had simplified navigation to the point where it did not require a Wrangler to cope, the point being that whereas the sailor could happily take fifteen or twenty minutes entering his various tables and making calculations to find his position the airman in the same time would be 50 or 60 or more miles from a calculated position that would thus be almost meaningless by then. So it was that I began to perceive the possibility of going, not for fighters but – shooting for the stars! – for flying boats.

With the end of course exams completed we were dispersed to one or other of the Elementary Flying Training Schools (EFTS); in my case it was to 25 EFTS at Belvedere, just outside Salisbury (now Harare), where I was posted to No 17 course that was due to start shortly, flying De Havilland Tiger Moths. In the week or two before the course got under way I was able to see something of Salisbury, a very attractive town, more so than Bulawayo; it had a sizeable business centre and everywhere wide avenues with brilliant masses of jacaranda trees especially in the residential areas where there were innumerable really beautiful houses in a temperate climate style, very English – the Southern Rhodesian climate is wonderful as although the country is within only some six degrees (south) of the Equator most of it is around four thousand feet above sea level and thus not too hot by day and pleasantly cool by night. I made contact with the Shell General Manager, HE Kinloch, who, with his family and their friends, gave me, from the start, some of that superbly generous hospitality the Rhodesians lavished on many thousands of RAF personnel in all parts of that beautiful country. There were frequent invitations, also, to spend weekends on farms and at the many gold mines.

The day came when we were issued with our flying kit – Sidcot suit, helmet, goggles, furry boots and warm gloves (not used for another year!) – and at last it began to feel like the real thing. We had also been interviewed by the Station Commander and I had for the first time boldly stated my wish to go on to flying boats at which it was smartly pointed out to me that I was in a single-engine stream and that was that.

The day after getting our flying kit, 9 July, we reported to Flights, in my case A Flight, where I met my instructor Pilot Officer Duval, a slightly older man with a firm but relaxed manner which inspired confidence – badly needed at that moment when we were all fairly wound up at the thought of what in those days was still a considerable adventure and wondering how we would manage. However, there was not much time for introspection because we were no sooner settled in the crew room than instructors started calling out the names of their pupils and we started awkwardly scrambling into our parachute harness, desperate not to keep the bloke waiting, and then waddled out with him to the aircraft, the heavy parachute banging against the backs of our thighs with every step.

The Tiger Moth was a biplane with two open cockpits, one behind the other, in each of which was a full set of instruments, joystick, rudder pedals and throttle lever – the instructor sat in the front cockpit and spoke through an ordinary piece of hosepipe into one's earphones, he having a similar arrangement in the other direction: it sounded just as though he was talking a long distance away along a sewer and the result was rather uncertain communication, particularly in the nervous early days.

For the first flight the instructor did the engine starting drill and it was only after two or three further flights that Duval would call out "Deller, get the fan turning, will you" and I would go out and have the engine running ready for him. That first flight was a turmoil of experiences; the thrill of really being airborne in this tiny machine, with the roar and vibration of the engine and trying to hear Duval in the sewer telling me what he was doing and pointing out the landmarks and me trying at the same time to see where all the instruments and controls were situated in the cockpit – no time to admire the view or even fully react to the excitement of the first flight but rather the somewhat daunting feeling that this was it and a huge amount of effort, tension, hard grind and no small amount of luck would be my lot in the next weeks and months if I was to reach the goal that all of us so desperately desired – those pilot's wings on the left breast.

The next thing to learn was the effect of the controls: in normal flight quite small movements were needed in order to make the aircraft climb, descend, bank and turn and I found that it took a little while before my anxiety to do the right thing allowed me to relax and handle the controls lightly. Gradually the whole performance began to be a bit more natural as, with Duval keeping up a running commentary (often not too flattering!), we practised for hour after hour taking off into the wind, flying straight and level – so difficult; while looking at the compass to see whether I was straight on course the noise of the airflow would change – "Watch your airspeed, the nose is too high!" – back on the level the aircraft started to veer gently to the left – "Your left wing's dropping, keep her level!" – things soon got a little better – "Watch out for other aircraft, don't keep your head in the cockpit!" This last is a most salutary warning because it is a curious and universal fact, both at sea and in the air, that although sea room and airspace appear limitless, if two ships or aircraft are even only vaguely in the same area there seems almost invariably to be some malign influence drawing them together, even to the extent of actual collision.

Then it was the landing, by far the most difficult part. Having checked the exact spot where one was to land one would get the aircraft in position, downwind from the airfield at about a thousand feet, turn in towards the airfield, set it at the right approach speed and rate of descent, keep it coming on down, with a touch of engine if the speed started to drop or a little nose-up if going too fast, then at about 100-150 feet, by means of stereoscopic vision, co-ordinate one's approach to earth with a gradual easing-up of the nose (slight backward pressure on the control column or joystick or just stick) thus losing speed so that the aircraft reaches stalling speed (at which there is no longer sufficient lift to support the aircraft) at the exact moment that the earth is contacted, the nose having been raised just high enough to ensure that the wheels and the tailskid touch the ground together – a 'three-point touch-down'; the tailskid, scraping along the ground, was the only form of braking. Insufficiently effective stereoscopic vision, preventing that essential judgment of the rate at which the ground is approaching, was the prime cause of many aspiring pilots' failing. My own great weakness was, always, a tendency to land with the tail too high which almost always produced a bounce – or several! This was the cause of a scary moment a little later.

This drill – take off, climb to 1000 feet, turn left across wind then downwind to the right point for the turn, again to the left, across wind, start the descent then turn left again on the approach path, continue the descent and land – known as circuits and landings or more generally, 'circuits and bumps', was the staple activity of those first few hours. We were all absolutely desperate to be able to fly and even at night one often heard someone – sometimes more than one – going through the drill in their sleep.

So as to get us used to handling the aircraft more freely we were introduced early on to aerobatics and spinning. The latter is vital training for every pilot; if an aircraft is allowed to stall in flight it will in most cases go into a spin – one wing or the other will drop sharply and the aircraft will turn over into a steep spiral dive which requires a special drill, varying slightly according to the type of aircraft, using control column and rudder in the right sequence, to cause the machine to straighten up and come out of its dive. (It must be stressed such a procedure would never be adopted with, or tolerated by, a heavy aircraft.) In order to induce the spin one throttled the engine back, held the nose firmly up while everything went quiet, speed dropped off steadily and there was a horrible feeling that the aeroplane would drop away from under one; then at the stall, over she would go and one was looking straight down at the earth as it spun round and round and got rapidly nearer and nearer. Personally, I never entirely got over the sinking feeling at the stall and the sigh of relief when the aircraft came out of the spin.

Aerobatics, on the other hand, were a slightly nerve-tingling experience when first demonstrated by the instructor and tended to need a deep breath when one tried the tricks for the first time solo. In 'looping the loop' the drill was to dive fairly steeply at full throttle until the correct speed was reached, then pull firmly back on the stick (but not so hard as to produce a high-speed stall) while the aeroplane climbed smartly to the vertical – the outlook being first the horizon then empty sky – then over the top of the loop, upside down with bits of rubbish, dust etc., from the bottom of the cockpit falling past one's face, starting the dive, still upside down and throttling back to avoid over-speeding the engine, then spotting the horizon and the earth that seemed to arrive within one's vision like a curtain falling before finally, stick still held back, gently pull out of the dive, becoming right way up and, if the loop had been perfectly executed, feeling a small bump as the aeroplane hit the disturbance from the slipstream at the point where the climb was started – great fun.

A slow roll was rather more difficult. To start with it was vital to have one's Sutton harness pulled really tight – in the loop the centrifugal force at the top of the loop kept one firmly in the seat but, in the slow roll, when inverted one was hanging on the harness with nothing underneath but the earth far, far below and if the harness was too loose one could, in the worst case, find one's feet and hands out of reach of the rudder bar and stick and thus be unable to right the aircraft, which could be very dangerous. The big trick in rolling was to keep the nose pointing always at the horizon: in a roll to the left one held the stick over to the left and as the aeroplane rolled round one had to mix the functions of the stick and rudder to keep the nose on the horizon – for instance, a quarter of the way round the rudder had to be used to keep the nose up while the stick was used to steer the thing, then half-way round and upside down the nose had to be kept up by pushing the stick forward (instead of the normal way, backwards), while still keeping it hard over to the left. Eventually with luck, one would find oneself, with intense surprise and delight, right way up and still pointing to the same spot on the horizon.

The real joy was to link these manoeuvres. For example, one might do a slow roll and, on coming out level again, pull up the nose to about vertical and, as airspeed dropped off until the aeroplane was just about to stall, kick on the left rudder so that the machine would fall away to the left (a 'stall turn' or 'Immelmann turn') in a dive that would give sufficient speed to pull up into a loop, then at the bottom go straight into another loop and at the top do a half roll to finish up straight and level again. If it worked well one had an exhilarating feeling that the whole sky was one's playground. But it was vitally important to keep a look out all the time for other aircraft and to bear in mind that in a succession of loops there was always a progressive loss of altitude so that, as happened on my course much later on, the last loop was indeed the last and not much was left to pick up.

All these activities, some boring, some exciting, were of course initially experienced with our instructors and the overriding goal of everyone, pupils and instructors, was to achieve first solo – the first time one actually piloted the aeroplane all by oneself. By the time we had started to accumulate five or six hours dual instruction one or two of the brightest began to go solo; this increased the already acute state of anxiety in the rest of us to do the same. I was plodding on, still doing quite well some days, then losing it again as everyone did. Duval was a great support and did not, like some instructors, rant and rave when the wretched pupil did the same stupid thing for the n'th time. Finally, after 9 hours 45 minutes total dual instruction I had really got it and Duval wanted me to have a pre-solo test (a routine check with another instructor who observed but did not instruct) but the sacred weekend break loomed and there was no time. However, on the following Monday a twenty minute check flight with Duval showed – to our intense relief – that I had not lost it, so Sergeant Chaldecott took me up for a thirty minute check including two good landings. As I taxied in he said I could go solo – he climbed out, removed the stick from the front cockpit and waved me off. After ten hours and thirty-five minutes (including the thirty minute test) there I was, taxying out in sole control, turning into wind then stopping to check that all was clear on the ground and up above. A very deep breath, throttle firmly pushed to fully open, then bounding across the grass with increasing speed, a gentle pull back on the stick and I was off, climbing away independently into the blue Rhodesian sky – first solo! Then a swift descent from euphoria to concentrate on the approach and landing – aircraft nicely positioned at a thousand feet downwind from the airfield, pointed accurately into wind as indicated by the orange windsock on the far boundary, gently descending at a steady airspeed, there's the edge of the airfield, rushing under the aeroplane about 30 feet below, gently ease the stick back, back, back, speed dropping off, keep the stick back with nose not too high, then a firm bump, wheels and tailskid together, the aeroplane rumbling and shuddering to a stop – the best landing I would ever do in a Tiger Moth!

That was the start of real flying training in the sense that, with a mixture of dual and solo, we were really learning to pilot the aeroplane freely around in the sky while endlessly polishing up our steep turns, climbing turns, powered approach and landing, glide approach and landing, forced landings and so on as well as aerobatics and low flying – this last was particular fun as there were large uninhabited areas of thin, low bush, mainly level, where we could hurtle along at the Tiger Moth's blistering speed of about 90 miles per hour which looked very fast at a height of some 30 to 40 feet.

One particular exercise, which the instructor hated and I realised why, was the important one of restarting the engine in flight (assuming, in real life, that it had stopped for some fairly minor cause that did not put it totally out of action). Understandably it was practised – once only! – with an instructor who, having selected a suitable field for a forced landing in case the engine did not restart, climbed to a safe height, throttled back the engine, held the nose up and switched off the ignition whereupon the propeller stopped turning and there was a horrible silence as the aeroplane hung in the air; then it was put into the steepest possible dive and, when speed had really built up and the earth seemed remarkably near, the aircraft was heaved sharply out of the dive, the ignition being switched on at the same time, and – nothing! We were still high up so, down into the dive again, holding it until the aircraft was shuddering with the speed, then sharply pull out and, with a jerk, the propeller suddenly turned and the engine burst into life – the sense of relief was very marked.

One of the more enjoyable exercises was cross-country flying to practise navigation and map reading. The Rhodesian landscape was not cluttered up with innumerable landmarks as it is in Europe and with the generally superb visibility it was not unduly difficult to find one's way even though handling a map and jotting down one's log in the breezy open cockpit while at the same time checking the compass course and flying the aeroplane made for a busy time. One of the best trips was to the forced landing ground at Hunyani; this was the private landing ground of a delightful farming family called Davies and the exercise was to carry out an actual forced landing drill after which one taxied – with all the assurance of one's twenty-odd hours solo flying – up to the farmhouse to be welcomed and given a delicious tea. After a little chat one climbed back into the aircraft, one of the family swung the propeller and so off home with an agreeable feeling of having achieved some form of graduation as a pilot.

On returning from another cross-country flight, instead of landing dead into wind, I carelessly touched down at about ten degrees off the wind to the left; I had also, as so often, landed with the tail too high so the aeroplane bounced and bounced and bounced, each time being carried by the wind more and more to the left while, the tailskid not having contacted the ground, the speed remained quite high. Within seconds I was bouncing with some velocity straight towards one of the maintenance hangars and the Chief Flying Instructor's office and at that moment I made the first one of two absolutely split-second decisions in my flying career that on both occasions saved my life and those of many others. I banged the throttle fully open, dragged the trusty Tiger Moth off the ground in a steep turn to the left and flew between two hangars at about 20 feet, then up and over the roofs of the huts just behind the hangars, in which part of the course were having lectures; apparently they all rushed out to see what had happened, particularly as there were some power cables just behind the huts and I have no idea to this day whether I flew under them or over them. An interview with Duval and the Flight Commander followed after I managed a good landing and returned one unexpectedly intact Tiger Moth to the flight's complement. I thought – and showed it – that I would be grounded, my longed-for flying career finished, but I was assured that I need not look as if I was about to be hanged but that I must firstly watch the windsock and secondly get that tail down on landing.

Near the end of the course we did our first night flying, quite a dramatic experience, swooping along the line of goose-neck flares (cans, filled with paraffin, with a long spout into which cotton waste or some such was stuffed and set light to) then soaring into the blackness of the night sky and turning immediately to flying the aeroplane on instruments since at night there is of course little or nothing in the way of external references by which to judge what the machine is doing. The standard RAF blind-flying panel consisted of six instruments, including airspeed indicator and altimeter and we had a great deal of training in flying entirely by the indications of these and the compass, firmly disregarding the often misleading physical sensations; in the air this was done, accompanied by another pilot, by pulling a folding hood over one's head so that nothing outside the cockpit was visible, a miserable and confusing experience since one had to battle constantly to convince oneself that the instruments were telling the truth and that, though it felt like it, one was not about to turn upside down with nil airspeed. On the ground the blind-flying training was done in a Link Trainer, a little mock aeroplane with just a totally-enclosed cockpit containing stick, rudder and throttle control and the blind-flying panel, the whole thing mounted on bellows so that it could follow the commands of the controls by turning, banking and pitching forward or backward (descending or climbing). It was moderately realistic and by the time one had undergone thirty minutes of exercises directed by the instructor who was sitting outside and watching the plot of one's actions and errors, the atmosphere inside was like a Turkish bath. It is said that a pilot somewhere in England was the only man to have been shot down in a Link Trainer; he was in the middle of an exercise when the station was attacked by an Me109 fighter which put a bullet through the Trainer's bellows – these promptly collapsed with a rude noise and deposited the little aeroplane on its foundation – probably an apocryphal tale but too good to miss.

Flying round over Salisbury at night, with its pattern of bright lights that amazed most of the fellows on the course just out from blacked-out Britain, was very enjoyable with the cool night air blowing away the heat of the day. The landing, too, was a minor drama the first once or twice, coming down and down towards the string of flares and then, in the last few feet, emerging into the brilliant illumination from the big portable floodlight. Unfortunately shortage of time prevented us from going solo which was a great disappointment.

By this time we were enjoying our last hour or two of Tiger Moth flying. We had a selection interview, with the Chief Ground Instructor, for commissions and then settled down to the exams in the ground subjects; these lasted two days and were followed by a monumental end-of-course party with all the instructors, from which we had by no means recovered, before setting off for two days leave prior to moving on to the next stage – Service Flying Training School (SFTS).

Forty-eight hours' generous Rhodesian hospitality had not prepared us for the shock of learning, on our return to the station, that almost the whole course had failed the navigation exam. It was completely inexplicable and apparently caused ructions at Rhodesia Air Training Group headquarters. Notwithstanding we were shipped off ignominiously back to the ITW at Bulawayo that we had left a month and a half earlier and joined a considerable number of others from the other two EFTSs who had similarly failed. After two weeks further navigation lectures we re-sat the exam and all passed, with immense relief. Though we did not know it, this was but our first experience of being b***ered about by the service.

Into long trousers

Back in Salisbury we prepared to move to one of the SFTSs, in my case a single-engine school, No 20 SFTS, at Cranborne, a pleasant suburb on the other side of Salisbury from Belvedere, where we were to fly Harvards. Under RAF regulations service aircraft could not be flown by anyone under the rank of sergeant, so while we were at EFTS we LACs were given our white armbands but only as Acting Sergeants Unpaid; as such we lived in the airmen's mess and hurried to meals grasping our precious enamel mug and knife, fork and spoon which we washed up afterwards in huge baths of hot water heated by wood – even now the smell of wood-smoke still recalls the vision of a jostling crowd of airmen dunking their 'irons' in the murky water and then tucking them into their breast pockets.

Once at SFTS we became full sergeants and started to enjoy the relative comforts of the Sergeants Mess. We were interviewed by a panel consisting of the Group Captain commanding the station and three other senior officers. I produced my customary surprise by stating that I wished to fly flying boats and was greeted by a quite polite reminder that I was at a fighter school. Meanwhile I got the camp tailor to sew my white sergeant's stripes onto my shirts – just in time, in fact, to be told that I had been selected as an officer-cadet and was to remove my stripes, have a thin blue line sewn onto my white armband and move into the Officers Mess. I lost no time in shifting my kit into my new bedroom which I was to share, very happily, with another trainee pilot, John Huggins, son of the Prime Minister of Southern Rhodesia, Sir Godfrey Huggins.

Sir Godfrey was quite a character. He was one of the small band of pioneers who had struggled up from the coast through hundreds of miles of rough country at the end of last century and in about 1900 had planted the Union flag on the spot where the capital city Salisbury was to be established – they were some of the very first Europeans to penetrate to the land of the Matabele and the

Mashona (these days called Ndebele and Shona respectively). Sir Godfrey was very deaf and was in the habit of protecting himself from hostile debate in the House by simply turning off his hearing aid. He was a very astute politician and succeeded, against all odds, in procuring Dominion status for Southern Rhodesia (as it was originally named in a compliment to the great pioneer African developer, Cecil Rhodes). He was also a generous host and I was fortunate to join many tennis parties at his beautiful home.

It was great being in the mess after the many months of somewhat basic comfort in barrack rooms and good food but rather roughly served and eaten. John and I had a very agreeable room boy, Inchenga, who did all our chores, laundry, button-polishing, everything, and without being told. The mess itself was very comfortable and spacious with good food well served, even a cold table!

A few days before this we had heard, to our enormous relief, that we had all passed the re-set navigation exam and were thus clear to start our SFTS course, flying the North American Aviation Harvard, a very smart-looking low-wing monoplane with an enclosed cockpit and a 550 horsepower Pratt and Whitney Wasp engine. It was altogether a tremendous step from the much-loved Tiger Moth; with a retractable undercarriage, brakes, a controllable pitch propeller (airscrew) and equipment for bombing and gunnery (one fixed forward-firing machine gun in the starboard wing) it was an entirely different animal and the first flight was very exciting as an introduction to real 'grown-up' flying.

Unlike the Tiger Moth the instructor sat in the rear seat and being seated, as pupil, in the front seat gave one from the start a much greater feeling of being in control, even under dual instruction. My instructor, Flight Sergeant Mace, agreeable but firm, suited me well – my second bit of luck in that department. At first the cockpit was a bewildering mass of instruments, levers, gauges and so on but the layout was logical and it was not hard to learn where everything was and what it did.

The takeoff, at first, was quite electrifying: on opening the throttle fully one could feel every one of those 550 horses and the aircraft really leapt very powerfully into the air and things happened quickly – undercarriage to be raised, then flaps up while checking the correct airspeed for climbing and at the same time watching for other aircraft on the circuit. The landing also was more rapid – throttle back, flaps down, check airspeed, undercarriage down then quite a steep angle of descent so that the ground approached very smartly and the final backward movement of the stick, to settle the machine down in a three-point landing, had to be steady as well as prompt; a sharp pull back caused the aircraft to stall and the original Harvards with which we started, having round wing tips, would drop the right wing which then scraped along the ground, if you were lucky, or else dug in and spun the aircraft round (a 'ground loop'), damaging the undercarriage as well, if nothing worse.

These wing tips, which were removable, were also, with wartime shortages, hard to get, so every one damaged cost the clumsy pupil a fine of two shillings and sixpence (25p, but worth a lot more then). As with the Tiger Moth, one of our first exercises was dealing with the stall. This was even more unpleasant than with the Tiger because, to induce it, after throttling the engine right back one had to hold the heavy nose up at quite a high angle, with the aircraft hanging uncomfortably in the air, and then, with only a second's warning in the form of shuddering, the right wing – normally – would suddenly drop and the aircraft would go into a spin unless instantly checked, which there was not always time to do; indeed, so sharp was the stall that, even though one was fully prepared, one invariably got one's head banged hard on the side of the cockpit canopy as the aeroplane rolled over. Shortly after we started our course the station began to get supplies of some neat square wing tips, that had been developed by the RAF at Boscombe Down experimental establishment to improve the stall, and when these replaced the round wing tips the Harvard was no longer a vicious machine though it still called for careful handling, as was necessary in order to prepare us for flying much more demanding aircraft on squadrons later on.

After four days of the normal diet of 'circuits and bumps' I went solo – in 5 hours 40 minutes, fairly average. The excitement and satisfaction of being able to take off and roam the skies – within the limits of the exercises written down in the authorisation book – but entirely on my own was something that is hard to put into words, so agile and powerful did the machine feel, with the blue sky above and all around. The rainy season was approaching and on many days quite large numbers of big rounded clouds developed, often rising to four or five thousand feet, and with my newly acquired freedom of the skies I had tremendous fun practising medium and steep turns, diving and climbing round those great white heaps. There was, however, much more to the course than this and low flying, stalling and spinning, taking-off and landing across wind, practice forced landings, formation flying and aerobatics – both dual and solo – alternated with intensive work in the classrooms on navigation, armaments, signals, meteorology and airmanship.

Formation flying was amusing and not nearly as difficult as might be imagined; the trick was to watch very closely the aircraft on which one was 'formating', making small corrections by rudder, ailerons and elevators and slight movements of the throttle, all done instantly as soon as the slightest deviation was perceived – the consequence of losing one's place in the formation was a lot of fairly delicate manoeuvring to get back on station. It was excellent training in precision flying and if well done was very satisfying.

With the much greater engine power compared with the Tiger Moth's 130 horsepower the Harvard was much more exciting in aerobatics although at the necessarily higher speeds the controls became fairly heavy and in the slow roll the heavy engine made it a bit difficult to keep the nose on the horizon – mine nearly always turned into barrel rolls, a term that is self-descriptive! Loops also required considerably higher speeds and there was a marked loss of height between each loop if one was doing a succession of them. As we were all frequently entertained by the many generous families in and near Salisbury there was a great temptation, with our shiny new confidence as pilots, to go and 'shoot up' their houses doing loops, high speed low passes or steep turns round the house at low level – a hundred feet or less. It was, rightly, strictly forbidden but many fell for the temptation; on the next course to mine a young Rhodesian found himself still going straight down on the last part of a second or third consecutive loop as he hit the ground at some two hundred miles an hour – little remained apart from a pair of shoes and a bit of mess on the engine six feet down in the earth. Steep turns low down were also very dangerous and in several instances fatal; either the aeroplane was yanked into the turn too sharply at high speed, causing it to stall and spin in or, while gazing at the admiring throng below, the pilot let the speed drop off – easy to do in a steep turn – and ran out of altitude.

Other less drastic ways of damaging aeroplanes abounded. The undercarriage lever, which was moved backwards immediately after takeoff to raise the undercarriage, was close to, and rather similar to, the mixture control lever; once or twice on most courses a pilot would mistakenly grab the mixture control, pull it smartly back into full weak mixture, thereby stopping the engine and causing the aircraft to crash-land in the sewage farm next door to the airfield. Damage all round was minimal but apparently the smell was awful.

Parallel with ourselves a number of larky Greek Air Force officers were also doing a similar course. Their speciality was landing with the undercarriage up, scratching the aircraft's belly and bending the airscrew blades right round the engine. To obviate such a happening there was a very loud horn in the cockpit which went off if the throttle was closed without the undercarriage being lowered: watching on the ground one could hear the horn clearly from a mile away as yet another of the Greeks blithely descended to his belly flop.

Night flying in the Harvard was quite straightforward and once one had gone solo there was often time between circuits to fly around a bit as long as one got in the authorised number of landings in the time allocated. After dark the air was cool and balmy and it was a glorious sensation to sit in shirtsleeves with the canopy fully open roaming around in the black night sky, entirely alone and master of the elements. Inevitably there was the temptation to exploit this feeling of power and two or three times, when I spotted a car moving along a road down below, I switched on the powerful landing light and dived down out of the night aiming the light fully at the car, pulling out of the dive at a couple of hundred feet – this must have added to the impression because the Harvard had no reduction gear between engine and airscrew so the latter turned very fast and on pulling out of a dive made a terrific noise like tearing acres of calico. Not perhaps the friendliest of things to do but high spirits were, and are, an important ingredient in a military pilot's make-up, albeit needing to be under proper control.

The rainy season was by now almost with us and more and more of the huge tropical thunder clouds put in an appearance. One evening, in particular, remains in my memory; in the hope of getting in some night flying before the storms broke we had started early and the experience of flying round in the dusk with those great clouds visible all about and huge flashes of lightning shooting from them on all sides was a most dramatic and beautiful one.

By daylight, too, those big storms could cause trouble: when they were close the winds blew strongly from every quarter every few seconds and on one occasion, when I was trying to land in these conditions, the first attempt failed so I went round again and after touching down the winds almost made the aeroplane dance and it could be controlled only by a combination of little bursts of engine and vigorous work with the rudder, as a result of which I finished up in the station's football field, but undamaged.

On another occasion I was coming in to land just after a heavy storm had passed and the entire airfield was a huge sheet of glassy-smooth water. In those conditions it is exceedingly difficult to judge one's height in the last fifteen or twenty feet of the approach: I was still on the descent path when I suddenly realised I was only two or three feet above the surface so pulled sharply back on the stick – too sharply because the aeroplane, which still had the round wing tips, instantly stalled and dropped the right wing-tip on to the watery ground. A quick burst of engine and opposite rudder straightened the aeroplane up and fortunately the layer of water had saved the wing tip from damage and me from a two-and-sixpence fine. But I always thereafter bore in mind the danger of misjudging height when landing on glassy water – a lesson I once carelessly ignored, much later, with what could have been fatal consequences.

By now we were nearing the end of the first part of the course (Initial Training Squadron) and wings exams were looming after which, if we passed, we would be fully fledged pilots – two wings on the left breast! – and ready for the final part in the Advanced Training Squadron (ATS). At this time I had learned that each of the two single-engine schools was normally allocated a place on No 1 School of General Reconnaissance at George in Cape Province, South Africa; the course there was a special preparation for service in Coastal Command in the UK – where the flying boats operated! A condition was a high pass in the navigation papers in the wings exams so I applied for this coveted place and set myself to do my best in the navigation work. One other pilot also applied and it was arranged that if we both got high marks there would be a 'run-off' in the form of a further, more advanced, navigation exam.

In the event I passed out top of the course in the wings exams and managed 91% in navigation; the other pilot also did well so we both sat the extra navigation exam, in a state of high tension. Fortunately the marking was done quickly and I won, so it was with much glee that I set off forthwith for five days' wings leave at the Victoria Falls with several of the others.

Five days of moderate pampering in the Victoria Falls Hotel were a tonic after the hard work and stress of the course, stress because, apart from the effort of learning to preserve one's life in the unnatural habitat of the air, there was the drive not only to do well but, most basically, to avoid the fate that was perpetually waiting just offstage of being found unsuitable as a pilot for some reason that could show up unforeseen at virtually any stage of the course.

Although the dry season had only recently ended and the Zambesi was still low, the Falls were nevertheless a stunning and beautiful sight; the majestic sweep of the great waters to the edge and the plunge in huge clouds of perpetual spray to the bottom of the immense gorge surely were nature at its mightiest and induced a profound sense of awe. For me this was specially acute because many years before, when I was a boy, I had seen a wonderful and very moving film of Livingstone's life in which the Falls, of course, seemed of almost mystical significance; to stand there, deep in Africa, and think back to that courageous man and his journeying through the perils of the unknown in this dark and strange continent was an unforgettably emotional experience.

The Falls, if I am not mistaken, were in Northern Rhodesia (now Zambia) and we crossed over the Livingstone Bridge back into Southern Rhodesia to spend a day in the Livingstone game reserve where we were able to walk about, with a degree of circumspection, among the kudu buck, eland, zebras, elephants and giraffes; the giraffes, we were told, had to be watched because they could suddenly charge and inflict severe injuries by kicking forwards with their front legs. Safely on our way back to the hotel we stopped on the Livingstone Bridge to lean on the parapet and gaze down about 120 feet at the huge rush of water from the falls just two or three hundred yards up the gorge. While we were thus absorbed the native sentry at one end of this great steel bridge came to attention to start his patrol; the African soldier was, and doubtless still is, very proud of his calling and its rituals and drills and this fellow produced the desired stamp by leaping about a foot in the air and landing in his big boots with such a resounding, clanging, crash on the steel roadway that we had the momentary impression of being about to plunge into the foaming waters far below – it really shook us.

Back at Cranborne we moved into the Advanced Training Squadron for the final part of our flying training, still on Harvards. My instructor was a Flight Lieutenant Leach, very congenial and quite a lad in his way; he longed to get away from instructing and on to operational flying and in desperation reinforced his numerous pleas for a posting by various heinous acts such as low flying between the hangars and streaking at low level over residential areas of Salisbury with the airscrew in fine pitch, producing the notorious Harvard whanging calico-tearing noise. I don't know whether he ever succeeded.

When doing low flying under dual instruction the practice was for the instructor to sit in the front seat instead of behind the pupil as was normal. The low-flying area was a vast flat plain sparsely covered with scrubby bushes and trees only some 15 or 20 feet high. Leach would start off by saying "When I look out of the cockpit I want to see the tops of the trees just passing the wing tips." He would then repeat "lower, go lower" as we flashed over the very near earth and my sole consolation was that he was in a good position up front to see any slightly bigger tree in our way – until he suddenly lowered his seat to the bottom of the cockpit where he could not even see ahead over the instrument panel but was still saying "lower, go lower"!

We also continued to practise formation flying – solo by now – but were also introduced to more advanced activities such as mock attacks on other aircraft, air-to-ground firing and high-dive bombing. For the practice firing there were targets set up at about a thirty-degree angle, in an uninhabited area of land well away from town and we dived down at a fairly shallow angle, aiming through the reflector gun-sight mounted behind the lower part of the windscreen, and at the correct distance pressed that inviting button on the control column to fire some 200 rounds from the single machine gun and then pulled up smartly; it was very easy while concentrating on one's aim to fail to realise how dangerously low one was getting. Even with the greatest care and application it was surprisingly difficult to get even a few shots on the target.

The real excitement, though, was high-dive bombing. The aeroplane was taken to three thousand feet and was then rolled over into a dive that was as near as possible to vertical. Speed built up very rapidly and a short but highly concentrated period of activity involved aiming the machine directly at the ground target, watching the altimeter unwind at breakneck speed until 1000 feet at which point one pressed the bomb release button to drop the small practice bomb and, simultaneously, started pulling out of the dive which had by then reached down to only some 500-600 feet and up to about 300 miles per hour; this had to be done with appropriate rapidity but not so fast as to produce the Harvard's nasty high-speed stall and it always caused a momentary blackout through the powerful G-force. The normal exercise was to drop eight bombs and by the time one had gone through this fairly tense performance eight times one experienced quite a degree of fatigue. The only fatality occurred when a pupil was in the middle of his dive and a bird hit the landing light in the leading edge of the port wing; at such high speed the light was forced in, and the in-rushing air blew the whole wing apart and the aircraft went 'straight in'.

The end of the course came just before Christmas, with many farewell parties given by our numerous kind Rhodesian hosts. As fully fledged pilots we celebrated the finish of our almost nine months marathon with, in my case, a total of 178 hours 30 minutes flying and a final assessment as 'above average' – the RAF uses four levels of assessment: below average, average, above average and exceptional. I wondered, would I ever achieve that final accolade? Meanwhile there had been some delay in the formal announcement of our commissions, but, as they had been confirmed to us in person I decided not to wait around, so emerged as a shiny new Pilot Officer with one half-stripe – my third commission, or fourth if having a Secret Service code identification can be considered to be a commission.

On 21 December came the departure for the GR School at George. I joined all those from the other flying schools who were to take the course and met a number of friends I had known at earlier stages of our training. Salisbury station was packed with those who were going to George, and others who were posted elsewhere, and all the numerous friends we had made among the people of Salisbury; I was being seen off by the Prime Minister and Mrs Huggins, the Kinlochs, Crawfords and many others, some of whom had come in from outlying farms and mines to see off others as well. It was all very cheerful, hilarious even, but with a strong undercurrent of sadness, as we left behind so many very kind people and they, I think, may well have wondered how many of our number would survive the operations in which we were moving on to participate.

Early the following morning we reached Bulawayo where we had four hours to do some shopping and look up old haunts – it seemed a lifetime since we were taking our first ground-borne steps towards becoming what we now were, competent Royal Air Force pilots. It was one of those backward glances in life that give one a feeling of elation but, at the same time, of humility bearing in mind the huge variety of pitfalls on the way.

Later in the morning the train departed again, pulled by a magnificent Garratt locomotive, literally two engines in one. The scenery was rather dull bush but we had many cheerful parties that livened things up. At one stage a twin-engined Oxford training aeroplane flew very low alongside the train and then proceeded to 'shoot it up', no doubt as a farewell to some friends on the train. Overnight we travelled at a sedate pace through Northern Transvaal and awoke next morning to very pleasant scenery on the way to Johannesburg. Unfortunately there was only a twenty minute stop in Johannesburg so all we could do was gaze briefly at the impressive skyscrapers and other prosperous-looking buildings in the first major city I had seen since leaving Cairo back in April. I still remember the sight of beautiful green, cultivated countryside in the evening sunshine, but the whole of the next day, by contrast, we plodded through the Great Karoo desert, the monotony only slightly relieved by distant views of blue hills and mountains – the Drakensberg.

At last, at 0510 on Christmas Day(!) we arrived at George. What we saw of it on the coach journey from the station to the camp was quite a surprise; very many of the buildings and houses were Georgian, totally unlike the colonial styles to which we had become accustomed, and there was greenery and pretty gardens everywhere. The town of George had in fact been established, I believe around the end of the eighteenth century, to house George III's mistresses, their households and other hangers-on whose presence in England was an embarrassment to the monarch.

Visions of Coastal Command – at last

No 1 School of General Reconnaissance had originally inhabited the RAF station at Thorney Island, near Portsmouth, but it had obviously become too vulnerable once the Germans were established in France and it was therefore removed, lock, stock and barrel, to South Africa. The airfield was grass, situated above some substantial cliffs – very convenient as it turned out – so our aircraft took off straight out to sea and the scenario was thus very similar to what we should expect at an operational Coastal Command station. One aspect of this was that, with no initial tracking over land where the first few minutes of navigation would be by map reading, we were immediately over the sea and immediately on to dead reckoning, the only form of navigation, apart from astronomical navigation, that we would use over the sea operationally in the absence, for obvious reasons, of any radio aids.

Dead reckoning is navigating by use of a compass, a watch and a means of ascertaining the wind speed and direction or, in the case of marine navigation, the speed and direction of any currents; if the heavens are visible it can be backed up by astronavigation using a sextant. Over the open sea the navigator uses an Admiralty chart which has nothing on it, except lines of latitude and longitude, a compass rose, a scale of nautical miles up the side and lines of magnetic variation. He plots a line leading to his objective, a convoy or whatever, which is his track and has a compass bearing; the wind will tend to blow him to one side or the other of his track or, if dead ahead or dead astern, will increase or decrease his ground speed. In the former case he must plot a course that will get him to his objective in spite of the wind, and the compass bearing of that is the actual compass course the pilot will fly – in the latter case the compass bearing of track and course will be the same but the estimated time of arrival will be either earlier or later than that calculated using only the distance as measured along his track and the airspeed of the aircraft, uninfluenced by the wind; depending on the strength and direction of the wind the speed of the aircraft over the ground, the ground speed, will be either greater or less than the speed of the aircraft through the air, the airspeed, unless of course there is no wind. Normally the wind changes frequently and for accurate navigation the navigator must check the wind regularly and amend the pilot's compass course accordingly. The pilot's part in all this is absolutely crucial. He must fly an accurate compass course at the exact airspeed and the exact altitude used by the navigator in his calculations; an error of one degree (1°) in the compass course flown could lead to a significant error in one's landfall if left uncorrected during a long flight.

The course consisted of ground instruction in advanced navigation, advanced meteorology, radio procedure, radio direction-finding, practical reconnaissance techniques, aerial photography and ship recognition, together with a large number of day and night navigation exercises, in which one was the sole navigator, a twitchy business. It was made even more nerve-wracking at the start because, in order to accustom us to coping with a 'scramble' we were given just five minutes after the briefing to collect our heavy bag with charts, almanacs and instruments including sextant, get ourselves out to the waiting aircraft, chart and instruments out, first track plotted, met wind (ie as forecast by the met people, not observed) applied and course handed to the pilot who had by then already taken off.

It was all high-powered stuff and the lecturers were almost all operational pilots on rest – interesting for us new boys, our first contact with the men who had actually 'done the business'. There were one or two civilian specialists also – the met lecturer was one of the top people from the government Meteorological Office in the UK. It was fascinating work and one of the most absorbing subjects, to me, was ship recognition; the school had a collection of solid models of warships of a scale such that when they were placed on the lecture room platform and viewed in silhouette from towards the back of the room, the effect was exactly as if the real ships were being viewed from a distance of seven miles. We had to learn the distinguishing features of every battleship, battle cruiser, aircraft carrier, cruiser class and destroyer nationality in the British, American, German, French, Italian, Russian and Japanese navies. In addition we learned about the various cruising dispositions of different fleets so that if, during a reconnaissance, we came out of a cloud and spotted three cruisers in line abreast we would know that they were probably part of the A-K line screening force of battleships and attendant lesser units which we would have to identify by name so as to enable our own fleet to know the size of guns and the speed capabilities of the ships they were to face if they could be brought to battle. The responsibility on an aircraft captain in such a circumstance was tremendous; on the accuracy of his identification could depend whether the admiral would put to sea and what the composition of his fleet should be. A case in point was the Battle of Matapan on 28 March 1941. It was known that an Italian fleet of unknown strength was at sea somewhere to the east of southern Italy and a Sunderland flying boat of No 230 Squadron, based at Alexandria, spotted part of an Italian destroyer screen and, shortly after, the whole fleet. On this sighting report Admiral Cunningham (later Viscount Cunningham of Hindhope) put to sea from Alexandria and, guided by the aircraft's regular reports of the enemy fleet's position, course and speed, engaged the Italians and inflicted such heavy damage on them that they never again ventured out from their home base. The Navy brass was never entirely happy that a mere junior RAF officer or even a sergeant pilot could call an admiral out to sea with his fleet but they made a great effort to reconcile themselves to the fact, although they much preferred that the junior officer should be a naval one, in the Fleet Air Arm of course.

The aircraft in which we flew the navigation exercises was the Avro Anson, a twin-engined machine equipped for two pilots, a navigator and a wireless operator; the navigator doubled as bomb-aimer and the wireless operator was also the gunner, when necessary. It was a prewar type, dating from the early 'thirties, designed largely for an anti-submarine role in which its limited range and small bomb-carrying capacity rendered it somewhat ineffectual in practice. In an age when land aircraft had fixed undercarriages hanging in the wind the Anson was one of the very first British aircraft whose undercarriage retracted into the wings after take off, thus greatly reducing drag. Although it was later mechanised, in the early version like those at George it was raised and lowered by some one hundred and thirty turns of a small handle placed at a strange angle right down on the floor on the left side of the second pilot's seat; the undercarriage itself was heavy and the airflow tended to hold it down also, so the effort involved by a necessarily contorted body during some three or four minutes of continuous cranking can be imagined. As there was no second pilot the job generally fell to the unfortunate wireless operator, with the pilot urging him to get the thing up quickly so that the very sluggish old 'Annie' would climb a little more smartly.

One of the bugbears of all wartime aircraft operating was shortage of spares, particularly in a non-operational area such as we were in. At one stage a particular problem developed with the Anson's radial engines in which the seven cylinders were arranged in a circle around the central crankshaft and propeller shaft. The exhaust from all the cylinders was collected in a pipe, forming a ring at the rear of the engine and this started to burn out in all the aircraft, red-hot exhaust gases rushing out through the splits and holes into the wings, with their several petrol tanks, presenting an unfavourable situation. Exhaust collector-rings being totally unobtainable, the only solution was to remove the burnt-out rings and fit short stub exhaust pipes to each cylinder; this meant that the streamlined cowlings surrounding the engines to reduce their drag also had to be removed, so the resulting extra drag reduced the already low cruising speed of the aeroplane to a figure not all that far above stalling speed, while the racket from the stub exhausts was absolutely deafening. It was then that the location of the airfield at the edge of a high cliff was greatly valued because the aircraft, barely airborne, were able to float off the edge and gain a precious few knots for the climb by a few seconds shallow dive. Otherwise the Anson was a steady old thing with quite a reasonable amount of room inside, but it had a very individual vibration from the engine and this upset some people. On one trip I had to practise with the bomb-sight which involved lying on one's stomach in the nose of the aircraft and after a little I began to feel a bit queasy, the only time I have ever felt even faintly ill in the air.

It was thought necessary that we should keep our hands in at flying and for this laudable purpose the school provided two very small two-seater aeroplanes in which we could have had a lot of fun, but the pressure of time on the course was such that many students did not fly at all; I did at least get ten minutes' dual and thirty minutes jolly pootering about the sky on one day.

There was considerable pressure on accommodation with fifty-strong courses and within a few days a number of us were moved out to hotels in the town. I landed up in the Criterion, a pleasant modern hotel which proved to be comfortable and gave us excellent food. Two others joined me and we very quickly became great friends. Duggie Lumsden was from Hawick and had been assistant organist of Carlisle Cathedral; he had a huge sense of humour – everything was good for a laugh. Frank Haddon had been a City of London policeman and had a wonderful, slightly cynical Cockney humour, very quiet and paralysingly funny. We set each other off the whole time and I have never laughed so much so continuously in all my life.

Fairly early on in the course the usual rumours started to circulate about the chances of a home posting – nobody wanted to go to the Middle East – and about the sort of operations we were likely to go on to: torpedo bombers, anti-shipping fighters, long-range reconnaissance and anti-U-boat aircraft, including among these last, flying boats! And it became fairly clear that flying boat postings, if any, would be only two and they would go to the students who passed out at the top of the course. I, of course, at last saw the glimmerings of a possibility that my dream, born in the eastern Mediterranean more than a year ago and nurtured all through official discouragement since then, might actually come true. Duggie Lumsden was also desperately keen to get on 'boats' and the image of such a prize made us even more serious in our work in the air and on the ground.

I did not find any of the work really daunting although from time to time I felt the pressures of navigating in the air; the exercises were deliberately made very intense and my mathematical phobias once or twice reared their ugly heads briefly. Meteorology appealed to me immensely and, as already mentioned, ship recognition struck an instant chord from my contact, albeit brief, with the Navy and things of the sea. In the two months of the course I had a total of 48 hours 35 minutes on air exercises, mostly by day until towards the end when we did three night navigation trips which were a trifle hairy for the navigator. By then we were already swotting hard and had started with one or two exams in the lesser subjects. The tension built up relentlessly, slightly relieved at one point when Duggie, Frank and I learned that we had been posted home. The final rush of exams was really hectic and then, suddenly, it was all over and we waited on tenterhooks for the results. Throughout all our flying and ground training there was understandable pressure to get us through to the squadrons as quickly as reasonably possible while maintaining the very high standard of our instruction and in those final two or three days at George the examiners must have burned gallons of midnight oil marking all the papers to get the results with the absolute minimum delay.

I finished with an 'above average' for the air exercises and 84.5% in the ground subjects against a course average of 79% (the high course average is explained by the fact that all those on the course had been selected from the top end of the pilots passing out from the Service Flying Training Schools in Rhodesia). I was third from the top and Duggie fourth but, as the top two were very young – only quite recently out of school – Duggie and I got the cherished recommendation for flying boats, the last step but one, the actual posting to a squadron! The Chief Instructor's comment was "A very reliable navigator who will develop into an excellent GR pilot", surely, I thought, a useful boost to my chances of really getting on to 'boats.

Two days hectic activity followed, ploughing through all the normal formalities of leaving an RAF station, saying goodbye to the local people who had been good to us in our very limited leisure time and – a huge priority – filling a big suitcase with tinned fruit, tinned meat, chocolate, dried milk, butter, dried fruit, a dress-length or two – all the imaginable things that were so short at home. Then the last of those hilarious station parties for which the railways always seemed to have allowed ample time before the train finally left with everyone aboard – just. The high spot of this occasion was an impromptu duet between Bill Kendal, the ship recognition instructor (and a former England rugby forward) and one of the course members, Courtney-Cox, a very smooth operator; both had turned their caps back-to-front to look like First World War German aviators and did an hilarious act "Vee go to bomp Lon-don" – we were all very young at heart in those days and anything was good for a laugh. So it was that on Saturday 28 February 1942 we said goodbye to those tense eleven months of basic training and departed for Cape Town, a ship and, God willing, home.

UK here we come!

Yet again, as had been the case with every move except the first one from Bulawayo to Salisbury, I was landed with having charge of the party. As soon as we arrived in Cape Town I had to see the Embarkation Officer but got no definite information and we all went off to a big transit camp which was quite comfortable compared with some other accommodation we had suffered in the past months. The CO of the camp actually gave us a welcoming party which heartened us a bit after the disappointing lack of news on our sailing – we were all very much in that classic overseas RAF syndrome whose despairing refrain was "Roll on that ******* boat!"

For the next four days there was total silence from the embarkation people and we had the chance to see something of Cape Town by day and, most enjoyably, by night. It seemed a handsome and quite friendly city with the first really top-class shops I had seen since Cairo and it was a good opportunity to collect some of the better things to take home. Then on our sixth day in Cape Town it looked as though some definite news was on the way, but yet again it was "Sorry, nothing yet." Finally, on the Saturday, just a week after our arrival, we were told to be ready to leave early the following morning. We packed in great excitement and left for the docks early to be told on arrival that only the NCOs were to go on the *Dempo* and that we should go back to camp and wait for yet another day and another ship.

The next day, Monday 9 March, we left the camp at 1300 and went on board the *City of Exeter*, an Ellerman Line ship of 9000 tons, capable of 13-14 knots. Frank Haddon had been allocated to another draft so, in the event, only Duggie Lumsden and I of the George triumvirate remained. At 1700 we sailed and headed straight out to sea leaving Cape Town rapidly receding astern and looking very beautiful in the evening sunshine against the massive backdrop of Table Mountain. It was an extraordinary and quite emotional feeling to be at last leaving the continent of Africa, where so many experiences had come my way, after something like a year and three-quarters.

The ship had passed the first bloom of youth but was quite comfortable even though very crowded; she had brought out over a hundred wives and children of the last British families to be evacuated from Burma. We were to sail unaccompanied as far as Freetown in Sierra Leone, through waters where German U-boats were known to be operating and we did not envy the captain his heavy responsibility. On the first day out, as officer in charge of the party I was interviewed by the captain and first officer and was asked to arrange for the members of our party to stand watches as anti-aircraft machine-gunners and anti-U-boat lookouts as well as helping the ship's officers in the event of trouble. We were all rather pleased to have some degree of regular responsibility instead of just sitting around waiting for the enemy to produce a surprise.

A very agreeable social atmosphere developed quickly, partly in a conscious effort to keep at bay thoughts of our perilous situation. Of course we all carried our life jackets and little emergency bags with us wherever we went. Many of us became quite adept at looking after and amusing some of the small children, and their mothers. The most moving recollection I have of that voyage is of Divine Service each Sunday morning, led by the ship's captain and held in the for'ard lounge. Looking out at the open ocean ahead and singing "Eternal Father, strong to save . . ." I was terribly conscious of all those innocent women and children most truly 'in peril on the sea'.

Eleven days out we were ploughing steadily ahead as usual, quite, quite alone, over a calm, sunny sea when the first officer told me quietly that the wireless operator had picked up an SOS from a ship somewhere in our general area. The word quickly got round because the first officer and the gun's crew, with life jackets on, closed up to the big 4.7-inch naval gun mounted on the after deck. An hour or so later we sailed through traces of wreckage and, a little later, two empty rafts. Later still we sighted something sticking up in the water, possibly an up ended boathook or spar, but at first it looked uncomfortably like a periscope. Attendance at boat drill was even more prompt and seriously observed from that day on. Even though something of this sort was hardly unexpected, nevertheless when it came it was a shock but all the passengers were very calm, outwardly, and nobody gave any sign of panic. Soon after this we sighted land and thankfully entered Freetown harbour to await the assembly of the convoy that was to take us home.

We wondered whether we should hear any news of the ship that had evidently gone down but nothing was forthcoming. We spent a whole week in Freetown, gazing at the town but unable to go ashore. It was very hot and humid with minimal breeze at any time so anyone who had suggested deck sports would have had little response; we spent quite a lot of time watching boys diving for coins that we threw to them and haggling with the numerous bumboat men, mainly for the wonderful fruit of which the best were the enormous pineapples. We had frequent parties after sundown – when the children had been put to bed – and watched the progress of sundry shipboard romances. With each day the number of ships in the harbour increased and it was heartening to see trim-looking warships of the Royal Navy among them.

Then one morning we woke to feel the throb of the ship's engines and, rushing out on deck, we were astonished to see the African coast receding and ourselves in the midst of an orderly assembly of columns of ships with the warships of the escort way out on the wings of the convoy. A few of the ships were passenger liners like ours but most of the others seemed to be the classic 'three-island' type of tramp ship – high fo'c'sle and high poop with bridge, accommodation and funnel amidships; we were not therefore surprised to learn that we were in a six-knot convoy and were going to take a long time to reach home!

Mercifully the long voyage was quite uneventful and the only real excitement as far as Duggie and I were concerned was catching an occasional glimpse of the unmistakable silhouette of a Sunderland patrolling some miles from the convoy. After a few days they left us as we were beyond their range and when, after many, many days, we saw them again we knew, what the weather had already told us, that we were nearing home waters. Finally, on Sunday 11 April, I was on watch early and was very moved to see a real home sunrise, the red sun shining through the haze and sending a pallid orange light across the grey waters. At 3.15 in the afternoon we passed Ailsa Craig, having parted from our naval escort during the morning, and anchored at five, off the Tail o' the Bank, really home at last after almost exactly two years crowded with experiences of a variety that it was not given to everyone to meet. How lucky I had been so far!

The following morning the ship was towed up the Clyde past the great shipyards alive with the clatter of riveting, with merchant ships and warships taking shape and more crowding the river so closely that we squeezed past a huge aircraft carrier with only about eight feet to spare. It brought that aspect of the war into immediate focus for us, reinforced after disembarkation by our first experience of the blackout in Glasgow, followed by a seemingly endless night journey in a crowded, blacked-out train which appeared to stop about every half-hour in desolate places where the wind whistled dismally round the train and the only human sound was the snoring of the passengers within.

From Euston we were ferried efficiently through town to Waterloo where we had breakfast and I had a brief family reunion. In that short glimpse of London it just seemed a little more drab than when I had left it en route for Romania; there was only the odd gap between buildings to hint at bomb damage. Our draft was quickly on its way to Bournemouth to No 3 Personnel Reception Centre which consisted of a number of requisitioned hotels that had been stripped of everything except lights, loos and baths and 'furnished' with lockers and beds, officers for the use of. However the weather was by now very pleasant and an English spring at the seaside convinced us that we could be very much worse off, as indeed we were to be three weeks or so later. Meanwhile, though, we spent our time quite agreeably, having been joined by a number of our friends from George; we had a few lectures, including a very interesting and sobering one on escaping, rounded off by a sergeant air-gunner who related how he had been hidden by a French farmer's wife but was one day seen by her children who talked at school – she subsequently died under torture.

Sensibly the authorities of the Centre gave us a good deal of leave and I thus had the opportunity, at last, to tell the family as much of the detail of the past two years experiences as the Official Secrets Act would allow. They, of course, also had their stories to tell, including some severe bombing with a direct hit on the block of flats where my mother and sister lived; it seemed very odd to me, in uniform in a fighting service, to hear two women calmly relating such potentially lethal happenings.

All too soon, early in May, we were moved to Harrogate, a so-called Personnel Transit Centre. We arrived at six o'clock on a chilly, dismal, drizzly morning; the 'Vichy of the North' appeared less than welcoming and the Grand Hotel where I and a number of others were billeted gave the impression of having been subject to even more in the way of official vandalism than those in Bournemouth. Here the atmosphere was very different from No 3 PRC; we were constantly subjected to the sort of 'bull' that all wartime RAF officers seem to have experienced at one time or another (obviously designed to 'put them in their place') such as being marched in large groups through the street under the command of some wingless type bawling orders at us. While we evidently could not be trusted to move independently in a manner becoming an officer we would nevertheless be expected at any moment to prepare to take up operational responsibilities which required that we be respected by others while necessarily having respect for ourselves – a curious mode of official behaviour unimaginable in the Navy or the army.

Happily we did escape occasionally on leave and after some six weeks at the 'northern spa' I was spending a family weekend with a cousin at Aldermaston when, in the middle of Sunday lunch, a policeman on a motorbike rushed up to the house with a telegram ordering me to return to Harrogate as I had been posted to RAF Station Lough Erne (later renamed Castle Archdale), together with Duggie Lumsden – wonderful news. I knew of course, that it was a flying boat station! At that moment I could not help thinking back to that hot afternoon in September 1940 in Alexandria when I had been walking down to the harbour and had been stopped in my tracks by the deep diapason that I took to be the sound of several motor torpedo boats under way, only to see, next moment, a magnificent Sunderland flying boat rise majestically above the massed warships and head out to sea. And then, months later, the first and many subsequent affirmations to sceptical senior officers of my determination to get on to 'boats, the great efforts to pass well in the ground subjects, the final accolade at GR school and now, the almost unbelievable climax, on Sunday 28 June 1942, my posting to a flying boat squadron!

Beginnings of a marine aviator

Back at Harrogate Duggie and I learned that we had both been posted to 201 Squadron at Lough Erne and it felt good to be, at last, members of an operational squadron; we were told later that 201 had started right back at the beginning of the First World War as No 1 Squadron of the Royal Naval Air Service (the RNAS joined with the Royal Flying Corps to form the Royal Air Force on 1 April 1918). We crossed from Stranraer to Larne and then via Belfast to Lough Erne where we arrived on Thursday 2 July. The first impression of this, a wartime RAF station with no frills, was of a mass of large and small Nissen huts set in really beautiful countryside on the edge of the lough, an enormous sheet of water about ten miles long, obviously ideal for flying boat operations. Our quarters were quite comfortable and the mess was huge; there was not only 201 but two Catalina squadrons, newly formed, that were working up to go overseas. There were numerous Canadians and New Zealanders and an army officer-navigator on one of 201's aircraft, who wore the observer's flying badge (an 'O' with a single wing) on his army uniform – very curious. The Group Captain commanding the station was 'Slasher' Pearce, a forthright and cheerful character with a boxer's nose and a prominent jaw sticking out beneath a short and ancient pipe.

The next morning we met the Squadron Commander, Wing Commander Crosbie – very agreeable – and the Flight Commander, Squadron Leader Gordon Pirie, a breezy, humorous live wire. We were both impressed, particularly when we were told that there was every likelihood that we should go on a captain's course in a month's time. They told us to look round the station to get our bearings and, in particular, to go into one of the vast maintenance hangars to look over a Sunderland that was undergoing a major overhaul.

We made our way through the usual clutter of buildings and huts that make up an RAF station down to the hangars occupying two sides of a very large concrete area at one end of which was the slipway sloping down into the water. We opened a door in the side of the maintenance hangar, stepped inside and just gasped. The huge Sunderland, resting on the wheels of the temporary beaching gear, literally towered above us. The cockpit windows were nearly twenty feet from the ground and the top of the fin and rudder no less than twenty-seven feet above ground level. The propellers and engines were much bigger than anything we had been close to and the wings (known as the mainplane) measured 112'9" from tip to tip. Even more impressive was the cathedral-like interior into which we stepped gingerly to avoid the numerous and mysterious bits and pieces that were being worked on. The whole thing appeared so vast that the thought that in a month we should be on the way to taking charge of one of these monsters shook us, as they say, rigid. Thoughtful but very excited, Duggie and I walked down to the slipway and looked out on the great expanse of water, sheltered by some small islands, where the squadron's aircraft swung peacefully at their mooring buoys; it was a tremendous feeling to be at last part of an operational Coastal Command squadron after a whole year and a half of training.

Next morning I was detailed to go on board one of the aircraft to watch a taxi-test in which the aircraft would be taken out to open water where the various tests on the engines could be carried out. The mooring buoys were not strong enough to hold the aircraft if the engines were running at more than tick over speed and, as a flying boat had no brakes, once under way it had to keep going ahead; if the engines were run up to full power on test the aircraft picked up speed through the water very rapidly so a lot of sea room and a very sharp lookout were necessary. I went out to the aircraft with the crew in a fast motorboat, always referred to as a dinghy, and climbed on board through the for'ard door on the port side, just below the cockpit. With everything in place the interior was even more impressive than it had been in the aircraft on maintenance the previous day.

I climbed up a narrow companionway to the flight deck and the pilots cockpit. The visibility was excellent and, although there was a great array of flying controls, engine controls, instrument panels, gauges, switches, bomb-setting gear and many others, it was all so spacious, well lit and clearly laid out that it was not nearly as intimidating as it had appeared at the very first glance. I was told to stand behind the captain's seat to watch the basic procedure of unmooring, taxying, testing the engines, returning to the buoy and mooring up. Each aircraft had a normal crew of ten: two pilots, a navigator, two engineers, three wireless operators, a rigger (expert on the aircraft's structure or airframe as it was called) and a 'straight' air-gunner – all the rest of the crew except the pilots and navigator were also qualified air-gunners, but the 'straight A/G' was the expert on the guns themselves and the turrets and their operating gear. I soon noticed that there was a very free interchange of the numerous duties involved in operating the aeroplane and keeping it in good running order – and tidy. Each crew had its own aircraft and, mostly, its own ground crew and they all took a lot of pride in keeping it on the top line and ready for operations. In fact a normal crew had within it all the qualifications necessary to maintain the aircraft, and do up to minor inspections, when operating on detachment remote from base.

While we were still on the buoy the two outer engines were started and run slowly while the buoy pendant was cast off and we were under way. As soon as the captain could see his way clear through the islands the two inner engines were started and we taxied out into open water, quite like a big ship, at some 15 to 20 knots. There was a brisk breeze and the water was choppy on top of a slight swell so the aircraft pitched up and down noticeably and every now and then a bigger wave would thump against the bows and fly past the cockpit in a rush of spray.

Both the captain and the second pilot kept a continuous lookout all round the aircraft for other traffic on the water. Then, with a good clear stretch of water ahead the two outers were opened up to medium power and the two magnetos on each and the airscrew pitch controls were tested: with all well the engines were opened up to full takeoff power to check that they were delivering maximum boost (supercharge) and revolutions (2650 per minute); instantly the whole aeroplane began to shudder under the tremendous power (1050 horsepower from each engine) and race forward over the water – the two pilots had a busy fifteen or twenty seconds checking the engine instruments, watching where we were starting to go, very rapidly, and steering the machine while switching each magneto off in turn. Immediately he was satisfied the captain throttled back the outers and then went through the same procedure with the inners. By the time he and the engineers were clear that everything was in order we had covered a good distance and we turned round to port to taxi back to base. With a land aircraft this very vital testing can be done with the brakes on and without the aircraft moving an inch, but a flying boat has to move freely in the water as already mentioned.

Approaching base the inner engines were stopped and we moved cautiously in towards the mooring area, using the two outer engines to steer the aircraft. As we came up to the buoy the rigger climbed out over the bow on to a tiny ladder hung on the side of the bow and clung on with one hand while in the other he held one end of a ten-foot long thick rope, called a 'short slip', the other end of which was looped on a bollard. The captain nudged the aircraft slowly up to the buoy, using minute bursts of one engine or the other to steer but not increase speed and with the buoy right by the port bow the rigger slipped his rope-end through a wire loop on the top of the buoy, grabbed it like a flash on the other side and handed it up to the other bowman who rapidly took a turn round the bollard, thus temporarily securing the aircraft. The two engines were stopped and while the rigger and his mate completed the mooring to the buoy the rest of the crew put on the engine covers, closed water-tight half-doors and left everything secure to enable us to go ashore. I felt I had already begun to be at home in these magnificent aircraft.

On my way back to the mess a smart young sergeant pilot saluted and said "Excuse me, sir, is the name Deller?" and there, by incredible coincidence, was Clive Davies, whom it may be remembered, I had last seen as a young trainee in Shell's wartime headquarters at Lensbury Club, Teddington more than two years before. Sadly we had only a few moments to express our mutual astonishment and pleasure as he was on his way to join his crew for a taxi-test.

On operations, at last

Three days later on Tuesday 7 July in the evening I was appointed to aircraft *W* as third pilot and the very next day at lunch I met the navigator and, very shortly after, the captain, Flight Lieutenant Sanderson, a cheerful and relaxed character known as 'Shiner' because of his bald head; he told me to pack immediately as we were to leave that evening for Mount Batten, Plymouth, on our way to Gibraltar!

Having put some kit together I went with the second pilot, Flying Officer Duggie Gall, out to the aircraft, *W4036*, a Mark III Sunderland newly delivered from the makers, Short Brothers of Rochester. On board there was just time to meet the remaining members of the crew as they bustled about getting *W* ready for departure. Then we taxied out, turned into the westerly wind and at 6pm, with the heavily laden aeroplane roaring and shuddering initially, then, once we were planing on the step of the planing bottom, settling to a smooth run at increasing speed; it appeared to take itself off as the backward movement of the control column was so slight – no heaving the aircraft off the water by main force. After takeoff we climbed steadily away into the westering sun, the engines were throttled back to give a climbing speed of 110 knots, the vibration lessened and the tension in the aircraft relaxed perceptibly. Getting almost thirty tons of aeroplane into the air with 4200 horsepower involved a busy and highly concentrated forty-five seconds, and sometimes even more, and in those seconds almost anything could go unpleasantly wrong in spite of the best of maintenance, because in wartime the heavier aircraft were operated at the absolute maximum of their capability and their high stress was reflected in the stress experienced by the crew, most of all by the captain.

As soon as we had reached our cruising altitude and had turned south towards Plymouth the captain, who had been highly amused to learn that the last thing I had flown was a single-engined Harvard, put me in the left-hand seat and let me fly the aeroplane all the way until the approach to Mount Batten. It was a very wonderful and thrilling experience to be actually piloting one of these great Sunderlands that had been my beacon of endeavour for so long. Such a big aircraft naturally seemed a little ponderous in its response to the controls but these were so beautifully balanced that only minute movements were needed to maintain correct heading, speed and altitude and it came a lot easier as a result of all those uncomfortable hours learning accurate flying on instruments in the Link trainer.

It was dusk by the time we reached Mount Batten and as I stood between the pilots' seats I watched intently as the captain checked the harbour area for any obstructions, particularly shipping, decided which part of the harbour to use for his landing and, turning on to the heading for the approach, throttled back the engines to reduce speed, set the flaps and then, at about 700 feet, settled the aircraft on a level descent. When the 'step' touched the water, the engines were throttled right back and the aeroplane settled rapidly in a whirl of spray followed by a great impression of peace and almost silence. We taxied in to a buoy to which we were guided by one of the station's fast launches and, after all the mooring-up and 'putting the aircraft to bed', I came ashore feeling myself to be really part of an operational crew at last.

On detachment to Gib

Next day we were up very early for a takeoff at first light with an eleven hour flight ahead of us. While the second pilot went out to the aircraft with the crew to get everything on board ready for departure the captain took me, with the navigator and the first wireless operator, to the operations room for my first experience of briefing. It was an impressive place, with the Ops Room Controller, who stood up from his desk to greet us, in front of a huge wall-map of the whole area from the south of England to Gibraltar marked with such things as convoys, submarine exclusion areas (where our own submarines were operating and any sighting should therefore be presumed to be friendly), U-boat sightings and so on. Over the map was mounted one of the standard RAF ops room clocks with curious multicoloured segments marked on the face, the significance of which I never succeeded in grasping. Then there was a large board showing details of all the aircraft operating or due for an operation, including our own – "Sunderland W/201, captain F/Lt Sanderson, transit and A/S (anti-submarine) sweep Gibraltar, take off 0500z (ie GMT), ETA 1600z." Several WAAFs were busying themselves with signals, maps and so forth, not to mention the inevitable cups of tea. Our trip had been ordered by Group headquarters by signal known as a Form Green; the report compiled at the end of an operation was a Form Orange and there were several others, for example Form Purple which, if I remember correctly, reported the aircraft availability state of the station.

The Squadron Leader, Ops Room Controller gave us details of expected enemy U-boat and fighter activity from the French west coast bases, weather en route, a convoy that might be met on the way and a warning to be on the lookout in the later stages of the trip for unmarked, black-painted Messerschmitt 109 fighters that were rumoured to be operating from Franco's Spain. The navigator collected his charts and details of the code letters and Very light colours to be used in different periods to identify us as friendly to our own forces and shore stations; for flying over the sea there are of course no maps as such and as mentioned earlier, all navigation was done using Admiralty charts which showed only lines of magnetic variation, lines of latitude and longitude, a compass rose and, if any land was near, a mere outline of the coast with names of points and ports, and details of shoals and lighthouse codes. The wireless operator meanwhile had been given his call sign, radio frequencies to use and two homing pigeons, in special boxes that could be made temporarily watertight so that their flight capabilities would not be impaired by getting splashed while the crew were, hopefully, climbing into their emergency dinghy, rapidly, before the aeroplane sank.

Before we arrived aboard the aircraft the crew had collected an impressive quantity of rations, the second pilot had checked the bilges for any water (that would add undesirable weight to the aircraft and would therefore have to be pumped overboard by a small petrol engine-driven pump mounted in the leading edge of the starboard mainplane) and inspected the eight depth charges suspended on their trolleys in the roof of the bomb room from whence they would be run out under the mainplane if they were to be dropped. The three powered turrets and their seven machine guns had been given a thorough check by the 'straight A/G' and, with some 2300 gallons (about ten tons) of petrol in the ten tanks housed in the huge mainplane, the aircraft was in all respects ready for departure.

Plymouth Sound is a very large area of water, clear of obstructions except for a low breakwater across the greater part of the entrance; the preferred takeoff direction, if the wind is from the right quarter, is straight out to sea, leaving a sufficiently long takeoff run to be sure of clearing the breakwater. As we were thundering across the glistening water I noticed that Flight Sergeant Hodge, the first wireless operator, was in a state of extreme tension. It was only afterwards that I was told that he had been the only survivor of a crash in which the captain had underestimated his takeoff run and had smashed into that breakwater – this was his first takeoff at Mount Batten since that terrible experience.

We actually cleared the breakwater by about seventy feet and set course for the Bay of Biscay and Gib on a beautiful summer morning. This was the real thing at last, suspended aloft with the steady roar of the engines and the hiss of the airflow that kept us aloft, the view ahead of limitless ocean and sky and the feeling of an entire crew quietly and efficiently playing their part in operating this great aeroplane, ready to go to their stations in quick time if we had the chance to spot a U-boat or were faced with attack by fighters – in fact a serious atmosphere with the quiet tension of a potentially tricky job to do.

Soon after takeoff, when the interior of the aircraft had been blown clear of petrol fumes, the captain gave the all clear for smoking and in no time the air was full of the mouthwatering smell of bacon and eggs being cooked on the double Primus stove in the galley by the off duty crew who then relieved others at their posts so that these could go below to the wardroom. Here there was a bunk either side and a table in the middle where cutlery (part of the aircraft's standard equipment) had been put out. Sunderlands were unique among operational service aircraft in having this roughly ten-foot-cube space below the flight deck where it was possible to get right away from the job for a meal and a little relaxation – the advantages of such a break on a ten or twelve hour trip had been sensibly taken into account by the high-ups who set the original specification for the aeroplane. This, together with the fully-equipped galley complete with sink, draining board and plate rack, put the Sunderland in a class of its own, particularly when, with its great operational flexibility, crews could find themselves having to live aboard in some remote location or, as on exposed stations such as Bowmore in Islay, during prolonged gale conditions. A proper little yacht-type lavatory, with a lock on the door, put the finishing touch to gracious living; indeed, some two years later, I did hold a cocktail party on board my aeroplane.

Just now, however, I was very much the third pilot. The practice was for the pilots to change over every hour or hour and a half; something like 80% of enemy sightings were made by the pilots and with the intense concentration a change of place or, with three pilots, one period off in three helped to reduce fatigue. So it was that I found myself in turn in the second pilot's seat and then, big moment, in the captain's seat, responsible for the minute corrections to the automatic pilot that had to be made from time to time to maintain the extreme accuracy of airspeed, altitude and course that was vital for accurate navigation over the vast empty ocean spaces.

Every moment of that first long operational flight was an intense thrill for me and when, after nearly eleven hours, we came in sight of the huge hump of the Rock and exchanged recognition signals with the Europa Point Signal Station I had to pinch myself to realise that this, after so much anticipation, really was *it*. We landed out in Algeciras Bay and taxied in to the harbour and on to a vacant mooring buoy. The heat was terrific and we were glad to get ashore for a shower and a change into tropicals. A very short sortie into town after dinner to get the flavour of the place was enough as we had learned that we were scheduled for an $11^1/_2$ hour anti-submarine sweep the very next day – $22^1/_2$ hours flying in two days – so this was life in long-range flying boats!

We were accommodated in single rooms in a large concentration of Nissen huts among which were a number of very large black packing cases. At about half past three next morning I was astonished to be awakened from a deep sleep by the noise of an aircraft engine being run-up on test apparently just outside my window; on looking out I was even more astonished to see, right there, a complete Spitfire with engine running and a fitter in the cockpit. Similar sounds were coming from all round the place. Totally mystified I went off to sleep again and eventually woke up hoping to see just what was going on; the answer was nothing, no sign of an aircraft or even of a packing case.

As we subsequently learned, in bits and pieces, the Spitfires were to be taken in aircraft carriers to a point reasonably near to Malta and flown off to complete their trip. Such valuable ships could not be put at risk under the intense enemy bombardment that Malta was enduring and against which the Spitfires were to be deployed. General Franco being such a good friend of Hitler, although not openly allied, Spain was a haven for Germans gathering intelligence of the Allies' activities and intentions; some of these people were established in Algeciras, across the bay from Gib, from where they were able to observe in detail through binoculars. Our packing cases were the key element in a brilliant plan to hide the Malta Fighter Reinforcement Scheme from German eyes. Each of the packing cases contained a complete fighter, ready for action, needing only to have its wings fitted and be fuelled and armed. The cases had been brought from the UK by ship, off-loaded and positioned among the Nissen huts after dark, then opened up for the fitters to make the final assembly and carry out the ground test. Immediately after this the complete aircraft were taken down to the docks, loaded aboard the aircraft carriers (HMS *Eagle* and USS *Wasp*) and struck down below into the hangars – all this before daylight returned! We had been detached to Gib to reinforce the Sunderlands of 202 Squadron and some Catalinas providing protection for the carriers by anti-submarine sweeps ahead and by close escorts.

We took off early in the morning and spent the next $11^1/_2$ hours flying a huge pattern, covering a considerable part of the northern area of the Mediterranean east of Gib, so designed as to give the maximum possibility of sighting any U-boat that might be in the area. A similar pattern was being flown simultaneously by another Sunderland in the southern part of the area, thus together sweeping the centre and flanks of the first part of the aircraft carriers route towards Malta.

The Wing Commander Flying at Gib at that time was a rather formidable character called Wing Commander Case, known universally as 'Uncle Case'. In appearance and behaviour he bore an astonishing resemblance to Captain Bligh, of the *Bounty,* as portrayed by Charles Laughton! Actually he did have a more human side as I discovered many years later when we were both fairly lit-up at a post-war reunion of members of what has always been called The Flying Boat Union.

Again on personalities: I accompanied my captain to the briefings in the ops room at North Camp and it is an intriguing thought that we may well have been briefed by a prewar architect who was then Squadron Leader, Ops Room Controller – none other than our very dear post-war friend John Atkinson!

We had two days free and this gave us a chance to look round the extraordinary British outpost at the bottom end of Europe that is Gibraltar. Unfortunately, it was not possible to cross over into Spain, for fairly obvious reasons, but the town itself was fascinating, very similar in many ways to places like Cairo and Alexandria that I remembered so well – brilliant sunshine, innumerable cafés and bars, bright colours everywhere, hundreds and hundreds of service people, prominent among them of course, the Navy and, equally prominent, the no-nonsense naval police parties. At night the place fairly hummed and in very many of the cafés there were superb bands consisting of extremely cheerful but emaciated Spaniards who produced a tremendous atmosphere of care-free gaiety that was such a contrast to the blacked-out country we had left only two or three days before. Wandering from bar to bar we came across a variety of interesting people: I remember one RAF air-gunner who told me, very quietly, that he had just crossed over from Spain having been smuggled along some sort of amazing chain of brave people all the way from somewhere in northern France. He also commented bitterly on the conduct of many American aircrew who could not resist blabbing about their 'adventure' even while they were on the way, putting their rescuers in such danger that some chains apparently refused to handle them.

Our next job was a cross-over patrol, rather like a very much extended 'X' with the two ends closed, between a point off Cape Bon in Tunisia and the vicinity of the south coast of France. This was to form part of an anti-submarine 'barrier' ahead of one of the carriers, *Wasp* or *Eagle*, on her way towards the flying-off point for the Spitfires en route to Malta. We spent over thirteen hours in the air, about half in the dark; this was my first experience of a night takeoff and it was quite something. The aircraft was blacked-out, all portholes covered, and there were just dim orange lights for the pilots' and engineers' instrument panels and the navigator's plotting table and the radio set. Pitching up and down on the black water as we taxied out into the bay it was quite hard to see the three small lights, each mounted on an anchored pram-dinghy, that constituted the flare path - very different from the double lines of goose-neck flares or electric lights that the 'wheely boys' enjoyed on their runways. The lights were some two hundred yards apart so the total flare path was about four hundred yards long. The drill was to taxi far enough (perhaps 1000 yards or more) downwind from the first light for the aircraft, on turning into the wind, to be aimed at the distant light and be well up on the step on reaching it and leaving the water by the time the third light was passed, thus enjoying the 'guidance' of each of these 40 watt bulbs during the critical stages of the takeoff. Distances are very difficult to judge on the water in pitch darkness and it needed all 'Shiner' Sanderson's skill to judge how far to go downwind before turning for the takeoff. The latter was fairly dramatic, hurtling at approaching 100 miles an hour into the blackness with the roar of the engines, the rapid thump, thump, thump of the waves hitting the hull, the occasional big one making the whole aeroplane shudder, the intent figures of the pilots dimly silhouetted against the faint orange cockpit lights and the bright red glow of the exhaust collector rings on the engines. The Sunderland's engines had their nine cylinders mounted radially, ie in a circle behind the propeller, and the exhaust from the cylinders was collected in a ring pipe which also formed the leading edge of the cowling used to streamline the engines and reduce their wind resistance; under full takeoff power these rings became extremely hot and, at night, glowed bright red. Many months later one of my wireless operators, having asked if he could stand between the pilots' seats to watch my takeoff at night, suddenly, at the critical moment of the takeoff run, shook my shoulder and pointed wildly at the engines – he thought they were on fire!

Throughout our patrol we kept a wary eye open for Vichy French fighters who, a few days before, had attacked a Catalina, damaging it and gravely wounding the captain who managed to bring the aeroplane home in spite of having refused the morphine we always carried, in the mistaken belief that it would make him drowsy and incapable of landing his aircraft safely. We saw no fighters nor did we see any submarines yesterday, this day or on subsequent days; I was to learn that this was the commonest experience among anti-submarine aircraft crews, not only in the Atlantic and the Med but everywhere else as well. Intelligence from captured enemy submarine crews provided some consolation, in time, as they evidently feared aircraft specially because of the speed with which they could approach and deliver their attacks; as a result the submarines would frequently submerge if they knew or suspected that aircraft were about, thus being forced to their much lower underwater speed and possibly losing a convoy or missing a rendezvous.

We did a thirteen hour daylight trip providing part of the escort for a damaged sloop, HMS *Lowestoft*, under tow towards Gib; then more than twelve hours on another sweep ahead of one of the Spitfire-bearing aircraft carriers before setting out for home on an uneventful 11 hour run to Mount Batten, carrying a heavy load of 'brass' in the form of high-ranking naval and army officers and one RAF aircrew sergeant, an escaped prisoner of war. We also had another sort of cargo, having been briefed by the mess to collect good things from the plenty of Gibraltar. Before the war my father had bought wine from a City firm called Mayer, Sworder from whose Gibraltar branch we bought cases and cases of wine and, particularly, sherry which were subsequently concealed in the Sunderland's capacious mainplane, down among the fuel tanks. On arrival back at Mount Batten we vigorously waved away the approaching Customs launch, explaining that we had secret equipment on board, which was true but apparently did not always keep the Customs at bay. We also bought quantities of fruit and I remember wondering idly whether I might be mugged by some of the 'erks' eyeing me as I walked up the slipway with a huge box full of bananas. Incidentally it should be mentioned that the Sergeants Mess also benefited from our excursion to the sun.

On arrival back at Lough Erne, to an understandably enthusiastic welcome, our tried and trusty *W* was due for a 90-hour inspection and, as a fitting close to a quite remarkable fortnight, I was able to watch as the aeroplane was taxied carefully up to the warping buoy just off the end of the slipway where airmen in heavy waterproof overalls waded out up to their chests floating out two huge legs, each with two oversize pneumatic-tyred wheels, which were up-ended and fitted into strongpoints in each side of the hull and under the mainplane; a small steerable trolley was mounted at the after end of the keel and a heavy cable was attached at one end to the keel and at the other to a massive mobile Coles crane, acting as a tractor, which slowly hauled the aircraft backwards up the slipway while a line from the bows to the warping buoy was equally slowly paid out to keep the aircraft in a straight line until the wheels were firmly on the concrete.

Three days later the exact reverse of the procedure was carried out and the aeroplane was refuelled ready for a thorough air-test of the whole airframe (ie the entire machine minus the engines) and the engines. The whole crew went out to check every bit of each man's responsibility and no sooner were we on board than 'Shiner' turned to me with a broad grin and said "This is your chance, you can do all the taxying and part of the flying!" And so it was that on Monday 27 July 1942, exactly one year and three weeks since my very first flight in a Tiger Moth – air experience – I was manoeuvring a Sunderland flying boat out through the islands then running up the engines on the usual pre-flight test and finally turning the aeroplane into the wind, opening the throttles to full power and, with a little initial help from 'Shiner' to control the very strong pull to the left due to engine torque and to keep the aircraft correctly balanced while running on the water – nose not too low so that the bows dig in, not too high so that the aircraft takes off too early and drops back with a possibly damaging bounce – then off the water with just a minute backward pressure on the control column and climbing on to a left-hand circuit – all as I had so carefully watched it done throughout the past fortnight.

On the downwind leg of the circuit at 1000 feet I looked intently out of my window to judge where I should turn across wind to throttle back the engines, set the propellers in fine pitch while losing height to 700 feet for the final left turn on to the approach, setting the flaps at two-thirds out, keeping the airspeed constant with the two inner engines and losing height steadily with the aircraft level in the landing attitude all the way down until I felt the point of the planing bottom touch the water, throttled the engines right back and eased her down off the step as she settled quietly in the water and I settled back in the seat, unbelievably relieved and elated while the surrounding multitude of three beamed congratulations. By the end of another two successful takeoffs, circuits and landings immediately following, I really felt I was on the way – and so, by way of many tribulations, I indeed was.

After all that let it not be said that all was earnest endeavour. In such a big mess the atmosphere was extremely social and often hilarious. A particular favourite as an evening pastime was 'liar dice'; we used a large round table for this and normally there would be ten people taking part – those familiar with the game will get some idea of the level of excitement from the fact that we had two pots circulating simultaneously and concentrating on our pot while keeping half an ear on what was happening with the other one, due to arrive within seconds with its own challenge, took some doing. Whoever was first to lose all three 'lives' bought a round of the magnificent Dublin-brewed draught Guinness that the mess imported in 50 gallon barrels, so, as the evening wore on the mood became less and less restrained.

On Coastal Command stations one aircraft with crew was always, day and night, 'on strike' (ie to be airborne within one hour of the operation order in the case of flying boats.) One night we were 'strike' crew but the weather was so bad that ops told us there was no likelihood of our being called out. Suddenly, about two hours and several pints of Guinness into a game of liar dice, the tannoy boomed out "Crew of strike aircraft *W* report to the ops room immediately." Consternation! – we gathered ourselves and our wits together as best we could, staggered through the filthy weather to ops, got briefed, dinghied out to the aircraft, climbed aboard soaking wet, got under way and, out in the rough and stormy lough reached the flare path just in time to receive a message "Operation scrubbed, return to moorings!" I suppose we should have made it but it was a relief not to have had to have a go.

Convoy escort

On 30 July we flew an eleven hour daylight escort on a North Atlantic convoy. It was a fine, clear day and after some three and a half hours flying over the limitless expanse of empty water the radar picked up the first indications of the convoy and almost immediately we sighted a long smudge on the horizon which quickly resolved itself into one of the most astonishing, indeed awe-inspiring sights I had ever seen; it was a sixty ship convoy and the ships were ranged in ten columns on a broad front which must have covered about five miles and with probably more than three miles from front to rear. Several tankers were concentrated around the centre of the convoy for maximum protection while the rest were a mixture, mostly of modern and not so modern freighters but with some medium-sized passenger vessels also. At that stage of the war escort vessels were desperately short and this huge collection of ships was being shepherded, to the best of my recollection, by one destroyer, a frigate and three or four armed deep-sea trawlers – it was very clear why there was such great need for an air escort with such a vast area of sea to cover, several square miles in fact.

Having learned, in the GR course, all about the drill for operating with a convoy I was very interested to see it for the first time in practice. The all-important point to remember was that ships gunners were rightly suspicious of any approaching aircraft, even though the arrival of an escort was normally announced to all ships in advance by lamp signal or flag signal, albeit in heavy weather this did not always work very well; the cardinal principle for aircraft was to identify from a fair distance by firing off a Very light with the colours of the period and flashing the letter of the period to the Senior Officer of the Escort (SOE), in this present case in the destroyer, and then turn briefly to show the aircraft in silhouette to aid recognition. The one thing never to do was to fly close to or over the ships, the probable result of doing so was to be dramatically and tragically demonstrated the very next day.

As soon as the senior officer was satisfied as to our identity he flashed us instructions for the type of patrol he wanted us to carry out, we having told him how long we could stay with the convoy, and any special observations on the situation. At that time, and for most of the war, radio telephony (R/T ie speech) communication with naval ships was very unsatisfactory, mainly because of the weakness of our sets but also because the naval operators, evidently feeling that we were a long way away from them up there in the sky, turned up the volume on their powerful sets to the point where their speech was so overmodulated as to be almost unintelligible, largely just a meaningless roaring noise. So communication tended to be mainly by lamp and here the difficulty often was that senior officers of escorts did not fully appreciate how relatively short our time with them had to be: they were apt to indulge in lengthy exchanges in Morse by signal lamp while we wanted to get off on our patrol.

A further difficulty over visual communication was that there was no position on the aircraft from which the lamp could be trained for any length of time without being obstructed by some part of the aircraft's structure, given that the aircraft was moving fast and therefore had to be constantly manoeuvring to keep reasonably close to the SOE's ship. The most practical way was to fly a shallow arc ahead of the convoy, backwards and forwards: many pilots did the signalling themselves and thus were only able to operate until they had the ship on their beam and hidden by the engines and the mainplane. I preferred to get one of my wireless operators to do the signalling from the astrodome (a large hemispherical dome of optically-correct perspex through which sextant sights were taken and which gave a good all-round view). As the ship was well below us I had to fly my shallow arc with the wing tilted down somewhat so that it did not obscure the lamp's beam, the result being that the aircraft tended constantly to get nearer and nearer to the ship and this naturally had to be watched carefully. On the other hand the wireless operators were much quicker than the pilots as their Morse was better and they also were able to use a lot of shorthand with the naval operators. With either mode of operation the aircraft had to be constantly turning to fly back again across the front of the convoy and the turn always seemed to have to be made in mid sentence. The whole operation often seemed to be endless and it had within it the seeds of great danger; we were flying low down and at a low speed so as not to keep getting too far away on each pass and one was concentrating so much on keeping station that it was terribly easy momentarily to overlook the airspeed indicator, allowing the speed to drop so that the aircraft was in danger of stalling. At just two or three hundred feet altitude there was no hope of recovery from a stall and more than one aircraft was lost from this cause.

During our four hours or so with the convoy we flew our patrol as ordered by the SOE, the pilots and the gunners watching intently for any sign of U-boat activity, or signals from the SOE recalling us for further instructions. The great mass of ships ploughed steadily on and the escorts roamed round the fringes of the convoy. Every now and then one of them would suddenly accelerate off on a new course, no doubt in response to an echo on the Asdic underwater detection gear. On board aircraft *W* we rotated regularly between our various duties and rest periods; we had hot meals which would have had ration-bound earthlings eyes out on stalks and countless cups of tea and coffee were taken round to the people on duty.

Eventually the time approached when we were to be relieved by another of the squadron's aircraft and we watched closely for the unmistakable silhouette of the Sunderland with its very deep hull and big prominent tail fin and rudder. Before long there she was, easily seen in the dark green and dark brown camouflage (it was only later in the war that the boffins at Coastal Command reasoned that a white-painted aircraft would be less easily visible and in practice this was indeed so, even, remarkably, against a background of dark cloud). We had told the SOE at the start that we should be relieved by another Sunderland at a given time and we now returned to the head of the convoy and signalled "Our relief in sight. Goodbye. Bon voyage!" to which the SOE replied "Goodbye and many thanks!" Throughout the trip we had seen nothing untoward but our presence around the convoy would have had a worthwhile, possibly even vital, deterrent effect, as already explained (see page 74). Furthermore our very visible presence no doubt gave some boost to the morale of the escorts and the ships in the convoy, much as I remembered experiencing it half a year earlier in our home-bound convoy from Cape Town (see page 64). On leaving our convoy I felt a pang of sympathy, as I always did subsequently, for those men down below who still had days or perhaps weeks to go before reaching the safety of port while we, with luck, would be back in our comfortable mess in another four or five hours; this feeling was specially poignant when taking leave of a convoy in those terrible winter Atlantic storms and when, frequently, the convoy had been repeatedly attacked by massed U-boats, with many ships lost.

The homeward flight, the convoy having moved many miles nearer home and with a tailwind, was shorter than the outward trip and we landed back at Lough Erne in the late afternoon. On coming ashore and seeing and talking to people who throughout a whole day had been going about their earth-bound business I had a strange feeling of having returned from a quite different world, an emotion a little akin to that experienced on returning from sea.

Death by own hand – almost

The following day aircraft *P* was airborne to escort a convoy in home waters where enterprising U-boats had sometimes penetrated. At lunchtime in the mess a rumour was circulating to the effect that contact with *P* had been lost and as the afternoon wore on and merged into evening, still with no contact, it was announced that aircraft *R* would take off at first light next morning to investigate. Then, later in the evening, we learned that the headquarters of 15 Group, Coastal Command, under which we operated, had been passed a signal by Royal Navy Western Approaches Command (who worked alongside 15 Group) that they had received a signal from the convoy stating that aircraft *P* had been shot down by the convoy and that the sole survivor of the crew of eleven was the tail gunner. Everyone was stunned and, at the same time, burning with anger – the weather conditions had been poor, with thick fog, and the crew had done exceedingly well to find the convoy, only to be shot down for their pains!

It was evidently felt that the RAF could not allow itself to be put off doing its duty by casualties, however distressing, so aircraft *R* set off into the same thick fog and once more succeeded in finding the convoy. This time there was not much delay in hearing from the convoy – aircraft *R* had been engaged by gunfire and badly damaged, a forced landing close to the convoy had been attempted but the aircraft crashed. It sank in two minutes but a number of the crew got out into the water; seconds later the eight depth charges the aircraft had been carrying blew up. The ships brought some of the survivors out of the water still alive but the devastating force of the explosion had stripped virtually all the flesh off their bones and they died very quickly, among them my young friend from Lensbury fire squad days, Clive Davies, seen only briefly as a sergeant pilot just four weeks before, on the slipway. (see pages 8 and 68)

So within forty-eight hours the squadron had lost two aircraft and 21 aircrew. Everyone had his personal, private grief but the station and the squadron carried on temporarily in subdued mood, but otherwise as normal. One had read many times about the reactions of squadrons to casualties in the First World War and it was, in a way, heartening to witness and be part of exactly that same traditional reaction. I have to say that from the very start of my war service I found genuine and deep inspiration in those remembered tales of the courage and devotion of those who had gone before us in the service of the country.

I do not know how far the facts of this tragedy were established at the time but, some years after the end of the war, through having our children at the same nursery school, my wife got to know the manager of a society florists and his wife. One day in the course of conversation it emerged by chance that he had been the officer in charge of a detachment of army anti-aircraft gunners deployed on one of the ships of a convoy, a common practice where convoys were liable to heavy attack from the air and on one occasion the ships in this convoy, in home waters just returning from one of the notorious Arctic runs to Russia, had been in thick fog and had heard an aircraft coming very close; in the Arctic any aircraft coming out of the perpetual freezing fog was certain to be enemy and would be on the convoy so quickly that instant anti-aircraft fire was the only option. Evidently, and understandably in wartime, no one had thought to impress on the gunners that in home waters an unseen aircraft should be presumed friendly (although the big Focke-Wulf Condor four-engined reconnaissance bombers did search for and attack convoys from time to time). Hearing, but not seeing, aircraft *P* their instant reaction was to open fire with everything, which they did, to devastating effect. It remains hard to understand why the same dreadful error should have been made, in exactly similar circumstances, the following day, but in fairness the difficulty of communication among ships in thick fog, in conditions of wireless silence, has to be recognised. It was a most extraordinary coincidence that I should come across this very nice man and at least it gave me the belated comfort of a perfectly reasonable explanation for which I could not help having a deal of sympathy.[1,2] *(footnotes are on page 104)*

Two days after the loss of *P* and *R* we in *W* were detailed for an escort on a convoy which was to be met at first light, so we had a night takeoff and two and a half hours night flying in a total of just twelve hours. This trip was routine, though more good experience for me, especially the drill of identifying to the convoy in the dark with only a shaded Aldis lamp flashing the letter of the period and, understandably, no coloured Very lights that would have announced the presence of the convoy to an enemy all the way to the horizon.

Two more similar trips followed in the next nine days bringing my total of operational hours flown to one hundred and eighteen hours and thirty minutes – not bad for a beginner with just six weeks squadron service. Duggie and I were then summoned to the Flight Commander's office to be told to take three days leave before going to Stranraer to No 4 (Coastal) Operational Training Unit for our captain's course, reporting on 18 August. After the frustrating two and a half months following our arrival back in England things certainly had moved at a remarkable pace – third pilot to embryo captain in seven weeks, with quite a reasonable amount of operational experience under my belt!

(continued on page 97)

The author in February 1940 as deputy leader of the fire squad at Lensbury Club, Teddington, wartime headquarters of the Royal Dutch/Shell Group. Note the 'Free and Willing' armband on his left arm (see page 7).

Author's collection

Aboard the Sardinian Prince
Left to right: ?, Tommy Henderson, ?, Stan Riley, Reid (Shell Turkey), author, Tom Tigg.
Author's collection

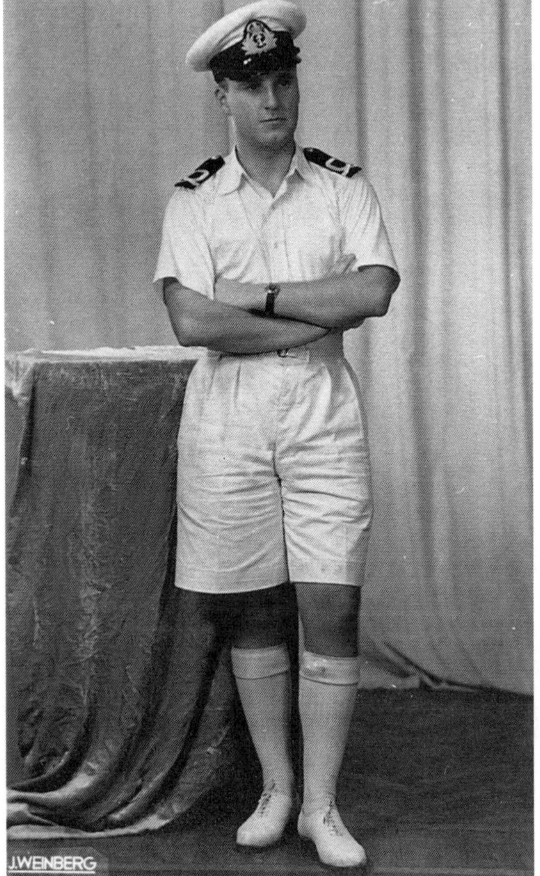

Alan Deller wearing the uniform of a Sub Lieutenant RNVR, HMS Dolphin *– while D/H5 in the Special Operations Executive.*
Author's collection

HMS Dolphin *in Piræus harbour, December 1940; the camera missed about five feet of the bow. The tarpaulin-covered heap for'ard of the main mast was the gun.*
Author's collection

Mk I Sunderlands of No 230 Squadron at moorings off the south coast of Greece, preparing to evacuate British troops.
Imperial War Museum, London (CM 759)

The author as Aircraftman 2nd class (AC2) at the Initial Training Wing, RAF Station Kumalo, Bulawayo, Southern Rhodesia (Zimbabwe).

Author's collection

A De Havilland Tiger Moth, the type of aircraft on which the author learned to fly.

Imperial War Museum, London (CH 2376)

A North American Aviation Harvard; note the flaps have been lowered to reduce speed to that of the photographer's aircraft. It was at No 20 SFTS, Cranborne, Rhodesia, that Alan Deller flew this type of aircraft.

Imperial War Museum, London (CH 621)

Mk I Sunderlands in formation, clearly showing the 'step' on the planing bottom, just below the rear edge of the wing.

Imperial War Museum, London (CH 35)

Mk II Sunderland undergoing major maintenance ashore, resting on two massive beaching legs – the starboard one can be seen below the mainplane – and the steerable tail trolley.

Imperial War Museum, London (CM 4872)

Mk III Sunderland up the slipway for overhaul, showing the beaching gear wheels and tail trolley.

Imperial War Museum, London (CH 16152)

Mk I Sunderland just starting its takeoff run.

Imperial War Museum, London (CM 842)

Mk I Sunderland in flight. The planing bottom, with its 'step' halfway along its length, can be clearly seen.

Imperial War Museum, London (CH 3210)

Mk I Sunderland on its mooring buoy: the bowman is reaching for one of the two main mooring pendants to then hand it up to his assistant who will mount it temporarily on a bollard while the captain keeps an eye on this vitally important procedure, during which the bow gun turret is retracted into the hull.

Imperial War Museum, London (CH 848)

Mk I Sunderland of No 210 Squadron escorting a fast troop convoy with battle cruiser escort.

Imperial War Museum, London (CH 829)

Mk II Sunderland of No 246 Squadron blown ashore at Bowmore, Islay, after the moorings parted during an exceptionally severe gale.

Imperial War Museum, London (CM 10191)

A Consolidated Catalina flying boat with one depth charge beneath each wing, probably on an exercise. The photographic aircraft is carrying dummy bombs.

Imperial War Museum, London (CM 2369)

The author and his crew at No 131 (Coastal) Operational Training Unit, Killadeas, Co Fermanagh, Northern Ireland.
Back row (left to right): *Sgt Warburton, Sgt Matheson, Sgt Owen, Sgt Dandeker*
Front row (left to right): *Sgt Moir, Flying Officer Allen, Author, Sgt Ellard, Sgt Jones*

Author's collection

Cocktail party aboard the author's aircraft S/230 at Mahé, Seychelles.

Author's collection

The author's aircraft being refuelled by Shell at Kisumu, Lake Victoria.

Author's collection

The author collecting official mail ("By safe hand of captain") from Flight Lieutenant Lancaster, Commanding Officer, Kelai advanced flying boat base, Maldive Islands.
Left to right: ?, Flight Lieutenant Lancaster, Flight Sergeant Ellard, Joe Eggett, ?, Author, Sidney Moorhouse (War Correspondent, Yorkshire Post).

Imperial War Museum, London

The Officers Mess, Addu Atoll, Maldive Islands

Author's collection

Mk III Sunderland S for Sugar *of No 230 Squadron RAF (the author's aircraft) at moorings at Addu Atoll, Maldive Islands. Passengers are being ferried out to the aircraft by one of the small, fast flying boat tenders – known universally as 'dinghies' – that served valiantly in every part of the British marine aircraft world.*

Imperial War Museum, London (CF 620)

Mk III Sunderland S for Sugar *about to leave the water travelling at about 95 knots (c105 mph) at Addu Atoll, Maldive Islands, the author at the controls. The four aerials on top of the hull are part of the early radar equipment.*

Imperial War Museum, London (CF 657)

Mk III Sunderland at moorings with a seagoing flying boat tender, a high speed launch (or HSL) widely used for flare path laying, rescue, towing, etc; their high superstructure rendered them unsuitable for ferrying crews and passengers as they would foul the airscrews when coming alongside.

Imperial War Museum, London (CH 10075)

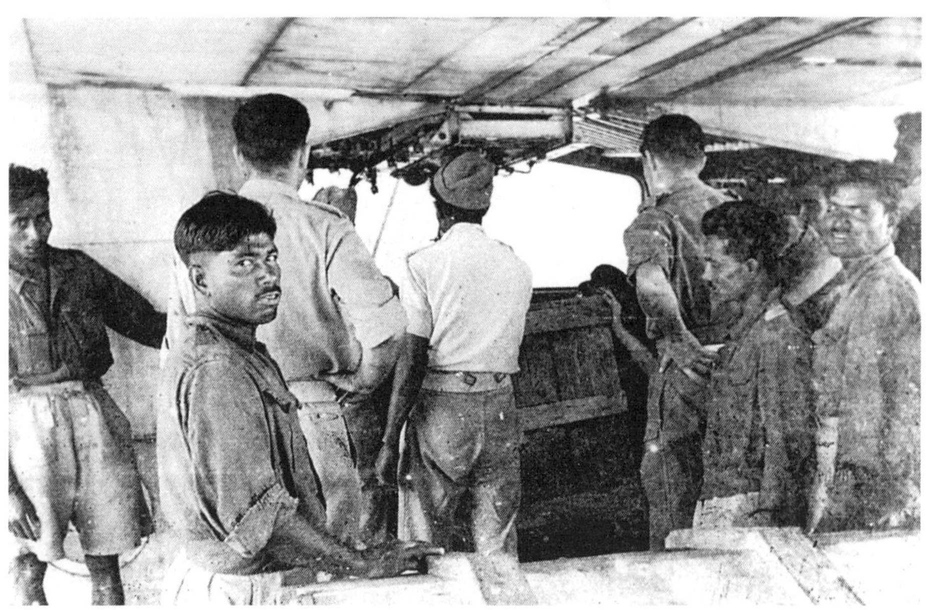

Sepoys of No 5 Inland Water Transport Company, Royal Engineers (Commanding Officer Major Corbett, third from left) watching the unloading of a half ton marine engine from the aircraft's bomb room, using the electrically-operated bomb trolley visible top centre.

Author's collection

All 510 officers and men of No 230 Squadron, Royal Air Force at Koggala, Ceylon, April 1945, prior to the departure of the advance half to Akyab, on the west coat of Burma. The boat is a Sunderland Mk V.

Author's collection

"Come full circle": the author standing beside a Tiger Moth at No 1 Reserve Flying School, Royal Air Force Volunteer Reserve at Panshanger, Hertfordshire, January 1948.

Author's collection

Captain's course – Stranraer

Arrived at Stranraer we found that five more of the George crowd were also on the course: Bob Russell, Charles Rodgers, Johnnie Cowle and the two Australians, Val Harris, one of the funniest men I had ever met, and Harold 'Jacko' Jackson. The Officers Mess was a remarkable folly, called North West Castle, situated right on the promenade. All the instructors were on rest from operations: one of them was 'Pissy' Parsons ex-95 Squadron in Freetown, Sierra Leone who had difficulty in explaining his sobriquet to his dear old white-haired mother, while another was 'Bismarck' Briggs who had flown the Catalina that found the ship in filthy weather; he made his regular checks on the ship's position by keeping in cloud and flying round until the anti-aircraft shells started bursting round him. My instructor was a pleasant, rather tense man called Flight Lieutenant Grunert.

While at Stranraer we would be having a certain amount of ground school, specialist flying boat stuff: drill when moving in harbours, rule of the road at sea, buoys and lights and some northern hemisphere meteorology, together with technical instruction on the equipment and operation of the Sunderland. But the main emphasis was on learning to fly the Sunderland and as a stepping stone to this we flew a somewhat antique twin-engined flying boat, the Saunders-Roe London. It had the great virtue of simplicity – it took off at 85 knots, climbed at 85 knots, flew the circuit at 85 knots and approached to land at 85 knots. Despite this I was not happy because my instructor was unrestful, constantly telling me what to do which thoroughly upset my confidence. I did manage to go solo on the Sunderland but had no real confidence about it and then one day I was flying dual in the London and had reached such a state that on the landing approach I was waiting for the chap to tell me when to check the descent, which he did not do and we hit the water with a tremendous smack, fortunately with no damage.

The next day I was moved over to join Duggie with his instructor on the Sunderland. After an hour and a half's dual the instructor called a dinghy and got off, leaving Duggie and me to alternate as first pilot for another two hours which went splendidly and completely restored my confidence.

Stranraer stands at the head of Loch Ryan, a large expanse of water, open to the sea at the western end and ideal for operating two or three flying boats on training flights at the same time, although we had to watch for the Irish mail boats sailing in and out of the loch; they were moored close in to the town, to one side of the area we used for night flying.

One morning near the end of our time at Stranraer I was flying solo in a Sunderland with a Canadian, Willy Fumerton, as the other pilot (we just had one engineer in addition, to look after the engines and do the mooring and unmooring). We were climbing out westwards over the sea past 'Paddy's Milestone', Ailsa Craig, when the engineer reported zero oil pressure in the starboard outer engine. In those circumstances the engine had to be shut down immediately because with nonfeathering airscrews the engine continued to 'windmill' due to the airflow driving the airscrew round and if the engine were to seize solid the airscrew would probably twist off, complete with the reduction gear, and fly through the air causing a greater or lesser degree of damage to the aircraft. So I shut down the starboard outer and returned for a three-engine landing. With two engines on one side and only one on the other there is naturally a tremendous force tending to pull the aircraft round in the direction of the failed engine but when cruising it can be counteracted by applying opposite rudder, helped by the rudder trimmer. Nevertheless, actually landing a big aeroplane in an unbalanced condition is not easy and the thought of having to do it one day is one of a pilot's less happy dreams. In this case I did actually manage a decent landing; it was a very valuable experience – and not my last.

Two nights later Charles Rodgers and I did our first night flying. It was a beautiful night with a brilliant moon and once airborne and on the circuit, we had a couple of minutes or so before turning in for the approach and landing to enjoy the spectacle of the moonlit hills contrasting with the black waters of the loch on which we could just see the three tiny specks of light that formed our flare path (see page 74). We each had two and a quarter hours flying in the first pilot's seat, with our cautious instructor in the second pilot's place, but solo would have to wait for another night, although we both managed well and felt confident.

The next night was equally fine, giving a clear view of the two Irish mail boats moored just to the left of our takeoff path and the blacked-out town of Stranraer over which we climbed away each time after takeoff – I say climbed but this aircraft, like the others we flew, was a veteran of the Mediterranean war, Greece and Crete evacuations and much more, and had since then done innumerable 'circuits and bumps' in the hands of apprentice captains; the performance of all of them was inevitably well below par and this one more or less staggered over the town and cleared the nearby hills by not all that much. Charles Rodgers and I again took it in turns to fly the aeroplane with the instructor in the other seat then, after about an hour he left the aircraft and we embarked on our first night solo flying.

From time to time throughout the evening we had all noticed a momentary very slight nudge to the left just as the aircraft left the water, but it was so slight and so irregular that it was disregarded – with big, complicated aircraft there were occasionally small niggles which usually disappeared with no harm done and cancelling a trip because of one would be highly unpopular. Charles did his four or five circuits successfully and then I took over for my first Sunderland night solo. Carefully lining the aeroplane up on a heading just to the right of the distant flare path I opened the throttles, got her running nicely on the step and then, at the moment of leaving the water, there was a distinct momentary leftward nudge before she dragged herself up over the roofs and the surrounding hills. Back on the water again that was my first night solo in the bag. I started the next run and as we left the water the port outer engine cut absolutely dead. With 2000 horsepower from the two starboard engines at full power pulling against only a thousand from the port inner (which from its position exerted minimum leverage) a violent swing towards the two mail boats began and was impossible to hold with the rudder. I realised that, even if there had been time to help by trimming the rudder, the dead beat machine on three engines would never clear the town whose waterfront, with our Officers Mess dead ahead, was approaching at around 100 miles an hour; we were by now well past the flare path and I shouted to Charles "I'm landing straight ahead!", throttled back the starboard outer to stop the swing, got her up to 150 feet, ran out the flaps to two-thirds and eased her down on to the water with the two inner engines, helped by the moonlight to make, actually, a decently smooth landing, coming to a stop less than 200 yards from the promenade.

Strangely enough, at that moment I felt completely calm even though the entire episode from takeoff to back on the water, with all its assessments and decisions, had occupied little more than thirty seconds. Our instructor, nervous at the best of times, was visibly shaken as he hastened back on board and we taxied back to the buoy. Charles, unable of course to do anything but watch and wait in the other seat, was steady as a rock, but what the unfortunate engineer – entirely in the hands of two 'sprog' pilots – must have gone through in those seconds can only be imagined. The instructor and the launch crew had seen a huge red fireball shoot out from the exhaust of the port outer engine at the moment of take off; it appeared that there was a fault in the carburettor which meant that as the aircraft accelerated on leaving the water the extra ram effect from the rush of air forced into the forward-facing air intake drastically upset the carburation – this had started off by correcting itself immediately but then deteriorated takeoff after takeoff until it stopped the engine completely – 1000 horsepower to zero in two seconds!

This was the second occasion in my flying career (see page 49 for the first) on which a split-second decision had enabled me, by God's grace, to save my own life and those of many others.

A dead cut, especially of an outer engine, at the moment of take off, at night and with nowhere to go is, I suppose, apart from fire in the air, every pilot's ultimate nightmare and all the boys naturally wanted to know what it had been like. For me, having gone through it and come out the other side, it was a great confidence boost and later experiences of engine failure were never as bad.

That was the end of flying at Stranraer for me and three days later, after a monumental party, we all set forth to Invergordon.

Captain's course – Invergordon

Actually the base was at Alness, some way from Invergordon and this was the name officially adopted later on. We got up at 6am and embarked on an interminable but gloriously picturesque train journey right across Scotland, eventually arriving at 10.30 at night. We were put in grim, untidy Nissen huts with no lights and just an antediluvian coke-burning stove in the middle which was, of course, empty. Night-time at the end of September that far north is cold and we managed eventually to scrounge some coke, but the stove was most reluctant to burn at all and we froze for the remainder of the night. Next day we had quite a long journey by coach (RAF pattern, noisy, no springs, insufficient/hard seats) to Alness itself where the ground school and the aircraft were based, on a wide inlet off the Moray Firth, close by the mouth of the Caledonian Canal.

On arrival at the base, we went through the usual formalities and learned something of the very intensive work that lay ahead of us. We also learned that next day we should collect our own crews and thereafter work with them throughout the course and then on to squadrons – quite a thought, nine of them! What would they be like? I made a good start that evening in the mess; I had been told to look for my navigator, Pilot Officer GH Allen and I found him standing by the fireplace, quiet, serious, medium height, immediately friendly – he gave me confidence.

Next day George and I met the rest of the crew, all sergeants. They seemed a sound lot, although with no flying boat experience, and we quickly plunged in at the deep end, going out to an aircraft with an instructor for my routine dual check halfway through the course. The machine was a newer model, a Mk III, and proved a bit of a handful on the water at first: the Mk Is and IIs we had flown at Stranraer had a fairly deep step halfway along the bottom of the hull (the planing bottom) designed to raise the after part clear of the water, thus eliminating its water-drag and making it easier to obtain the increased speed to enable the aircraft to plane over the surface of the water instead of ploughing through it, so reaching takeoff speed more rapidly. The turbulence behind the step helped the water to break away, but there was also a slight suction effect while the step was still deep in the water and this imparted a degree of directional stability in the middle stage of the takeoff run before the rudder had become fully effective with high speed. In the new Mk III the step had been greatly reduced to only about one inch deep, virtually eliminating the drag of the slight suction effect but also eliminating entirely the small contribution to directional stability. Thus it was that on this first outing with my new crew I was taken by surprise by the much greater tendency of the machine to swing to the left due to the torque effect of the engines at full power, specially once up on the step at speed, and to stop the swing getting out of control I had to abandon the takeoff and shamefacedly taxi back to have another go.

The situation during the latter stages of the takeoff in these advanced aircraft was quite tricky. Fully loaded the aeroplane would come up on the step, ie with just the forward part of the planing bottom in the water, at about 50-55 knots after which more and more of the bottom would be lifted out of the water with rapidly increasing speed until the aeroplane was racing over the water at some 70 knots (about 85 mph) with only about one foot depth and two to three feet length of the keel left in the water, and even that rapidly decreasing as speed rose steadily to 80 knots and on to actual take off at about 95 knots (about 115 mph). It was a bit like balancing a 30 ton heap driven by 4200 horsepower at around 100 miles per hour on a pinhead – have the nose fractionally too low and the machine would dig into the water and be held back, have the nose fractionally too high and the machine could come off the water at too low speed, stall and bounce back on to the water, possibly straining or damaging the bottom – and at the same time maintaining a straight line was also desirable although in some circumstances, as will be related, a flying boat could do, craftily, what a land aircraft cannot do – turn on the step and change direction in the middle of the takeoff run.

For the rest of that morning, with several successful takeoffs, circuits and landings, I quickly got the feel of the aircraft and came to enjoy its general improved agility and the superbly balanced controls making it a joy to handle in the air. During this first week we new captains were settling down with our crews and they, in their turn, were getting used to us and, most importantly, were being thoroughly inducted into the practice of their particular specialities as performed on a big flying boat and, furthermore, learning their duties in the marine handling of the aircraft – mooring and unmooring, use of the drogues, care of the bilges, refuelling on the water and so on, a new world for them. As well as the navigator I had first and second engineers, three wireless operators and a rigger (responsible for the aircraft structure). A second pilot and a 'straight' air-gunner (ie concerned solely with the aircraft's armament; all the other crew members apart from the second pilot and the navigator were trained air-gunners as well as having their own speciality, as explained earlier – see page 67) were to be picked up later. As a crew they were promising, but within a day or two some of them came to me and said they were not settling well with three others while they knew of three in another crew who were unhappy in a rather rough lot and would I agree to swap? I was not altogether surprised as the three complained of stuck out like a sore thumb so I got the agreement of the 'authorities'; a nicer, sounder, trio could not be imagined than our new acquisitions and we all settled immediately into a keen and harmonious team.

Flying was mainly navigation exercises to get us settled in as a crew, apart from some additional night-flying 'circuits and bumps' and practising full-glide landings (engines throttled right back in a near-45 degree angle of approach) and crosswind takeoffs and landings. On the ground we all had mainly brushing-up exercises in our respective lines of activity but, in addition, for the captains, navigators and wireless operators there was a fiendish but most valuable exercise in what was called 'The Madhouse'.

On three nights, after dinner, each captain would ensconce himself in a tiny cubicle with his navigator and one wireless operator in similar cubicles alongside. The captain had a dummy signalling lamp, dummy flight instruments and compass and intercom to the other two; the navigator had charts, chart table with all his navigation instruments, a coding machine and the recognition codes; the wireless operator had a dummy radio set. Everything was connected to the instructors' room from which the whole exercise was conducted: we skeleton crews were briefed as for a regular convoy escort sortie.

The cubicles looked on to a darkened space with a large dimly-discerned table and, very prominent, the chief instrument of torture – 'The Clock'. At takeoff time the clock started and we settled down to set the course being worked out by the navigator who also gave out the recognition letter for the period. Two minutes later, on glancing out of the window one saw that the clock had advanced to within half an hour of the expected time to meet the convoy; at the same time the wireless operator had received a signal in code altering the expected meeting point with the convoy – new course worked out by now, and set on compass by captain who looks up to see illuminated on the table a tiny model U-boat dead ahead – capt. announces decision to attack, orders flares dropped and tells navigator to prepare signal to Group saying "Attacking U-boat position so and so" (navigator to work out position and pass signal to wireless operator – captain worries "it ought to have gone in code"). Next moment U-boat disappears – captain to navigator tell wireless operator to send "U-boat dived, attack cancelled." Clock advanced twenty minutes while navigator still working out new expected time of arrival at convoy which suddenly illuminated on table eight miles ahead, captain sends recognition letter, Senior Officer of Escort flashes (little lamp beside model destroyer) "Carry out square patrol round convoy at five miles", captain to navigator to work out patrol meanwhile first course please. Clock seen advanced one hour, aircraft now on far side of convoy from SOE, suddenly an enemy cruiser appears some miles distant, aircraft too far to flash so, captain must decide to break wireless silence to report enemy, navigator told to draft signal giving enemy description and position (needed by Group and HQ also), captain to decide encode?, or in view of the urgency to send in plain language? Wireless operator to send . . . and so on at a hectic pace, a whole twelve hour sortie compressed into an hour and a half – wet rag stuff but a very valuable run-in to the real thing, applying so much that we had learned in theory.

On the other hand the flying became more interesting. We did two navigation exercises to the Faroes, with an instructor each time. The first approach to the islands was astonishing. They rose straight out of the sea as vertical cliffs that were unbelievably high; to check we flew close alongside the cliff tops and the altimeter read just 2000 feet! Even more remarkable was our approach to our destination, Vågar, at the head of a fjord that was itself about a thousand feet above the sea, its waters spilling over a sheer drop into the sea below in an impressive waterfall. It was quite extraordinary to fly in directly over the cliff edge and waterfall, very low so as to stop the landing run before actually reaching the town. The takeoff was in the reverse direction and the run was so short that we were barely off the water when we cleared the cliff edge and suddenly looked down a thousand feet to the sea.

The final exercise was a night navigation trip over the North Sea towards Norway with myself as captain with my crew and Bob Russell acting as second pilot changing over as captain part of the time. By this time George was proving himself a very steady and accurate navigator and it seemed quite an adventure ploughing out into the pitch blackness in the general direction of an enemy-occupied country. All was well until, after about three hours and a long way out, the first engineer reported a sudden complete oil pressure failure on the starboard outer engine with the oil temperature rising rapidly. I was flying the aeroplane at the time and immediately cut the throttle and switched off the ignition so as to slow the engine down as much as possible to prevent it from seizing with the attendant danger of the airscrew and reduction gear twisting off and chopping something. Unfortunately, as already mentioned, the Bristol

Pegasus engines did not have feathering airscrews where the blades could be turned edge-on to the airflow, thus stopping the engine from 'windmilling' as it continued to do in this case. I asked George for a course for home and he estimated that we had about an hour to go, so I trimmed the rudder to correct the swing being caused by having two engines working on one side and only one on the other and settled down to a rather suspenseful slog through the night.

The engines had been at cruising speed of 1700 revolutions per minute (rpm) when the oil pressure failure occurred and the starboard outer, when shut down, was windmilling at 1240 rpm. As time went on the revs slowly dropped as the unlubricated engine got hotter and tighter and by the time we picked up the Invergordon SE (radar) beacon (about 40 minutes out) the revs were down to some 700. We altered course to follow the beacon and at about 20 minutes out, with the revs down to about 300 we spotted a 'Pundit' just below – (Pundits were red lights in various spots all over the country that flashed a secret Morse code letter which, when checked against the briefing papers, would indicate their position) – very helpful in the total blackout. In this case the Pundit's location was Lossiemouth and George immediately reported that we were 30 degrees off course; obviously something was wrong with either the beacon or our receiver so, with my heart in my mouth, we altered to George's new course and soon afterwards spotted the flare path (the usual three 40 watt bulbs on pram dinghies). Instead of doing the regulation circuit before landing, with the starboard outer barely turning at 240 revs I came straight in and made my second three-engined night landing, decently done, only to be ticked off by the duty instructor on the flare path launch for not doing a circuit before landing. It was our first crisis together and I have sometimes wondered how the crew felt that dark night with their safety in the hands of their new captain.

It was clear next day that the people on the ground, as usual, reckoned the pilot had exaggerated the trouble and, with the tremendous pressure to keep the aircraft flying, they just filled the engine up with oil and started it up; oil pressure was still zero and when they opened up the oil filter it was full of white metal melted out of the bearings – so it was a very near thing. Meanwhile it was discovered that the SE aerials on one side of the aircraft had been bent, most probably by dinghy drivers hanging on to them to help them to get alongside in high winds, and that explained the false indication of the beacon. Thus captain, navigator and SE operator were all exonerated.

The last week was taken up with final classes, general clearing up and postings! We were to join a newly-formed squadron, No 246, operating Sunderlands at Bowmore on the Hebridean island of Islay, while Duggie was to go to No 230 Squadron based at Alexandria. We had been the closest of friends for a whole year and were sorry to part; at about that time we had heard also that the third of our little trio of laughter-makers at George, Frank Haddon, had been tragically killed, with all his crew, in a landing accident in a Hudson.

So, with a reasonably satisfactory assessment of 'Average' at the end of the captains course I prepared to set forth on operations with my own crew who were fast becoming good friends and a very competent team.

Footnotes:

Observations on the foregoing:

1. Although I was naturally not privy to the detailed chronology of this incident the account I have given is correct in essentials.

2. Technical note: there had been more than one or two instances of depth charges, supposedly in the 'safe' condition [ie not primed for action], exploding following a crash at sea. For the weapon to be primed a spring-loaded rod within the 'pistol' [the firing device] had to be freed to rotate, thus opening small ports through which the water could enter and, at a certain pre-determined depth, exert sufficient pressure to release the firing pin that would explode the detonator which in turn would set off the main charge – which in the case of the later Torpex-filled depth charge, was powerful enough to punch a hole in the immensely strong pressure-hull of a submarine at a distance of up to 19 feet; the spring-loaded rod was prevented from rotating by a spring clip which was fastened by a rigid link to the depth charge carrier; in the event of a very heavy landing, particularly a catastrophic one resulting in the break-up of the aircraft, the heavy depth charge could bounce on its carrier, thus disengaging the retaining spring clip so that the weapon became active and would explode if it fell into the water and reached the pre-determined depth. Shortly after 201's experience, and one or two others, the rigid link was replaced by a steel wire slightly longer than the distance between carrier and spring clip so that it could absorb a bounce without dislodging the clip.

Fourth Movement
(ii) Operations
Bowmore, Islay

After a week's leave in London and a few bombs – quite a strange experience after months of peaceful remoteness – we all met in good order in Glasgow and on the morning of 19 November 1942 took a MacBrayne's ferry down the Clyde and round the southern end of Bute to Rothesay and East Tarbert on Loch Fyne, very beautiful country even in poor weather. From East Tarbert a bus took us over the hills to West Tarbert where we took another MacBrayne's ferry for the trip to Port Ellen on Islay; this was a fascinating journey as the ship was loaded with cows, a car or two and numbers of people with produce, all of which chopped and changed at each of the numerous small stopping places, sheep replacing cows, poultry joining pigs and everyone treating it all as a jolly social occasion.

Then we were at the little town of Port Ellen where we disembarked and piled into the RAF's usual type of spring-less, hard-seated bus for the journey through the very beautiful, rather bleak Islay countryside with lovely hills and mountains in the distance. Topping a rise coming into the village of Bowmore we saw its distinctive round church at the top of the wide main street leading steeply down to the whisky distillery and the little harbour. Most striking, however, was the view of Loch Indaal, wide open to the sea to the left of us and, in front of us, the truly thrilling sight of six Sunderlands at moorings. This really was it at last!

The accommodation and the ops room were in Nissen huts on a small rise overlooking the loch, just on the far side of the village; the squadron office and the maintenance and marine craft sections, as we soon found out, were in the distillery which was closed for the duration of the war and held its (reputed) several million gallons of distinctive peaty spirit firmly under lock and key. We quickly found our way around and equipped ourselves with the wellingtons and oilskins that were semi-permanent wear in the swiftly changing and often quite violent weather with which we were to become all too familiar; the loch faced southwest so the prevailing wind came to us unobstructed.

Soon after we arrived we were told that we were to have a brand new Mk III aircraft (some of the other squadron 'boats were Mk IIs) which we should collect from Pembroke Dock as soon as it was delivered there from the makers. This was a tremendous boost to the whole crew and we could hardly wait to get our hands on the new boat which would bear the identification letter *K*. I immediately decided she should be called *Katie* after the lady in the song, popular at that time "who went to Haiti where she met a natie who taught her many things".

Meanwhile, however, there were many routine things to see to and to undertake, among them the job of duty captain at night in bad weather. This involved spending the night in a small hut close to the jetty in the small harbour and using an Aldis signalling lamp every half hour or so to illuminate all the aircraft in turn to see that they were all safe at their moorings. If the weather became severe during the night the duty captain had to contact the Flight Commander who had to judge whether conditions were bad enough to call out gale crews.

We did not have to wait long to experience Bowmore's worst in the way of weather. Early one day the met officer predicted gale conditions in which the violent wind and the rough sea would put a serious strain on the aircraft moorings; a gale crew – a pilot and three others (but never the navigators!) – would stay on board each aircraft to do whatever might be necessary to protect it from damage or loss: if the aircraft should start to strain severely at the moorings the pilot would start two engines and, each time a gust came, would open up the engines sufficiently to take the strain and then, as the gust died down, throttle them back so that the machine would not ride up on the buoy – all in all a tedious but vital job that could go on for hours or even a day or more. This time the crews were relieved after some five hours as the storm turned out to be quite a mild one. However the decision whether to put gale crews on board or not had to be taken in good time because if it were delayed and the sea became very rough it could become impossible to get the dinghies alongside the aircraft to put the crews on board – an unattended aircraft might then break loose and be blown ashore and damaged or lost.

It was very important that I should have a chance to become familiar with the features of the coastline in our operating area, effectively the Scottish west coast and the stretch round the northern part of Ireland to Lough Erne and beyond. For this purpose I did navigation trips as a passenger, first with a South African Air Force Lieutenant, Jack Lever, known as 'Soapy', a most engaging, humorous character who had served earlier as a wireless operator/air-gunner in light bombers in the East African campaign, and secondly with Micky Teare, a fairly experienced captain, a Yorkshireman with an amusing turn of phrase. These were two of an enjoyable company in the mess among whom was another captain, Anthony Squire, a laid-back humorous fellow, the son of the poet and writer Sir John Squire and a film director who liked to hide an interesting intellect behind an affectation of faintly amused boredom.

It was not until mid-December that, having now acquired a rather youthful second pilot and an air-gunner to complete my crew – ten of us in all – I was told to go to Pembroke Dock to collect our very own aeroplane. We arrived at PD early in the morning and as soon as possible went out to '*K* for Katie' — hull number EJ137, a fine new Mk III Sunderland built by Short Brothers at Rochester where the Sunderland had been designed originally and where they were still built on the original jigs and quite largely by the original craftsmen, producing a much better finished machine than those made by other firms at Windermere and Belfast. It was quite a moment to step inside my own boat and share the satisfaction being expressed by all the crew with this beautiful machine.

On Sunday 20 December, we made our first flight in her, an hour and a half stooging around in poor weather while we all tried to get the feel of things. All seemed well and she handled pleasantly in the air. The next thing to do was to collect all the mass of equipment laid down in the 'book of words': we all became rapidly immersed in a chase round to one place after another, armed, of course, with the relevant papers, to collect emergency dinghies, boathooks, Mae Wests, anchor and twenty fathoms of chain, engineer's toolkit, cutlery and crockery, Primus oven, plate rack, drogues, emergency ration packs, parachutes, sextant, Aldis lamp, Very pistol, six Browning 0.303 machine guns and one Vickers K machine gun – and so on, including a fog bell to be rung while under way through busy waters in fog! It was rather like commissioning a warship and emphasised to all of us the huge difference between operating in a land aircraft, where you flew whichever machine was available for that particular flight, and the flying boat world in which you and your crew literally made your aircraft your home as well as your chariot.

Our second test flight two days later was cut short after only forty-five minutes because of low oil pressure on one engine. We were getting a bit frustrated as we wanted to get back to Bowmore for Christmas and obstacles – inevitable at such a busy station as PD was – seemed to us to be deliberately put in our way, although the equipment people were admirable.

Next day was better as we were cleared for a four and a half hour navigation trip after a good test flight in the morning. We really started to feel at home with our aeroplane even though the weather was bad with a lot of turbulence which made things uncomfortable and hard work for the pilot – me! The following day was Christmas Eve and we rushed to get final equipment aboard in the hope of getting away later in the day; we did a taxi-test to ensure that all was shipshape, only to find that the starboard outer engine was running too fast on the tick-over which made manoeuvring on the water difficult. We returned to a buoy right alongside the old fortifications of the Royal Dockyard and awaited an engine fitter who would adjust the throttle control. In due course – and not a minute sooner – he came, did his stuff and announced that all was ready for a trial start of the engine; the moment the engine fired it roared straight up to 1500 revs swung the aircraft round to face the port wall and ripped her adrift from the mooring buoy. Only feet away from the wall I had to cut the roaring engine, leaving us completely helpless and drifting in the wind out into the main fairway, at which precise moment the Neyland ferry started to cross, moving directly into our path. Fortunately our frantic shouts had been heard by one of the many launches moving among the numerous other moored aircraft and we were taken in tow just in time and that definitely meant Christmas at PD.

Cheerfulness returned with a splendid party in the mess – one of the handsome and comfortable prewar RAF messes – a sharp contrast to our bleak Nissen hut at Bowmore. Christmas Day passed pleasantly enough with another party in the evening and on Boxing Day a leisurely recovery had been followed by some work tidying up the aircraft which had collected a lot of dirt from the coming and going of maintenance men and their gear while the numerous adjustments required by a complicated aeroplane were carried out.

On our way back to the shore in the late afternoon darkness and gloom, happily anticipating yet another party, I happened to glance out towards the west and noticed red flares being fired. The next moment I recognised a Sunderland moving slowly towards us under three engines and with one wing tip float missing; several of the crew were sitting on the opposite wing to prevent the float-less wing dipping into the water which would promptly fill it and cause the aircraft to capsize and sink immediately. I sent my crew off to shore in the dinghy and commandeered a pinnace, a big three-engined RAF flying boat tender, to go and take the stricken aircraft in tow. As I got close the captain called out that his aircraft was also holed and sinking as I had already guessed having heard in the distance the noise of his auxiliary power unit (he was Bill Statham, a Canadian, who had been on the captain's course with us) and as it would be useless, indeed a monumental nuisance, to put her on a buoy I decided to beach her on a sand bar I knew lay across the entrance to the inner harbour.

The coxswain of the pinnace was very sound and we started slowly towing the battered Sunderland through the darkness. All the while she was getting lower in the water even though her crew had had the auxiliary power unit pumping water out of the hull at its maximum rate. But towing too fast would have risked possibly slewing the aircraft, probably flinging the men off the wing into the water where they would have been difficult to find in the darkness, and causing the machine to capsize. I stood on the pinnace's deck conning the procession through the crowded aircraft moorings, trying to balance the need to get to the beaching quickly against the risk to the aircraft from rushing the job, keeping up a shouted dialogue with a very worried Bill and trying to quell my own considerable worries. It took nearly two hours from picking up the tow to finally landing her on the bank two miles away, with only the top of the hull and the mainplane showing as the tide rose. When I finally got ashore, around nine, all thoughts of a party had evaporated. But I got a pat on the back from the Station Commander next day.

I saw Bill later and he told me he had taken off for Malta early in the afternoon with a full load of spares for the Spitfires that were fighting the ferocious air battles over the island. As darkness was coming on one engine failed and another sounded shaky; with a full load of petrol for the long trip and the heavy spares he could not maintain altitude so with a heavy heart they pitched the precious spares overboard and turned for home. The main takeoff and landing area was in Angle Bay, a very open stretch of water some distance from Pembroke Dock itself; the water had been fairly rough in a strong wind and Bill had made a heavy landing, knocking a hole in the bottom, while at the same time a wave wiped off his starboard wing tip float. For some reason the station had not been able to get a launch and a flare path out to Angle Bay – maybe his radio had packed up as well, I do not remember – so he had had to plough his dark and lonely way, in a thoroughly shaky situation, for what must have seemed like two ages until I got the pinnace to him.

We finally got away from PD on a sunny morning and, after a picturesque flight up the Welsh coast, past snow-covered Snowdon and the snowy mountains of the Isle of Man, I brought the squadron's new aircraft in to a cautious landing at Bowmore. It was good to be back again and, now that we had our own aeroplane we seemed to be accepted – as we ourselves felt more and more – as proper members of the squadron. We also revelled in some clean clothes; we had had to spend longer than intended at PD and it was no use getting anything washed there as we did not know from day to day when we should be leaving.

The next day was New Year's Eve and quite a selection of the delightful local womenfolk were brought to the mess for a very vigorous dance, the party being conducted with the rectitude to be expected of a Scottish island community; but there was in fact enough to drink although sadly, on this island with eight distilleries, no whisky. As midnight struck I could not help looking back to previous New Years – last year in South Africa, the year before in hospital in Alexandria – as I wrote in my diary "Where next year? Ah! who knows?"

Operations – North Atlantic

We spent the first two weeks of January on numerous tests, in the air and on the water, to get all the equipment adjusted and to make sure we were all thoroughly conversant with every aspect of our aircraft and the work we were to do. Day after day we trudged down to the harbour in sweaters, sometimes two, wellies and oilskins, sped across the water often drenched with spray, stepped on board and settled to work, punctuated by breaks for hot drinks from the galley and chat among ourselves, all conducive to the welding together of the crew. Getting back ashore was frequently the most frustrating part of the day: not only were many other crews working on their boats but numbers of maintenance men – 'erks' as they were known, quite affectionately on the whole, throughout the RAF – also needed to be ferried to and fro among the aircraft and between the aircraft and shore; an erk who found he had forgotten a spanner had a long way to go to get it. The result was that one often had to wait what seemed like an age before a dinghy driver appeared to notice one and the whole area of the 'trots' (lines of buoys to which the aircraft were moored) resounded to despairing cries of "Dingh-e-e-e!" plus some verbal embellishment.

The engine fitters had the worst job of all the 'erks'. To get at the engines small platforms about a foot square, forming part of the leading edge of the mainplane, were hinged downwards to provide a firm foothold; if the front of the engine and the airscrew itself needed to be got at, light frames were hitched on to the little platforms and a light alloy plank, eight inches wide, was passed under the engine and located on the frames each side. On this minute support the fitter, clad in heavy and clumsy overalls against the cold, would sit, often at Bowmore buffeted by freezing wind and driving rain or even sleet, and do his vital work adjusting valve clearances, fitting new plugs and so on. The joyful thing about it was that anything, a tool or a spare part, dropped from frozen fingers fell straight into the water and was not seen again. We used to admire them for getting anything done at all but there is no doubt that the difficulties of servicing on the water in winter in an exposed location like Bowmore contributed enormously to the poor record of aircraft availability from which the squadron suffered for much of the time. Due, I am sure, to the superb efficiency and knowledge of my first engineer, Sergeant Matheson, who had been apprenticed at, and then worked for years in, a great Scottish lorry makers, our aircraft *K* had a very good record and in later months we were strike aircraft for three or four days at a time on occasion, no other aircraft being available.

Three weeks into January we were strike aircraft for the first time and the next day we were sent off on our first operation to patrol far ahead of a convoy which we in fact never saw. After nearly twelve hours we reached land which, to our horror, we recognised as St Kilda, nearly 100 miles from Islay. George, whose navigation had hitherto been spot-on, was absolutely shattered and it did not look good as a start to our career with the squadron. In Coastal Command it was routine for the navigator's log and charts of every operational sortie to be sent straight to Group Headquarters where it was minutely analysed by the navigational experts. George's log was found to be absolutely correct and it was obvious that there was something odd about the aircraft that had never shown up before. The compasses had originally been swung most carefully so we took to the air to make a radio compass check; over two hours and twenty minutes we flew backwards and forwards over Bowmore on a series of accurately flown courses while the radio loop aerial inside its streamlined housing on top of the hull just above the navigator's position was rotated to pick up accurately a radio station whose position was known precisely and the readings compared with the courses as shown on all the aircraft's magnetic compasses. The correlations were exact on every course flown – absolutely nothing amiss! So it was agreed with Group that we should do another op and see whether the thing had cured itself.

A day later we set forth in atrocious weather to escort a convoy. Our SE (radar) packed up on the way out and after extended searching we failed to find the convoy although we had our first real experience of being buffeted around in the air without respite while a few hundred feet below the wind was tearing great shreds of foam off the tops of immense rolling dark browny-grey waves. Understandably keen to get home we were stunned to find ourselves approaching land about 60 miles away from where we should have been. It was a dreadful feeling, especially for poor George. There was nothing for it but to do another tedious airborne check of the compasses. To eliminate any chance that some radio anomaly was the cause we flew the same courses over Bowmore, this time using the astrocompass which was aligned each time on a single heavenly body, in our case the sun, whose position relative to the earth had been precisely determined by sextant. Again everything checked perfectly; George's navigation had once again been checked and indeed praised by Group.

The next day we were sent out, together with Jack Lever in his aircraft *F*, to do a sweep flying parallel tracks to try to spot survivors from a torpedoed ship. Once again the weather was appalling, so bad that visibility was almost nil and the huge waves swamped any tiny indication there might have been on the SE that a raft or lifeboat was down there. I decided it was useless to persevere and turned for home, landing just after dark after eight hours uncomfortable flying. We had made an absolutely accurate landfall – the gremlins had gone, never to return – a complete mystery!.

Jack had evidently decided to stay on and as the weather became even worse the CO decided that the flare path should be positioned over on the far side of the loch where there was some slight shelter but which meant that the first flare was very close to land at a point known as Black Rock. We were in the mess after dinner when someone rushed in and shouted "Soapy's on fire!" We all dashed outside and were transfixed by the terrible sight of a huge fire, seemingly on the far shore of the loch, with the great aeroplane an eerie red silhouette against the flames. We knew he must have his depth charges on board and for a few seconds we watched in horrified suspense for the certain explosion; it came in seconds and although it was nearly a mile away we involuntarily ducked, partly from a wholly irrational fear but mainly in horror at the scene and the thought of our friends as, two or three seconds later, the huge 'whoomp' of the explosion reached us. All of us joined whatever transport was to hand taking people from all over the station in the hope of being able to do something to help.

We reached Black Rock in about ten minutes. The fire was out and the scene, in the stormy darkness, was unbelievable. The aircraft had landed literally just yards short of the water on a twenty-yard strip of grass between the road to Port Charlotte and the rocky shore and, incredibly, had stopped absolutely dead. The shock had evidently ruptured the fuel lines and fire was instantaneous; the explosion of the depth charges a couple of minutes or so later had literally consumed that great aircraft. The two wings had been somersaulted and lay upside down with the wing tip floats pointing to the sky, the four engines had been thrown forward on to the rocks and beyond that not the tiniest fragment of the aeroplane or anything in it remained.

We quickly heard that Jack Lever and his young Canadian second pilot, 'Johnnie' Johnson had been flung through the windscreen. Jack was considerably cut about the face and had been hustled by two other crew members to the far side of a tiny hillock to escape the explosion they knew was imminent. The Australian wireless operator had been trapped by the set falling on him and Johnson and the other seven went back inside the inferno to try to get him out and were caught in the explosion. By the time we arrived Jack had been taken away by ambulance and shortly after there was a call for volunteers to move one of the engines so that they could get at 'Simmo' Simmonds, the second engineer, whom they recognised by the big black and white woollen scarf he always wore. Soon after that 'Johnnie' Johnson was found – he was intact except that his face was badly smashed. Of the others nothing was visible in the darkness although one or two hardy souls thought they had seen some pieces. The CO decided that nothing more could be done until daylight and that all ground personnel, together with all off-duty aircrew, would parade at Black Rock next morning to clear the site.

Next day was fine and clear and it was immediately obvious that the eight aircrew were distributed far and wide. People's reactions varied: I observed, but did not pick up, a breast bone and collar bone with a tattered bit of RAF issue blue shirt attached and then moved to where I found nothing worse than a dead sheep; George had seen a sergeant with two legs under one arm and looking briskly for anything else he could find – and so it went on. At one point, in mid-morning, the youthful squadron Medical Officer told me with evident relief that he now had nine heads. I do not know how the other aircraft crew reacted but we, of aircraft *K/246* were somewhat thoughtful as we were due to be strike aircraft the next day.

As it happened we did not fly again for six days by which time we had had the full military funeral of three of the dead, including 'Johnnie' Johnson. We paraded in the square down by the harbour and marched in a slow procession up the steep, wide main street of Bowmore village to the round church at the top of the hill where the three now rest in a small plot in the corner of the tiny cemetery reserved for service and Merchant Navy dead, a quiet spot that looks out over the waters of the loch and the low hills beyond.

The court of enquiry found that the cause of the crash was, inevitably, pilot error by Jack. He had had an exceedingly difficult trip and when he eventually spotted the flare path it was so dark all round that he did not appreciate how close it was to the land; in addition the very strong wind no doubt led to a steeper descent than normal, while on this trip he was flying a Mk III (instead of his usual Mk II which was on 40-hour inspection) and I always had the impression that the Mk III had a slightly greater rate of sink on the approach to landing than the Mk II. Although the court refused to accept that an error had been made in siting the flare path so close inshore we felt the the duty captain was right in his contention that that was the prime cause.

Weather – the principal enemy

Meanwhile my promotion to Flying Officer had come through, but it was unmarked by anything except a gale that was unusual even for Bowmore. Gale guards were put out on the aircraft – this time it was the turn of the second pilots to be in charge – and very quickly the storm blew up to the point where the outer engines had to be started up in order to ease the strain on the moorings (see pages 105-06). These conditions continued into the night when at times the aircraft's airspeed indicators registered over 70 knots wind speed. The following day and night saw only minor fluctuations and the sea by this time was so rough that there was no question of getting alongside to change the crews over. Eventually, after nearly sixty hours, during fifty-four of which the pilots had been continuously in the seat, opening and closing the throttles as the wind speed altered a little either way, the gale eased to a high wind but the sea was still mountainous; from the shore we could see the aircraft pitching violently without ceasing and half hidden by perpetual clouds of driven spray. At last the weary pilots could now relax a little but all the crews had run out of food and they had had to break into the emergency rations in the aircraft's inflatable rescue dinghies. At least they had a modicum of warmth from the big paraffin heater that was part of each aircraft's equipment. The crews were finally taken off after seventy-two hours of continuous, scary, cold, uncomfortable duty but not a single aircraft broke from its moorings.

At the beginning of February we were, as seemed quite normal, strike aircraft, and on a stormy night the squadron received an urgent request from Group to go in search of a minesweeper which had broken down some 300miles out in the Atlantic; apparently the Navy were particularly anxious to rescue this vessel and a powerful Admiralty tug had been despatched to find it – we were to direct the tug to the minesweeper when we had found it. The weather was appalling and the CO, having stressed the importance of the job at our briefing, came down with me to the harbour where we stared out into the black night and a vista of raging sea. He said "Alan, do your best to get off but if you decide the conditions are too dangerous I'll back you to the hilt." Muffled in sweaters, wellies, oilskins, warm scarves and anything else we could find we stepped into the dinghy and set off, with the squadron's best coxswain driving. The moment we got beyond the harbour wall the weather really hit us: so as not to get the dinghy swamped the coxswain had to keep crabbing out towards the aircraft – some half a mile away – keeping the little craft head-to-sea while maintaining a safe low speed. We were thrown about and drenched by each successive wind-driven wave; the trip, which would have normally taken three or four minutes at most, in fact took us a good twenty minutes; George and Danny, our first wireless operator, and I leapt one by one aboard our faithful *Katie*, cold and wet as were the rest of the crew who had everything ready, having somehow managed to get a foothold on the mainplane and remove the heavy canvas engine covers without one or other or both being blown overboard.

I started all four engines on the buoy so as to ease the job of the bowmen unmooring the violently pitching aircraft and then, by keeping her at a small angle to the wind, crabbed across towards where I could just see the three little pram-mounted 40 watt bulbs that were our flare path. At that period of the war the standard takeoff drill was to open up the outer engines to full power and delay opening up the inners until coming up on to the step so as to avoid the inner propellers being damaged by hitting water and spray thrown up by the aircraft's bows in the early stages of take off. So this night, having lined *Katie* up with the distant flare path and set the gyro-driven direction indicator to show the exact bearing of the takeoff run, I opened up the outers and immediately the aircraft was battered and thumped by each wave, many of them going solid green right over the top of us while the windscreen wipers, at full speed, tried with limited success to cope with sea and rain. At about 35 knots I pushed the inner throttles right forward and nothing happened; the engines were full of water and were just ticking over. I was determined to have one more shot to see if we could get off. The only remedy was to turn off the flare path and do a 180 degree turn so as to go downwind when the waterlogged engines could be allowed to clear themselves. The natural tendency of the Sunderland was to face very firmly into wind and on a night like this to get it to turn right round needed the full power of both the starboard engines. The first attempt failed and while halfway round the wind and sea were forcing the starboard wing up and the port wing down so that the port wing tip float was under great strain, largely under the raging water; loss of the float would have meant immediate capsize and sinking, a very dangerous situation. I let the aircraft swing back into wind and with rudder urged it a bit farther in the other direction so that, when the starboard engines were once more opened up to full power the swing gathered just sufficient extra momentum to push the aircraft past the into-wind point and slowly round to face downwind. An additional dimension to the danger of this manoeuvre arose from the considerable speed through the water built up by the starboard engines at full throttle with the aircraft beam-on to the sea and that port wing tip float at its most vulnerable.

While all this was going on the noise was indescribable. It has to be remembered that, unlike civilian aircraft, military machines had no insulation, so we were effectively flying in a tin can; with every thump of the waves the whole aircraft shuddered, the sea poured down off the hull and the airscrews made a weird 'whanging' noise as each heap of water and spray hit them, while the wind howled unceasingly. It was a fraught five or six minutes and the momentary relative calm while we were going downwind was welcome although the combined activities of constantly adjusting the outer engines to overcome the aircraft's urge to turn round again into wind, running up the inners to clear them, checking our heading by the gyro direction indicator and trying to guess, in the total darkness, how near we were getting to the rocky head of the loch, made that calm very relative. However when we turned into wind there was the flare path where it should be and, taking a deep breath, I opened up the outers and, just as we were nearing the first flare, the inners, and they responded! Once we were up on the step we thundered on into the darkness, everything thumping and juddering, the engines roaring and we pilots bouncing up and down so much that we repeatedly hit our heads on the cockpit roof.

It was an enormous relief actually to get off the water although the slow climb to get the heavy aircraft up to cruising height at 1000 feet was laborious in the extreme: in the very rough air a rate of climb of 50 feet a minute would be nurtured by carefully riding an up current, only to be lost seconds later by hitting a down current, then once again making a minute backward movement of the control column for just as long as one could feel the slight extra lift from another up current, easing off in anticipation of the next loss of lift so as to avoid losing a couple of knots of air speed and the twenty or thirty feet of altitude needed to regain it. After half an hour of this we reached a thousand feet and I thankfully engaged the automatic pilot in the much calmer air.

Twenty minutes or so later the darkness began to look even darker and suddenly we were hit by a roaring squall. I disengaged the automatic pilot and began a full-scale battle. The aircraft was literally tossed about, one wing down then the other, suddenly seeming to hang in the air then banged upwards by an up current that rattled everything on board, then turned 30 degrees off course and all the while certain of the blind-flying instruments giving crazy readings from one second to the next – airspeed going from our cruising speed of 110 knots (we were very heavy) to 80 knots and then up to 140 knots, rate of climb one minute negative 500 feet a minute, next second apparently climbing although the seat of my pants – the only reliable guide in those conditions – told me that we could not be. Then, as suddenly as it had started the storm ceased. I began faintly to discern a difference between the slight lightness of the next lot of storm clouds and the very black small gaps between them but before I could make for one of these gaps we were suddenly flung around again to such a degree that retaining any sort of control of the aircraft needed the most intense concentration of all the senses and a mixture of firmness and gentleness on the controls; this time, too, we had hail – it sounded like millions of stones being shot onto a corrugated iron roof and was so deafening as to be momentarily almost disorienting. Then, just as suddenly, it stopped. We went on like this for half an hour while I steered as carefully as I could to avoid what looked like the worst storm clouds: I reported every change of course to George who somehow managed to plot it on his chart – I had to use the gyro direction indicator as the magnetic compasses were swinging wildly as we hit each squall – in fact the aircraft had become so heavily charged with static electricity that the wireless operators were getting shocks off the set and had to earth it while a most spectacular aurora effect developed on the airscrews so that each was surrounded by a shimmering circle of reds, greens, blues etc. and at the same time the front gun had a dancing flame on the muzzle and one of the crew told me on the intercom that I had St Elmo's Fire hovering on the tip of my nose.

After an exceptionally busy half hour I saw the sky begin to lighten with the approaching dawn as we thankfully moved clear of the squalls into calm air and the autopilot took over while I tucked into a plate of bully beef sandwiches and a mug of hot chocolate. We could see that all the paint had been removed from the leading edge of the mainplane by the hail and later, when we got back home, we found that not only the mainplane but the entire hull forward of the cockpit was polished bright, every vestige of paint having been blasted off by the hail.

When we reached the position given for the minesweeper there was no sign of it so we started a square search and on the second leg we came upon it and were greeted by enthusiastic waving from the crew. I signalled that we would leave them and go in search of the tug that was on its way and would then guide it to them. In fact we found the tug quickly about 40 miles away and gave it bearing and distance to the minesweeper to which we then returned and reported an estimated time of arrival of the tug. Thereafter I went back to the tug every half hour and gave it a check bearing and distance; on the last occasion the tug signalled "Have minesweeper in sight. Many thanks" and we said our adieus, returned to the minesweeper, signalled "Tug has you in sight" and, with a signal of thanks from them, turned for home. On reporting at ops for debriefing I was told that the Navy HQ in Liverpool had signalled congratulations to the squadron. But I never did fathom out what a minesweeper was doing 300 miles out in the ocean.

The eyes of the convoy

At this time – February, March, April of 1943 – the Battle of the Atlantic was moving towards a climax, as was revealed after the end of the war, and we regularly went to ops for briefing on a convoy escort job to find a note on the operations map beside the convoy symbol saying "25+ U-boats in contact". It was an awesome thought that one was about to undertake a significant share of the responsibility for the protection of the ships in that terrible situation. I remember particularly one night when we were to be with the convoy at first light so were about to make a night takeoff. On the way to the aircraft in the dinghy, when some three or four hundred yards away in the dark, I saw quite clearly the black silhouette of the Sunderland, looking just like a huge whale and with that characteristic high tail fin and rudder. I suddenly was acutely aware that I was shortly to take that great machine into the air and go out over the ocean to help to guard a part of the nation's lifeline. It was the only time I ever had that feeling, not in any way of fear but simply of being deeply impressed, emotionally, by the very fact of flight and by the responsibility for a big aeroplane, my crew and a job to be done whatever the odds.

The weather in the North Atlantic at that time was very mixed and in March and April there were some of the worst storms in living memory. On the other hand, if we were lucky the met conditions could be quite good and it was a dramatic experience, after three or four hours flying over empty ocean, perhaps with predominantly heavy cloud, to see in the far distance a broad shaft of sunlight streaming down to the water and illuminating the lines of ships forming 'our' convoy; it always brought a small lump to the throat thinking of all those men exposed, month after month, to often acute discomfort and the ever-present threat of a ghastly death.

At other times the ocean presented a very different face. On one occasion we were sent out to try to shepherd together a convoy that had dispersed in ferocious weather because it was too dangerous to steam in close company in virtually nil visibility and with the ships difficult to control. On our way out conditions were gloomy but not too bad, then, when we neared the position of the convoy, there was a spectacular deterioration – thick, turbulent clouds came down to about three hundred feet, the aeroplane was hurled about so violently that we were all strapped in for safety, no question of the automatic pilot of course. There was a weird, slightly orange glimmer in the all-pervading gloom and the sea was unlike anything I ever saw, before or since – enormous waves, each covering a huge area and approaching 90 or more feet from trough to crest, were partially obscured by sheets of wind-driven spray and water. From time to time we came upon a ship and we attempted vainly to make contact but all, freighters, escort vessels, liners large and small, were wallowing in and out of walls of water, rolling literally almost on to their beam-ends, It was inconceivable that they should not capsize and how people could survive conditions like that, perhaps for days on end, defied imagination. At the same time, flying the aeroplane in the unceasing hectic turbulence, and often seeming to be no more than a couple of hundred feet or less above the towering waves, needed a lot of care and concentration; I flew it for 6¾ hours, strapped in my seat, until we came out of the really bad weather on the way home, having accomplished very little of use. I then handed over to the second pilot and asked for a good hot meal; when the delicious aroma drifted up to the flight deck and I went below to the wardroom I discovered that the entire crew had been almost prostrate with airsickness and, apparently, as two of them were cooking my meal they had to take it in turns to rush to one or the other galley hatch to 'feed the gulls'!

Over the ocean enemy long-range aircraft, Focke-Wulf Condors, were a rarity and mostly avoided combat so our two principal enemies, which caused many losses, were weather and engine failure. I had always been interested in meteorology and from time to time would send coded weather reports during flight; there was strict wireless silence on operations, except for enemy sighting reports or emergencies, but up to three met reports per sortie were permitted since up-to-date information on the weather approaching the British Isles and Europe was obviously vital, particularly for the bomber boys. We had set out on a convoy escort job in fine weather but expecting to meet a warm front (a line of separation between cold air and relatively warm air coming along behind it) near or over the convoy. We were approaching a typical warm front cloud build-up and I sent a signal describing it just before we plunged into thick cloud and heavy rain which I again reported; after some three-quarters of an hour we came out into some trailing cloud, diminishing, and then sunlight – the back of the front – so off went the third report. We still had not seen the convoy but within ten minutes we received a signal from base "606-1" which was RAF code for "Return to base – immediately". I forthwith abandoned the sortie and ploughed back through worsening weather that was really thick at Bowmore and within about five minutes of mooring up cloud and rain were right down to the deck, closing the base completely. Back in ops we were told that our reports had shown that the front had advanced much faster than expected and was threatening to close our base before we could get back, hence the recall signal. In fact every other flying boat base on the west and south coasts had already closed some time before we reached Bowmore so we made the last shelter by some twenty minutes – thanks to those met reports.

Quite frequently during those winter days, while we did not fly high enough to suffer that bugbear of the bomber boys, icing of the wings, we did get icing in the carburettors; the suction in the venturi of the carburettors meant that there was reduced pressure and consequently reduced temperature which, combined with near-freezing or freezing air temperature and a humid atmosphere, caused ice to build up in the air intake and progressively strangle the engine. The Bristol Pegasus engines had a clever mechanism which ensured that a shortage of air for the engine, for example due to high altitude or icing, was automatically corrected by further opening of the throttle; at a given point of throttle opening the setting was reached beyond which it was not safe to operate the engine in weak mixture (the economical regime for cruising) and the mixture controls on the engine control console would 'trip out' to change over automatically to rich mixture. The normal air intake for the carburettor was just below the engine in the airscrew's slipstream but it was possible to switch over to another intake within the engine nacelle that supplied warm air to the carburettor; this got rid of the icing but as warm air is less dense the engine lost a small amount of power which was compensated for by an automatic opening of the throttle which in turn meant burning more fuel. The squadron engineer, 'Buck' Ryan, started complaining that we were using too much fuel because we were using warm air too frequently; we pointed out somewhat forcefully that it was better to use a bit more fuel than to end up in the drink but he remained unconvinced, so I said to him "OK Buck, come out on a trip with me and see for yourself!" By and large those in ground occupations were reluctant to fly but Buck, to his credit, said he would. We went out on a long Atlantic patrol and about five hours out, in clear air and at a thousand feet, the engineer reported zero outside air temperature. I looked at Buck and he said "No, no, stay in cold air" and even though the chances were that all four engines would very shortly stop and a thousand feet did not last long while trying to get the engines started again, I waited. Thirty seconds later one mixture control 'tripped out', followed immediately by the other three. Buck and I looked at each other, no word was needed. I called to the engineer to change to warm air and pump some de-icing fluid into the carburettors; the fans kept turning, comment was superfluous and no more complaints of high fuel consumption were heard from then on.

Engine failure was one thing that, by the grace of God, I did not experience over the ocean, although I did once have to come back off an exercise with the starboard inner backfiring like an artillery barrage due to a broken valve. On the other hand another of the squadron's captains, Ivor Brazenor, had a major engine failure while on a convoy and managed to put the aircraft down in a high sea close to one of the ships. All the crew got out but as the machine plunged head-on into a big wave he was thrown forward and smashed his head on the instrument panel; he went down with the aircraft.

Our longest flight on the squadron was a straight trip out to the west to search for some lifeboats from a convoy that had been heavily attacked. In the heavy seas out in the empty ocean a sighting was all but out of the question and we returned, having sadly seen nothing, after thirteen hours and five minutes in the air.

That was, in fact, our last operational flight with 246 Squadron. Shortly afterwards we were all thunderstruck to be told that the squadron was to be disbanded – at the height of the Battle of the Atlantic! – in order, so we gathered, to release ground crews to support the Bomber Command assault on Germany.

On 30 April we, with the other squadron aircraft, flew up to Oban where we handed over our much-loved *Katie* to a Norwegian squadron, No 330, and it was goodbye to the round church on the hill, the Nissen huts on the flat overlooking the loch with our proud aircraft at their moorings, and the occasional delicious suppers to which we as a crew were invited by Mr and Mrs Currie who ran the village bakery. Goodbye, too, to the splendid Sunderland as we were told that we were all to be converted to Catalinas – twin-engined American flying boats.

"Catalinas, for God's sake!"

By mid-May we were at No 131 (Coastal) Operational Training Unit at Killadeas on Lough Erne, close to where I had been on 201 Squadron, and were becoming familiar with our new mount. It was an ugly duckling that was clumsy to handle in the air, and on the water, compared with the Sunderland; it had one 0.303 machine gun in a First World War-style open cockpit in the bows and one manually-trained 0.5 machine gun in each of two Perspex 'blisters' aft of amidships with a limited field of air that left the rear, the most vulnerable quarter, completely unprotected; its marine equipment was minimal and designed, obviously, by people who had never seen a boat. It was noisy, had rudimentary cooking facilities and an Elsan chemical toilet as well as a pee tube that flowed out below a sort of trap door towards the rear that opened inwards to allow a highly inconvenient drift sight – yards distant from the navigator – to be fixed up and read from a prone position. On opening the trap door one was met by a reverse blast of air that usually also bore with it the results of the most recent use of the pee tube!

However it had two very reliable American Pratt and Whitney engines and could stay aloft for more than sixteen hours and even, with special tankage, for as much as twenty-four. This advantage was to some extent offset by the fact that, with poor streamlining and the eight depth charges hanging out in the breeze under the mainplane the machine cruised at no more than 75 knots so, while it could stay quite a long time with the convoy, it took a long time getting there and back.

Apart from the engines it was hated by all of us, pilots and crews; its one merit was that, approaching to land in a rough sea, it could be flown very slowly and then banged down into the water with a minimum of fuss whereas the Sunderland needed careful handling at the first contact with really rough water.

We also heartily disliked Killadeas itself, where there was an unpleasant culture of disdain for trainee crews – most of whom already had operational experience – that extended from the top right down to the lowliest airman. Our mood, in reaction to this, can be judged from the expressions on faces in some of the crew photographs. Two of us got some satisfaction by making a formal protest to the Chief Ground Instructor that produced some slight amelioration.

The flying on this conversion course involved the usual 'circuits and bumps', day and night, navigation exercises, air-firing and low-level practice bombing (at 50 feet). We also did several very useful Operational Flying Exercises (OFEs) which simulated actual operations – briefing, over-ocean flight and debriefing and included dropping two live depth charges. We were instructed to send a wireless codeword just before we dropped the DCs and on one of these sorties the signal was sent and the aircraft then disappeared and was never seen again. It was obviously vital to try to sort out the mystery so one of the most experienced pilots on the course, a really splendid Canadian, Ted Muffett, who had been a bush pilot in the far north of Canada, was sent out accompanied by a second aircraft: the required signal was sent and next second the crew in the companion aircraft were transfixed with horror to see the depth charges explode on the surface 50 feet directly below Ted's aircraft which disintegrated with the huge power of the Torpex explosive and disappeared in seconds without trace. Painstaking checking and research subsequently showed that our DCs had been fitted with faulty 'pistols' (see page 104, note 2) which caused the charge to explode on impact instead of setting it off at 25 feet depth where the water pressure would trigger it.

On another OFE Charles Potter was sent out, by prior arrangement with the ship, to do an escort on the *Queen Mary* sailing westwards independently at high speed straight into the teeth of an Atlantic gale. The lumbering Catalina trundled out against the wind and when Charles eventually caught up with the ship the Commodore instructed him to do a square patrol around her. The drill for such a patrol was to set off on the upwind leg, then turn 90 degrees to port to pass across the ship's line of advance, then turn 90 degrees to port downwind, 90 degrees to port again to cross astern of the ship and then start the next upwind leg. The Catalina set off to get ahead of the ship on the first upwind leg, thrashing along at its best 75 knots airspeed; after a quarter of an hour the *Queen Mary* was still there just off the port quarter and all Charles could do was to give up and drift back relative to the ship and patrol back and forth across her stern!

After seven weeks we passed out as fully trained Catalina crews and, thankfully, left Killadeas. I was pleasantly surprised to find myself assessed as a 'Good average' pilot and captain after a total of 97 hours 15 minutes flying on the course. Some crews were posted directly to squadrons but the rest of us were sent to kick our heels for weeks at Oban where we were billeted in a splendid seafront hotel which, however, had been stripped of everything – carpets, furnishings, light fittings etc – leaving only the most basic amenities. The only bit of joy during this period was a flight in a Sunderland with a highly-experienced pilot who demonstrated to us a special method of landing – the full-flap, full-glide procedure, an extremely valuable trick where a landing had to be made in a very confined space. (See Glossary page 186 for more details.)

How I learned my secret identity

During the weeks at Oban we were given a good deal of leave, much of which I used to renew acquaintance with a girlfriend from prewar. We first met for lunch at a West End restaurant during which I asked her what she was doing as she was obviously a civilian; she said "Oh, I'm in the War Office" so of course I asked what she was doing there and she replied "I'm afraid I can't really tell you." Imbued with wartime security consciousness I did not pursue the question. After a little interval she became momentarily pensive and then said "I suppose it doesn't matter my telling you, but I came across your file the other day"; she was obviously in the same organisation as I had been in 1940-41! Actually, the name Special Operations Executive (SOE) had not been revealed at that time, but after lunch she suggested I might accompany her to where her office was – it was 64 Baker Street and I realised that our setup in Cairo had been part of this much bigger, secret organisation. As time went on, information was slowly revealed about the activities in support of the French, Belgian and Dutch resistance which I guessed were centred on 64 Baker Street and when SOE finally became public after the end of the war I at last acquired the full identity of what had been until then just D/H5.

Back to war again

After more than a month waiting in Oban for a posting one of the other captains from 246, Ted Garside and I were so disenchanted that we set off under our own steam for No 18 Group at Pitreavie (the Training Group for Coastal Command) and talked our way into seeing one of the principal personnel people who, once he had recovered from his surprise at being bearded in his office by two junior officer pilots, listened to our tale of woe quite sympathetically and we came away feeling that we might have got something on the move. In the event it was another month before Ted and I were told that two crews were urgently needed for a Catalina squadron at Mombasa and we were to collect our crews and go at high speed to RAF Station Lyneham, right down in the southwest, where tropical kit would be issued and we would be flown out to Kenya immediately.

Lyneham was an enormously busy station that was responsible for ferrying numerous different types of aircraft out to Africa and the Middle East. Our two crews were to be distributed in penny numbers among some of the ferry armada. My little Scots wireless operator mechanic Jock Moir and I were allocated to a Wellington XIII torpedo bomber and we did a short hop in this to a satellite airfield nearby at Portreath. We discussed with the crew what drill we should adopt if we were attacked by German fighters during our daylight crossing of the Bay of Biscay; they clearly had no idea what we were driving at so Jock and I just left it and decided that we would take over as best we could if we got jumped by JU88s. This light-heartedness in ferry crews must have been fairly general because we later heard, unofficially, that, of the over 100 aircraft despatched on the night we took off, five failed to arrive at destination and this was apparently par for the course.

Our first leg was from Portreath to Rabat in Morocco and early in the morning of 19 November 1943 the 'Wimpy', bung-full of fuel, staggered off in the darkness, using the handy cliff at the end of the rather short runway to drop 20 or 30 feet to gain a little bit of extra airspeed for the climb. I suggested to the pilot that I might try my hand at some navigation but he demurred, pointing out that they had a standard procedure under which they flew in a general southerly direction until they were abreast of Lisbon, whose radio station they picked up on the directional loop aerial, and then shaped a course for Rabat to which they would be guided by a radio beacon. It all seemed rather haphazard, like the experience of Arjun Dandeker (Danny) my first wireless operator, who flew out in a Hudson whose pilot had such a hangover that, once airborne, he engaged the automatic pilot, told Danny to sit in the pilot's seat and call him if there was any trouble and retired to the rear of the aircraft to sleep; at one point two JU88s flew across ahead of them but took no notice, probably being on the way to deal with a Sunderland encountered a short while before.

Our two crews coalesced at Rabat, which was cold and wet, and where we spent four days in primitive quarters, in which we froze – not my idea of North Africa. Back at the airport we were weighed before boarding a Dakota; there was some concern about overloading because an ENSA party (part of the huge forces entertainment setup) travelling with us included an actress who, as I observed out of the corner of my eye, weighed 250 pounds – almost 18 stone – and big with it. She was fitted in and we set off in cold, wet weather past snow-covered mountains to a turning point at Gibraltar where we turned east and called at Oujda for fuel, finally landing at Maison Blanche in Algeria where we spent the night. On the way we had seen anti-aircraft fire (always known in those days as 'flak' – an acronym of the German portmanteau word for anti-aircraft gun: Flugzeugabwehrkanone) opened up on what was presumably an enemy reconnaissance aircraft – a taste of the war again.

Next day, after a very early start, we flew via Castel Benito and Benijna, names so familiar during the recent desert battle, to Cairo West airfield. Flying over the desert we saw many signs of the battles – wrecked tanks, occasional remains of aircraft and odd debris lying around in the sand. Finally, outside Cairo West, we found ourselves in a Personnel Transit Centre, very late at night, surrounded by howling desert and consisting of Nissen huts for messes, offices and so forth and, as accommodation, legions of bell tents on bare sand, the whole under the command of a truculent Australian wing commander. However Ted and I were not unduly worried as we reckoned we should be on our way to Mombasa any day, having been rushed out from UK and all across North Africa with hardly time to draw breath. We should have known . . .!

The days dragged on into weeks during which we went quite frequently into Cairo which Ted and our two crews found an eye-opening experience. I was able to look up several of the Shell people I had known three years before; it was quite pleasing to be able to show myself as an active participant in the war but frustrating to be prevented, naturally, from saying anything to satisfy their curiosity about what I had been doing in those earlier days.

Apart from a YMCA trip we all took to the Pyramids and Mohammed Ali mosque the only other feature of our sojourn in the desert was the recruitment of a second engineer to replace the one member of my original crew who had not wanted to come overseas with us. Our new man would never have won a beauty contest and had had an unhappy time with his previous crew somewhere in the desert, but we welcomed him and set about restoring his morale: he was an archetypal cockney, rejoicing in the name of Joe Eggett, and had been a window-cleaner in Kennington before the war. He had a typically sardonic sense of humour and at the same time cheerfully accepted a good deal of ribbing, not least on the occasion, many months later, when he put up a monumental 'black' (see page 165).

It was getting very near to Christmas and Ted and I were getting weary with the regular calls at the admin office to see whether there were any sign of our 'urgent' posting to Mombasa. With the grudging permission of the Australian CO we marched into GHQ in Cairo where a senior personnel chap – aircrew, we were cheered to observe – was clearly impressed by our tale of woe. He admitted that there was no sign of any posting for us so we had better gather our crews and go down to Nairobi to see whether they could fix us up that end. Things instantly started to move and, after a dismal Christmas, the 27th saw us all on board a BOAC aircraft that took us via Wadi Halfa, Khartoum (overnight stop), Malakal, Juba and Kisumu to Nairobi.

The following day I went with Ted to Air HQ East Africa where we were told that the Catalina squadron at Mombasa definitely had no need of any crews but that 230 Squadron, flying Sunderlands at Dar-es-Salaam, did have a requirement for two experienced crews – would we be interested? . . .Would we?!! It was arranged that the necessary contacts would be made to see whether we could be accepted. Our crews were naturally as excited at the possibility as Ted and I were – and I, of course, was particularly looking forward to seeing my best friend, Duggie Lumsden, again after a whole year.

New Year's Eve in the mess at Nairobi's Eastleigh airport was a dull affair but my minuscule interest instantly evaporated as I was told that Duggie had been killed that very day with all his crew except one who was in the tail turret. He had apparently been flying in cloud and had hit very near the top of a hidden 'kopje', an isolated 1000 foot hill inland from Dar. It was shattering news and rather took the edge off the confirmation next day, 1 January 1944, that we were posted to 230 Squadron.

"230 Squadron – enough said!"

On Sunday 2 January 1944 we were flown via Mombasa – where it felt as if we had stepped into an oven – Tanga and Zanzibar to Dar-es-Salaam where we were greeted, in a somewhat subdued mood, following Duggie's funeral, by an extremely pleasant crowd of people, including a number of Australians. It was almost three years since my first slight contact with 230 Squadron (see page 40) in Alexandria. The base was on raised ground overlooking a large area of water surrounded by palm trees except at the north end where it opened into the main harbour of Dar; this was our operating area where eight or nine Sunderlands lay at moorings. The town itself looked, from a distance, somewhat unlike the other African towns we had seen which were in territories colonised by the British and had a preponderance of corrugated iron roofs; Tanganyika had been a German colony before the First World War and the general impression of the buildings was of a heavier, more solid construction.

After two days of formalities and settling in I went with one of the Australian captains, Oxley ('Ox') Watson for a re-familiarisation check on the Sunderland. Three good takeoffs and landings were enough for me to feel completely at home and the crew and I were elated as we returned to shore, back once again on those superb machines, all thoughts of the wretched Catalina banished completely from our minds. A few days later we were allocated our own boat, aircraft *N*, hull number W6078; I was told that it had once been run up on a sandbank and, although it was perfectly safe, it had, as a result, a peculiar behaviour at takeoff, coming off the water and then going on, seemingly almost endlessly, at about six feet altitude before it could be persuaded into a far-from-agile climb. The next day I was sent off with a load of maintenance people and odd aircrew to join a couple of other squadron aircraft on detachment at Mombasa. The camp here overlooked a large expanse of water, an extension of the harbour, from which we and the Catalina squadron operated. In the evenings, sitting on the verandah of the wattle-and-thatch mess with a drink in our hands, it was interesting to watch the BOAC pilots bringing in and taking off their C-class 'Empire' flying boats, so similar to the Sunderland; their short takeoff run and the genteel hum of their engines contrasted sharply with the lengthy and thunderous departure of our own aeroplanes.

The leisurely evenings in the event numbered precisely five and, after two days' preliminary preparation and testing of the aircraft I took off very early in the morning with a big load of passengers on 'Operation Island', a regular commitment of the squadron which involved visiting a number of flying boat bases and military and naval outposts in the many islands of the western Indian Ocean, carrying mail and relief personnel and sundry high-ranking officers of the three services on their important business. For me it was a sudden launching into a completely different operational world, flying into strange and unfamiliar places, entirely responsible – with the crew – for our aircraft and deciding the number of passengers I could safely carry as well as the time of departure, all so different from the precisely regulated operations from one, or perhaps two, familiar bases back home in the North Atlantic.

That first day we flew to Diego Suarez in Madagascar. Cruising height on these trips was 5000 feet to be in cooler air and heaving *N* up to that height was quite a job and taught me a lot about that particular boat. We landed on a large lake, more or less rectangular in shape and surrounded by picturesque hills covered with every kind of luxuriant green vegetation mixed with the ubiquitous palm trees. With our officer passengers George and I were put up in an army mess where, after dinner, we sat out in the balmy evening air, heavy with the scent of bougainvillea, while a band of the King's African Rifles played jolly music and we drank long John Collinses. To finish the evening we went into the town where the warm streets, with an unmistakably French atmosphere, were filled with colourful people and colourful establishments, including Chez Georges where we ended up with a somewhat riotous finish to the evening.

Next morning we flew to a small island called Pamanzi in the Comoro Islands between Madagascar and the mainland of Africa. The landing area was a long strip of water between steep hills which were covered with masses of green vegetation and brilliantly-coloured flowers which seemed to blaze forth and hang from every tree and primitive shack as we drove from the little landing stage to the rickety but friendly mess; this was situated high up on one of the hillsides and the experience of sitting out on the small verandah in the warm scented evening with a rather warm drink and looking down on our aeroplane moored far below was one of the most delightful I had ever enjoyed.

The same afternoon we returned to Diego Suarez and refuelled ready for the five hour flight to the Seychelles the next day with 28 passengers. This was a trip we had looked forward to and it did not disappoint; the first sight of those rich green islands with the surrounding ocean changing from blue to dark green to

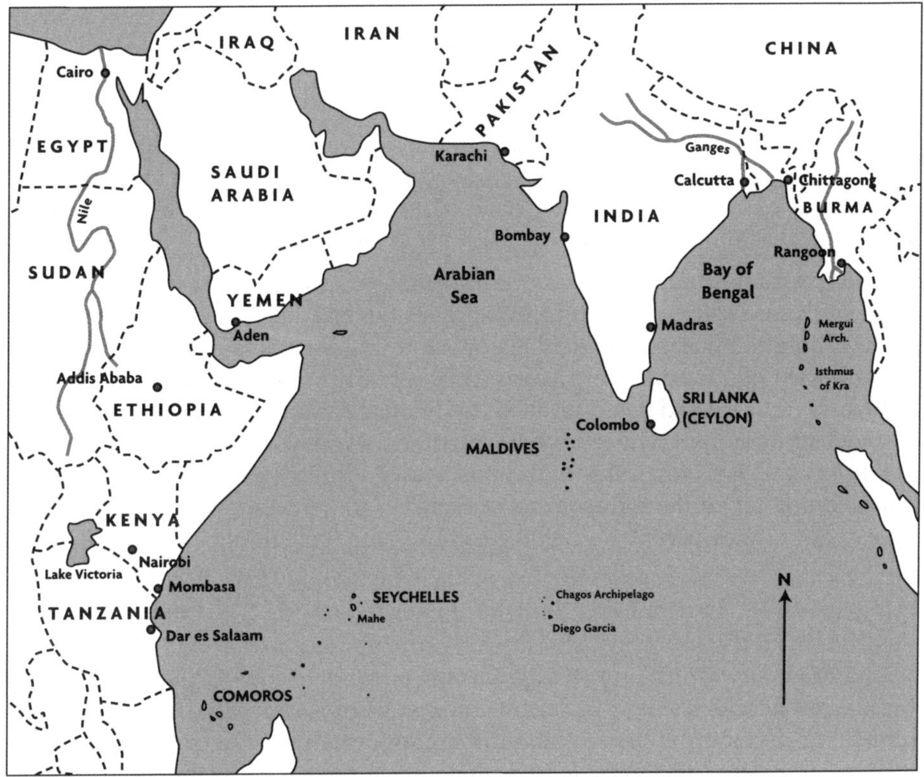

The Indian Ocean

On 27 December 1943 Alan Deller, and his crew, left Cairo en route for Dar-es-Salaam and a posting to 230 Squadron, flying his beloved Sunderland. Their area of operations would be the vast expanse of the Indian Ocean. 'Operation Island' (see page 124) involved delivering personnel and mail to flying boat bases and naval outposts on the islands of the western Indian Ocean, including the Maldives, Seychelles and Comoros. As a guide to the distance flown, it is approximately 3000 miles from Dar-es-Salaam to Colombo.

light green and then crystal clarity approaching the dazzling white beaches was simply stunning. There was a limitless choice of landing area in the sea off Victoria, the capital, on the big island of Mahé; with the clear water and brilliant light it was easy to miss the prevailing swell and I bounced on landing which annoyed me.

As we approached the shore in the dinghy we were met by the curious sweetish smell of copra, the main export of the islands; it pervaded the whole town and we quickly got used to it. Victoria was a typical African town – buildings entirely constructed with local materials, wood and palm-frond thatch, with everything wide open to the air, the heat being pretty intense – but with a distinct French accent in addition: the local dialect is a sort of French patois and the cuisine is mainly French colonial or creole. Our mess was built entirely of palm trunks and palm-frond wattle and was literally on the beach, a stone's throw from the water's edge. The whole atmosphere was lush and gorgeous; if this was the Seychelles we would happily stay here for ever! The local women were almost uniformly lovely, mostly exceedingly friendly and, regrettably, in very many cases carrying a particularly virulent form of VD.

Ever since we left Mombasa we had had occasional trouble with ignition on two of the engines and as we arrived at the Seychelles I had to declare the aircraft unserviceable. That meant no trip next day, so it was possible to give way to the enervating atmosphere of heavily scented flowers and humid heat for a little and the day finished with a very pleasant dinner as a guest of the Royal Navy shore base, together with the officers of a sloop that was moored out beyond my aircraft. The following day we all worked hard to get *N* serviceable again but the elusive ignition trouble persisted and the not entirely reluctant decision to stay on was inevitable, leading to another delightful evening, this time an open air cinema show followed by a really superb dinner as guest of a glamorous and amorous half-French, half-Seychelloise lady called Eva whose husband Philippe performed a close escort throughout the evening; she was a well-known hostess to all the British and French officers who were based in the Seychelles or called there from time to time.

Next day we finally got our mechanical troubles sorted out and I fixed our departure for early the following morning. Meanwhile I had invited a number of officers from the army and the RAF, together with the RN officers from the shore base and the sloop, to a sundowner party aboard the aircraft; the crew had helped to get everything tidy while George and I collected whisky, sherry and gin and tonic and a pile of attractive snacks from shore. Sundry marine craft ferried the guests out to the aircraft and we all managed to get into the wardroom with an overflow into the galley: the wardroom table looked marvellous with all the bottles and goodies arranged – even some modest flowers! – and the party went down extremely well. I have often wondered whether other Sunderland skippers had done anything of the sort – certainly no other military aircraft could adapt itself so simply to a temporary peaceful social role. The upshot was a trip ashore, maintaining a somewhat strained dignity, and a riotous procession of rickshaws to Eva's for dinner which, it has to be admitted, turned into a bit of a shambles.

Early in the morning of the following day I got my 28 passengers on board and set off for Pamanzi once more, marvelling, as we climbed away, at the sheer beauty of those islands. A seven hour flight took us to the equally lovely little island. As I taxied up to the buoy the port outer engine started backfiring, the same old ignition trouble again, so instead of going on, as scheduled, to Diego Suarez we stayed the night. Among the passengers was an army film unit, one of several that travelled round the many isolated bases in the Indian Ocean giving film shows for the lonely servicemen; on this occasion they offered to set up their projector in the town square and the Pamanzians had the first cinema show in their history, with the films projected on to the white wall of the post office.

The crew worked hard the following day and had the offending engine going to my satisfaction by the afternoon, but too late to make Diego Suarez before dusk. So, with few regrets, the whole lot of us sat out on the verandah of the army mess, drinks in hand, enjoying the relative cool of the evening and watching the shades of night creeping over the incredible floral beauty of this island whose only alien feature that night was my rather doddery old *N* swinging peacefully at her buoy.

We left Pamanzi for Diego Suarez at first light with 32 passengers and landed after two and a quarter hours with the local passengers ready for a quick disembarkation so that I could take off again at ten o'clock for Mombasa. We picked up one or two new passengers including a fairly elderly RNR Lieutenant Commander whom I invited on to the bridge to watch the takeoff. As mentioned earlier, the lake at Diego Suarez was more or less a rectangle. That morning the wind was blowing dead across the longer side that would provide the best takeoff run but which would necessitate my throttling back the starboard outer until we reached a speed at which the rudder had enough airflow to enable it to take over the job of countering the weathercock effect of the crosswind – but that would mean that poor old *N*'s takeoff run would be so prolonged, due to the reduced power early in the run, that she would never clear the huge palm trees at the end of the lake. I decided I would start my takeoff run dead into the wind along the shorter side of the lake with, of course, all four engines at full throttle and then, approaching the far side and well up on the step, turn the aeroplane – at about 70 knots (or 85 mph) – 90 degrees to starboard and continue the run along the longer side of the lake. This I did and old *N* lumbered along, coming off the water about halfway along the long side and then doing her usual trick of sticking at about six feet altitude while the palm trees came nearer and nearer. The unhappy naval officer was convinced we would hit them and crouched down between the pilots seats and in the next five or six seconds I had a very close look indeed at the tops of the palms as we struggled over them. There followed immediately a smart turn to starboard to avoid a hill just ahead and take to a shallow valley which shortly led off to port into another shallow valley near the end of which we had just sufficient altitude to clear the remaining hills and head out to sea. It had been a busy but very instructive three or four minutes.

A nice landing back at Mombasa ended an intensely interesting experience, far removed from winter flying in the North Atlantic. Nevertheless this 'Operation Island' was not just a jolly jaunt. Apart from ferrying everything from a Major General to a humble radio mechanic we kept an eye on shipping in the area so as to spot any unusual traffic as earlier on in the war Japanese submarines had operated in these waters and they, together with a number of German U-boats, were still active in the Indian Ocean. The weather was also a hazard, particularly in the Mozambique channel between Madagascar and the African coast. One night back in 1943 one of 230's aircraft was caught out there in violent storms and had got lost for some reason that was never discovered. There were no navigational aids as such anywhere in the Indian Ocean and so, although base at Dar-es-Salaam could hear their repeated messages on the radio there was no means of using these transmissions by radio direction finding (RDF) to plot their position. As time went on fuel was running low and the operators at base could tell from the quality of the Morse that some panic had set in on board and it was heart-rending to hear this and be able to do nothing to help. Finally all went quiet and no trace of the aircraft was ever found. One has to try to imagine how it must have felt on board – pitch black night, violent turbulence, no hope of a landing on a very rough, invisible sea, no idea of position but aware of mountains possibly not far away and, with fuel nearly exhausted, the knowledge that very shortly everything would, inescapably, stop. I have always felt great sympathy for the crew and, specially, for Archie Todd, the captain, with whom we had trained at Stranraer and Invergordon.

Meanwhile I had done no night flying for seven months so I drove old *N* round the circuit a few times. This hour-and-ten-minutes' refresher was fortunate because two nights later, not far out of Mombasa on patrol to PLE (prudent limit of endurance – fuel, not pilots!) I noticed smoke blowing back from the starboard inner engine. It was blue smoke which I guessed was from engine oil leaking onto the hot cylinders and, remembering from my early incarnation as an oil man that lubricating oil has a relatively low self-ignition temperature, I throttled back the engine and returned to Mombasa for a three-engine night landing, my third so far. It was rather embarrassing because I was a newly-joined pilot on the squadron and with the not uncommon tendency of ground staff to accuse pilots of panicking unnecessarily over mechanical shortcomings there was a noticeable atmosphere; this was reinforced when next day, after a thorough examination had apparently shown nothing wrong, I took the aircraft out on a taxi-test and came back, again reporting blue smoke from the engine. This time they removed the engine, took out the crankshaft assembly and subjected it to a magnetic particle test. This immediately showed up a tiny hair-crack in the propeller shaft which was invisible to the naked eye but, once oil pressure built up with the engine running, allowed oil to leak out and be blown back onto the hot cylinders. Not for the first, or the last time, I was vindicated for my stand.

In mid-February, my promotion to Flight Lieutenant having come through, I was recalled to Dar-es-Salaam to be greeted with the news

a) that my old *N* was to be replaced by aircraft *S* for *Sugar*, hull number EJ143 (and thus, like EJ137 *K* for *Katie* of 246 Squadron, a fine boat built by Short Bros at Rochester) and
b) that with the whole squadron I was to fly off in a week's time to Ceylon (now Sri Lanka).

This was a thrilling prospect for the whole crew, a beautiful new aeroplane and what should be a fascinating trip, not straight across the ocean, for which we did not have the range, but via Mombasa, Kisumu, Khartoum, Masira Island and Bombay to Koggala, a base on a lake in the southwest corner of Ceylon.

Squadron move

A great thing about travelling in one's own big aeroplane (granted, in this case, one borrowed from King George VI) is that one can pile aboard all one's kit and belongings with no problems of space or weight and set off each day at one's own chosen time. So it was that the ten of us took *S* into the air at 0800 hours on Wednesday 16 February in excited anticipation. After a quick call at

Mombasa we started to climb to get over the 9000-foot high mountains on the way to our first overnight stop at Kisumu on Lake Victoria. The 500 mile trip took us three and a half hours during which we climbed to 10,600 feet. As the principal role of the type of aircraft we flew involved flying at fairly low altitude the superchargers on the engines were geared to maintain full 'boost' (ie supercharge) only up to about 5000 feet, beyond which point the boost, even at full throttle, fell off progressively; this was my first experience of this and with the considerable turbulence produced by the hot equatorial air and the mountain currents I was too busy to pay much attention to the impressive scenery; but the arrival over Lake Victoria was marvellous – the enormous expanse of blue water glittering in the afternoon sun and surrounded by distant blue mountains made an unforgettable impression.

To prepare for the next day's long flight to Khartoum we refuelled in the evening and for me this was quite a thrill. The Shell fuelling launch was one of those 'Empire' fuellers in the stationing of which along Imperial Airways Empire routes I had played a very small part during my first months in the Aviation Department in St Helen's Court in 1935-36.

I made a very early start not only because of the long trip ahead but in order to avoid the loss of power at takeoff due to the intense heat later in the day; this was particularly important at Kisumu because Lake Victoria being at 3000 feet altitude the thinner air already reduced engine performance. There was virtually no wind and in order to avoid prolonged taxying to get into a downwind position I decided to take off downwind. The water was flat calm, conditions in which a flying boat is reluctant to 'unstick', so the attendant launch crisscrossed my takeoff path to make some sort of waves, though they were more cosmetic than useful; in any case we passed that part of the run long before the aircraft showed any signs of leaving the water so I resorted to the final trick in such circumstances and very gently and gingerly rocked the aeroplane back and forth to a minute degree – dodgy when travelling at approaching 100 miles an hour, at which speed this drill could very easily produce 'porpoising', a very rapidly increasing and uncontrollable fore-and-aft oscillation that quickly produced disaster unless stopped immediately by throttling back and aborting the takeoff.

At any rate we did get off and had a very interesting flight across Uganda and then the Sudan; the southern part of the country was a mixture of thin bush with small straggly trees and the vast swamp-lands or 'sudd' and as we flew pretty low we had superb views of elephants, giraffes, different sorts of antelope and so on until we reached the apparently endless and almost featureless desert, relieved only by occasional encounters with the White Nile, with its fleets of graceful feluccas and every now and then a partially submerged hippo. After eight hours flying, covering more than 1100 miles, we reached Khartoum, shimmering in the peak early afternoon heat. The Nile was glassy calm, a condition in which it is impossible to make an accurate judgment of height above water in the critical moments leading to touchdown; the appropriate drill is the night approach, a slow loss of height with the aircraft in the landing attitude until the keel touches water; not for me though! – I reckoned I would judge my height by the trees and buildings along both sides of the river and thus be able to pull off the rather smarter full-flap, full-glide approach (see page 101) in which one eased out of the steep glide close to the water and touched down neatly without the help of engines. Unfortunately the mirage effect of the terrific heat made the said buildings and trees look quite a lot further below me than was in fact the case and the next thing I knew was a hideous lurch forward as we hit the water at rather more than the recommended speed while the aeroplane was still coming out of the glide. In these circumstances aircraft have somersaulted to disaster and I was extremely lucky to get away with it, much chastened!

A somewhat better performance was put up by one of the squadron's Australian captains who came in shortly after us. He was KV Ingham, known as 'Ding', and he had a young Aussie second pilot, Les Connell and navigator, Noel Verney. We all retreated swiftly from the stupefying heat and settled in a comfortable mess. I had never until then exchanged more than a passing word with Australians and I was a little wary, wondering what would be their reaction to a 'pommy bastard'. In fact we all got on extremely well and by the time an evening of drinks had loosened tongues I got the impression that they were amused, and not put off, by my very English accent.

The following morning there was a very strong wind which had whipped the normally placid Nile into really rough water and at the same time had produced a thick sand haze which persisted as far as Agordat even though we had by then reached 11,300 feet while starting to cross the mountains of northern Abyssinia (now Ethiopia) en route to Aden, our next stop. At that altitude we passed comfortably over the mountains which were enormously impressive, viewed from above, bone-dry and a picture of dusty brown desolation. Passing Agordat, Keren and near-by Asmara I was reminded of the then quite recent war waged by Italy to conquer Abyssinia and looking at the place it made me wonder why on earth Mussolini had wanted it.

Once over the mountains we saw the Red Sea ahead and turned southeast, flying first of all over a string of quite dramatic volcanic islands and then along a dreary coastline until we reached Aden and its big harbour filled with every kind of craft including a variety of large and medium warships; it took a few minutes before I spotted an RAF launch and the mooring buoys which told me where to land, the first time I had put down and manoeuvred among crowds of other vessels. Having moored up we had a short time to look across to the town, all white and dwarfed by the hills behind, hills so arid and dusty-looking that it gave one a thirst just to look at them. However when we eventually got ashore we found ourselves in a comfortable mess with good food and those Sudanese servants who are so excellent after the rather rough-and-ready Africans. George and I were put in a huge bedroom together with 'Ding' and his second dickie and navigator; the Australians were fascinated by my neatness in arranging my gear and, in addition they somehow found out that, because my hands tended to get uncomfortably hot and sticky while flying in the heat, I wore the chamois leather gloves that were aircrew issue (together with silk inners and the solid brown leather outer gloves – all needed for warmth at high altitude and in cold climates). The result was a lot of good-natured hilarity and I think it was then that I acquired the nickname of 'Dixie' that remained with me throughout my time on the squadron. And it did not take long for ground crews to pick up on the glove thing so that, as I only found out much later, shortly before I left the squadron, I was known among the 'erks' as the 'kid glove pilot'!

Our next hop was to take us along the south coast of Arabia to Masira Island off the coast of Oman, a distance of well over a thousand miles, followed by an oversea trip of nearly 1000 miles to Bombay. Throughout these long distances there were no support facilities of any kind, apart from fuel at Masira, so 'Ding' and I decided to take a day at Aden to enable the engines to be thoroughly checked. That took the morning and in the afternoon we walked, seemingly for many hot and dusty miles along a flat road through flat, flat desert, into the little town of Aden. With all the service people wandering around the numerous shops full of 'tat' it was faintly reminiscent of the atmosphere in Gibraltar but indeed a pale and extremely seedy likeness. My only shopping success was in a small chemist's which boasted, apart from a few native remedies, nothing more exciting than a tiny stock of 'Mum' deodorant, of which I bought the lot. We all thought what a deadly hole Aden was and we lost no time next morning getting into the air. There was unbroken thick cloud as we climbed out eastwards along the coast of the Hadramaut but at 2000 feet we started nosing up through thinning cloud until we suddenly emerged into golden early morning sunlight that illuminated pink mountains in the distance to the north, the colour seeming to be reflected momentarily in the rolling carpet of cloud in between; it was quite literally breathtaking in its beauty and was one of those memorable moments that flying people uniquely experience from time to time and which accentuate the drama of moving through the lonely spaces of the air.

The later stages of the flight were on the whole less impressive although, apart from sandy beaches and a few villages and small towns on the coast, the incredibly wild and forbidding country inland was striking in its emptiness – it was not hard to imagine, much further inland, the Rub al Khali, the Empty Quarter. And so it was no surprise to find our destination, Umm Rasas on Masira Island, after eight hours and twenty minutes flying, offering nothing but sand and a few stone huts. We refuelled from a barge using a handpump; this took a long, long time which did not matter as there was literally nothing else to do so we turned in early to sleep on string beds in one of the totally bare stone huts.

After another early start we climbed to 5000 feet and flew comfortably for six and three-quarter hours over a glassy ocean in a direct line to Bombay which, with George's usual competence, we hit absolutely bang on after almost 1000 miles. Again, as at Aden, the harbour was huge and busy, with masses of varied shipping, but we were quite soon ashore and joined up again with the Australians for a very cheery evening in the Grand Hotel, our first experience of luxury since our farewell party in the Gymkhana Club at Dar-es-Salaam a week ago. We had a scheduled break at Bombay so the next day both crews split up and set out to explore the great city with its teeming crowds of people all mixed up in chaotic masses of noisy traffic, its heat and smells and its myriad shops filled with attractive goods of which we were soon to learn to be suspicious, the quality frequently failing to match the price even after bargaining. It was certainly a fascinating introduction to India and a final splendid evening in the Taj Mahal Hotel gave us a small hint of the fabled splendour of Indian life at the upper end.

Our final leg to Koggala, of some 1100 miles, took us just over eight hours in a fairly relaxed low altitude 'coast crawl' down the west coast of India and then across 300 miles of sea to the southwest corner of Ceylon. It gave us the opportunity to have a good look at India's coastal scenery, very fertile, with numerous towns and villages that gave an overall impression of faded white and pink and yellow while in the country areas there were also numbers of palm-frond wattle huts, often built on stilts in the shallow water along the edge of rivers and small lakes. We could see bullocks everywhere, pulling ploughs and carts and it was not hard to envisage the vast size of the Indian population even with such a brief aerial view of a small fraction of the country.

Fourth Movement

(iii) The Far East

Far East ops

We arrived at Koggala, journey's end, on 24 February 1944, after some 5000 miles and forty-two hours, ten minutes flying over eight days, during which we had come to know our new boat very well; it had performed faultlessly throughout. Just as we were coming in we hit a very heavy rainstorm with thick dark clouds, the first bad weather of the entire trip. We made landfall at the little town of Galle and it was not hard to spot the Koggala lake about eight miles east along the south coast. The first thing that struck me as we circled to get an idea of the geography before coming in to land was the number of islands in the lake: we had been told that landing and takeoff was always from south to north on the one stretch of water on which this activity was feasible and it was immediately obvious that a large island protruding on to this water from the right, just over halfway along its length, meant that our 'runway' had something like a thirty degree dogleg, as indeed proved to be the case when we got down.

The station itself was very large with an extensive servicing area and a concrete runway that was used frequently by a small Fleet Air Arm detachment; everywhere there were palm trees and lush undergrowth, away from the occupied areas, and the humid atmosphere and general impression of hot, hot dampness overwhelmed us from the moment we stepped ashore. Many of the offices and stores were in houses, mostly dotted about in among the palm trees and all-pervading greenery; they were very simple, made of plaster-covered brick or concrete, with roofs of rather similar tiles to those common in Mediterranean countries for example, while the floors were of concrete, the whole looking, smelling and feeling damp. Most other buildings on the station, including our quarters and the mess were built of palm-frond wattle on frames of palm trunks, the haunt of a variety of spiders and the occasional scorpion. Cobras often came into the quarters; my first wireless operator went into his room and spotted one asleep on top of his mosquito net from where it leapt down, wriggled out on to the verandah and sat there swaying from side to side with its hood extended and making a rather disagreeable hissing noise. Some 'erks' passing by got a big stick and beat it to death. The only quarter on the whole station that was mosquito-proofed was that of the Station Commander, Group Captain Mills, and those busy pests made the evenings everywhere else nearly unbearable, particularly during the monsoon.

We found that there were two Catalina squadrons in residence and it became very clear in the first few days that they and the operations room controllers were not at all pleased to have their long-established setup broken into by the rather more prestigious Sunderlands. Nevertheless, four days after our arrival I was detailed to give one of the squadron commanders a ride and he so much enjoyed looking round the aeroplane and handling it in the air that the trip ran to just over an hour. In fact both the squadron commanders were very decent men and quickly accepted us.

One of the first things we all did was to take a look round the general area, noting headlands, the odd lighthouse, river mouths, a few settlements that could hardly be called villages, in short anything that might be useful in future as a landmark when returning from a trip. This also gave us our first experience of turning thirty degrees to starboard on the step at 70 knots as we came to the dog-leg; we immediately saw, also, that the huge palm trees that came right to the edge of the lake ahead of us were a real menace because the whole takeoff run was not all that great and it meant that every yard would have to be used on a heavy takeoff in order to gain at least a hundred feet to clear the trees. The Catalinas, having a much lighter wing loading (total weight divided by wing area of aircraft), came off the water earlier than we would at full load and were not worried; we asked whether the nearest trees could not be cut and were told that the local people would object and a certain Admiral who was the wartime 'supremo' of the island had decreed that in all eventualities the wishes of the local populace must take precedence over any operational requirements – so the palms remained, as did a huge crocodile that was apparently the repository of the souls of the departed locals.

One day, some months later, air crews and maintenance people were busy on all the aircraft when suddenly the crocodile appeared, swimming between the two rows of moored aircraft, with his body almost submerged and his snout and horrid little eyes looking unbelievably sinister; everybody who happened to be up on the mainplane instinctively checked his foothold. We estimated that he was sixteen feet long. A while later he ate half of an unfortunate RAF officer who had fallen into the water and drowned.

Only a week after our arrival I did an anti-submarine sweep which involved a night takeoff so as to be in the search area by first light. At Koggala they had the luxury – there being no blackout – of a row of fixed lights all along each side of the takeoff area; this was fine except that on starting the run all one could see at the halfway point was a jumble of lights, foreshortened into an almost continuous line, apparently situated right across the takeoff path: it was only when, having boldly put doubts on one side and rushed at this apparent barrier, one arrived at the dogleg, the lights instantly resolved themselves into a continuation, thirty degrees right, of the nice double line of lights and one then smartly executed the high-speed turn on the step. During the day one could pick up the position of the dogleg quite easily by reference to the surrounding topography but at night, with nothing visible except a pile of lights, one had no exact idea of where to expect the dogleg until one was actually there, travelling very fast.

With a number of convoy escort jobs the squadron was quickly getting used to the operating conditions which, so far, were rather less arduous than winter in the North Atlantic; we had, however, been warned to remember lessons, treated rather lightly at ground school, on the sudden dangers liable to surprise pilots flying in the tropics. This was to pay off not many months later.

One of these early convoy escorts sticks in my mind. The convoy was a long way up the Indian west coast and I was required to remain with it until dusk by which time I would not have had the fuel to get back to Koggala, so it was arranged that we would come back down as far as Cochin, where there was a small flying boat base, and spend the night there. By the time we left the convoy we had been airborne for 10½ hours and it took another one hour and fifty minutes to get to Cochin for a night landing. At Cochin there were storms all round and it was pitch black. A small flare path had been set out but I could just see all sorts of boats moving this way and that across the flare path which I could only hope the boys down below would clear before my fuel ran out; by then we had been in the air for well over 12 hours. They eventually gave me a green light and I came in, only to get a frantic red at 300 feet; I opened up (ie set the engines to full power) and went round again and on my next approach got a red again, this time at 500 feet, not quite so fraught as 300 feet when a big aircraft is close to landing and has to be heaved up again with engines reset and flaps brought in, but bad enough. I had never seen Cochin in daylight and in the dark, with lashing rain and turbulence, it was extremely difficult to judge the required length of the approach from perhaps two miles away and as I was nearly down on the next attempt I realised that I was overshooting, so I opened up again. This time I had to make it and in fact got down on this fourth attempt, with less than a hundred gallons of fuel left which means perhaps a maximum of 20 to 30 gallons actually usable (economical cruising consumption was about a 120 gallons an hour).

Next morning we awoke to find ourselves on a lake with lush vegetation on every side, and no sign of the previous night's storm. We only had a 3½ hour trip back to Koggala so we passed a bit of time watching the numerous small native boats plying back and forth. One ancient bearded soul came alongside with his little boat loaded with huge stems of little sweet green bananas; we had a lot of bully beef left over from the rations so we bartered about a dozen tins for a couple of stems, one of which we suspended between the pilots' seats and, as we trundled serenely down to Koggala, we just broke off one banana after another and ate them with (fairly) guilty thoughts of our banana-less folks at home.

Westwards from Ceylon is a long, straggling group of coral islands, the Maldives, and here, once more, there were advanced flying boat bases. One was on Kelai, almost the northernmost of the group, about 500 miles west of Koggala, another, little used, was on the island of Mali, the capital of the group, the third was on Addu Atoll, the southernmost except for Gan close by (a Fleet Air Arm base), 500 miles south of Kelai and 600 miles southwest of Koggala. From time to time supplies, mail and relief personnel had to be taken to these lonely bases and mail and personnel brought back: the base personnel did a six month stint at what looked, at first sight, to be tropical paradises, but service comforts, boredom, heat and mosquitoes (carrying a particularly virulent strain of malaria) rather took the edge off the charm after a week or two.

Ted Garside had already been to Kelai once and I took the opportunity of flying with him on his next trip. The first sight of the islands, big and small, each with its lagoon fringed with glistening white sandy beaches overhung with palm trees and curving round to where white and blue waves broke over a coral reef, was stunning, so beautiful were they, set in blue sea fading to deep green and then pale green until the white beaches took over inshore. We just off-loaded our human and material cargo and returned immediately to Koggala to a night landing after a total of eight hours flying. It was the first time I had flown with Ted and, whereas I was always fairly tense taking off and, particularly, when landing – being somewhat of a perfectionist it had to be absolutely right every time (as, if I may say so, it mostly was!) – Ted, on the other hand, was completely relaxed, sitting comfortably back in his seat, for all the world as though just reading a book, and did a superb job every time – he was a fine natural pilot.

A few days later the ancient troopship SS *Manela* was nearing Colombo with the squadron's main party aboard, a month and a half behind us. (*Manela* and a sister ship had acted, even before the war, as occasional tenders to, and temporary bases for, various RAF flying boat squadrons.) Three or four of us flew out to escort the ship in, taking with us a good number of the ground crew who had worked so hard with us while waiting for proper equipment and spares. It was a very merry party with everybody waving to everybody else while we pilots tried hard to concentrate on avoiding the other aircraft as we circled about in a fairly confined airspace.

On a subsequent trip to Kelai which included an anti-submarine sweep, I was also carrying the station accounts officer, a very pleasant, somewhat older Australian who was terrified of flying. I chatted to him about how it would all go and took great care to do a smooth takeoff and a gentle climbing turn on to course. We were cruising happily along over a sunlit ocean when I noticed that a rocker box had come loose on one of the cylinders of the starboard inner engine; it was not exactly life-threatening but could produce more trouble in a little while so I had to tell poor old Harbutt – 'Harbottle' as we called him – that we were returning to base with a partially unserviceable engine. He was distinctly underwhelmed but cheered up, finally, as I had invited him up to the flight deck to watch what happily was the sort of landing that appears to be all done with a flick of the wrist.

Eleven days later, in the course of a rather tedious exercise to re-calibrate our directional loop aerial, I passed 1000 hours as a pilot, not quite two years after my first Tiger Moth trip – not exactly a helter-skelter rate of clocking up hours but not untypical of the effects of the vagaries of war with its frequent periods of wasted time.

Meanwhile a completely new organisation, Southeast Asia Command (SEAC), had been set up with Admiral Lord Louis Mountbatten as Supreme Commander of all Allied forces in the area. Hitherto the pursuit of the war in this area had suffered from the dead hand of India Command staffed, as it was, by unreconstructed peacetime officer-wallahs and those wartime officers who enthusiastically embraced the same comfortable approach to work. The setting up of SEAC, and Lord Louis' arrival to head it, brought an immediate wind of change and invigorating new spirit which spread rapidly, not least through Lord Louis' rounds of visits to the front line throughout his new command which featured his very effective 'turn' of getting all officers and men together, standing himself on an ammunition box or, in our case, an engine crate, and giving a breezy talk on how things were going to go from now on and his audiences part in the plan. It was stimulating stuff and he looked terrific in his beautifully-tailored tropical uniform and his naval cap, dripping with 'scrambled eggs', at a jaunty angle.

About this time 222 Group (the group controlling all RAF activity based on Ceylon) in Colombo held a big conference on anti-submarine tactics in the morning and in the afternoon we were able to sit in on a convoy conference where the masters of all the ships forming the convoy are briefed on the situation in the area of the convoy's route while the Senior Officer of Escort explains his plans, particularly the drill to be adopted in any emergency like a U-boat attack; this was exceedingly interesting for me with my background. In the tactical conference I made quite a contribution based on my experience of the major U-boat battle in the North Atlantic which was a good deal more recent than that of most of the others present: this was well received, even by the big brass. Presumably as a consequence of this I was summoned to the Station Commander's office: he said some very flattering things, which quite took me aback, and then urged me to apply for a permanent commission. I thought for a few moments and then thanked him for the compliment and said that I had a good job waiting for me with Shell and I would prefer to stick with that, which he quite understood; in the event it proved to be a wise decision, I think.

A heartening new phase of the war

Late in the evening of Tuesday 6 June, we heard on the BBC the thrilling news of the opening of the 'Second Front' this day. I wrote in my diary "Second Front started at last – big stuff! I wonder whether Christmas will see it all over." Well, I wasn't the only one. At that time the invasion of Europe was customarily referred to as the 'Second Front' as a result of ceaseless calls from Stalin and his deluded working class and middle class sympathisers to support the Russian front by forcing Germany to divert forces from the east to the west by forming a second front. This propaganda was quite effective at the time although we and the Americans were quite right in maintaining that to launch such a huge and risky enterprise in the weak and heavily committed position we were in in 1942 and 1943 would have been suicidal and would have put back our participation in the war against Germany not by months but by years. Stalin never accepted this and constantly criticised the (relatively) small quantity of war materials scraped up from our own desperately needed resources that we delivered at such terrible cost in men and ships by the Arctic convoys.

Meanwhile *S* was due for a 40-hour inspection and I taxied her very gently up to the warping buoy which was only about twenty yards from the slipway. A hawser was then attached to the aft end of her keel and was hooked up to a big mobile crane that hauled her round ready to be pulled backwards up the slipway and on to the hardstanding once the wading party had floated out and attached the two beaching legs, one either side of the hull, and the steerable tail trolley had been fitted close to the hawser attachment point.

The inspection and overhaul would take a good month so the whole crew was sent on leave; in view of the uncomfortable conditions in which we lived, and the debilitating effects of the climate, all operational aircrew were supposed to have three weeks leave every three months and we had just completed three quite busy months flying. George and I booked into the Grand Hotel in Nuwara Eliya which we reached after a fascinating train journey starting at sea level at Colombo and climbing to 5000 feet through lovely mountain scenery with brilliant flowers and rich greenery in the forest and the huge tea estates on which we could see hundreds of women picking the tea. Finally a taxi ride took us to Nuwara Eliya itself, at 6199 feet, where it was cool and fresh, wonderful after the months of coastal damp heat and allowing us to get into blues again. George persuaded me to try a round of golf, a game I had never played. It went really well, I got the hang of it quite quickly and decided to have a real crack at it. Next day we went out again and I could hardly even hit the ball let alone propel it in even approximately the right direction – no, it was not for me after all. So we walked and read and looked in vain (or at least I did) for some charming females but they seemed to be one of the many amenities unavailable for the duration. As *S* was due to be ready shortly, we had only ten days of actual leave, so we were soon back in the hot sticky atmosphere of Koggala – and, of course, *S* was not in fact ready. It was another month before the overhaul was completed because the highly corrosive water of the lake had attacked the bottom and six bottom plates and nearly 6000 rivets had had to be replaced. For some three weeks the unfortunate metal-bashers had lain on their backs under the aircraft, in roasting heat, drilling out each tiny rivet and carefully punching the new one in, a job that had to be done very thoroughly because even one or two slightly leaky rivets could let a surprising quantity of water into the bilges.

Meanwhile Ted and Jack Rand, with Johnnie Middleton, the Flight Commander, had been sent up to Assam to rescue a Chindit force in peril behind the Japanese lines in Burma. The Chindits were a special unit set up by the army, largely on the urging of a somewhat Lawrence of Arabia-style character called Brigadier Orde Wingate, to harass the Japanese and at the same time to 'keep a foot in the door' in Burma following the terrible retreat of the 14th Army in 1942. They flew in in gliders and were supplied entirely by air. The conditions under which they operated were extremely arduous – great heat, debilitating humidity during the monsoon, constant attack by leeches, rapid infection of wounds and the unrelieved tension of coping with a wily and murderous foe. Air supply in the jungle had to be by aircraft landing on prepared airstrips – parachuted supplies would inevitably end up to a large extent adrift, landing in the jungle where it would be difficult and dangerous to retrieve them before the enterprising 'Nips' stepped in. In the monsoon, when the rain is unbelievably dense, heavy and incessant, it was impossible to hack the customary airstrips out of the all-enveloping mass of wet trees and undergrowth. After many bloody actions and the labour of incessant movement the Chindits had become dangerously hampered with some 500 sick and wounded men who would have to be evacuated by air if the force was not to be immobilised and overwhelmed by the enemy. They had managed, after almost unbearable exertions, brilliantly described by one of their number, Brigadier John Masters in his book *The Road Past Mandalay*, to reach the shores of Lake Indawgyi in central Burma where they camped, completely exhausted, scarcely any longer a fighting formation.

Southeast Asia Command (SEAC) decided the only way to save the force was for the sick and wounded to be evacuated by flying boat so our two aircraft were sent to a place called Dibrugarh on the Brahmaputra river in northern Assam. From there they flew hundreds of miles through and over hills up to almost nine thousand feet, completely blind in the massive monsoon clouds and rain, to the lake where they filled the aircraft with walking wounded, stretcher cases and stumbling sick men. Unfortunately Jack Rand's aeroplane was sunk early on by a huge tree trunk, probably a teak log, so Ted, with Middleton as passenger, got landed with almost the whole operation, successfully bringing out the major share of the casualties, plus some five or six frightened Japanese prisoners, over 500 men in all. Ted collected a well-earned DFC as did Middleton, who was in charge of the operation.

In Middleton's absence I was made acting Flight Commander, something I had not expected as a number of other captains had been longer with the squadron than I had. It took me a few days to get into the ways of RAF administration, after which I came to enjoy having a really responsible job to do and it gradually appeared to me that it was going well. This, however, me being me, did not prevent me from worrying myself into sleeplessness which, in spite of dosing with the only known remedy at that time, phenobarbitone, rapidly became effectively chronic. I was looking forward rather anxiously to some relief when Ted and Johnnie Middleton came back from the Brahmaputra, but that operation in fact dragged on for something like three months.

Meanwhile 230 Squadron was quite busy but in some difficulty. 222 Group in Colombo had been used, over quite a long period, to dealing with Koggala's two Catalina squadrons and it seemed to us that we were not getting as much operational work as we should. Our case, though, was weakened by increasing amounts of unserviceability in our aircraft: our engineering management could, I think, have been more effective but the main reason was lack of spares. When a squadron was moved away to a new base overseas it was provided with a spares pack that contained everything from washers to wings, including engines. Due to one of those ridiculous battles of protocol with India Command that were a hangover from the peaceful days of the Raj we had been unable to get hold of our spares pack, which was stuck in Karachi; one imagines someone in Colombo had sent the wrong piece of paper to requisition the pack's release and it was beneath the dignity of the sahibs in India Command to send it back for correction, or something like that.

At any rate, as a result our only source of replacement engines was Middle East Command; air operations in Europe demanded engines on such a scale that none were to spare for squadrons overseas, so a huge Maintenance Unit at Abu Sueir on the Suez Canal rebuilt engines that were worn out or damaged in crashes, welding a bit of metal on here and there where necessary and generally making the thing work as well as possible. With the best will in the world this was not the way to produce safe performance under the highly stressed conditions of operational flying. One of our aircraft had had a complete four engine change during a major overhaul and on its first test flight it came back after some 15 minutes with one engine completely wrecked; we could hear it from a couple of miles away, sounding like 10,000 tin cans rattling as the dead engine windmilled. It has to be borne in mind that a high proportion of our British engines were built in 'shadow' factories organised to supplement the parent engine factories and staffed almost entirely by retrained workers from other industries and recruits from outside industry, so the quality of the product could not be expected to match that achieved by the experienced 'originals'. When, on top of that, you had those engines patched up and rebuilt far from the parent factory the wonder was that the fans kept turning as regularly as they did – and all this, compared with the quality and reliability of the Catalina's American engines, made by well-fed workers to whom bombs and blackout were something you read about, only added to the embarrassment of our unfavourable showing in comparison.

In spite of such difficulties, however, we did manage to get some interesting flying. I remember particularly a day we spent 50 miles or so off Colombo taking part in a naval co-operation exercise with a small escort carrier, HMS *Begum*, commanded by Captain 'Jackie' Broome who, although I did not know it at the time, was not only a 'character' but had also had the terrible experience, while commanding the escort of an Arctic convoy, PQ17, of having to execute an order from the Admiralty to disperse the convoy, subsequently watching it slaughtered ship by ship by a concentration of German submarines and aircraft. On this occasion things were less fraught and his fighter aircraft flew busily all day in response to dummy enemy sightings we provided. At the end of the day, on a lovely sunny evening, we were stooging round about a mile off the carrier watching the last of the fighters landing on; with the last one safely down *Begum* flashed the signal "Would you care to land on?" I immediately replied "Here we come" and did a wide circle to port of the ship's port quarter and lined up astern of her, descending in the approved carrier approach fashion to what I judged to be about ten feet above the ship's flight deck; because of our large wingspan my keel actually passed over the port side of the flight deck while my starboard wing tip passed within about ten feet of the captain on his bridge – level with him – and the sailors on deck literally threw themselves flat as we approached. I was going pretty fast and so was able to pull up into a reasonably flashy climb away from the ship while Jock Moir signalled "Goodbye and good luck". I hope Captain Broome felt that I had responded suitably to his joking invitation!

This episode incidentally gave me a slight illustration of the way Fleet Air Arm pilots have to operate. The sea, in this case, was calm with just a gentle swell but even so the carrier's stern was rising and falling a good eight to ten feet as we came in over it and the thought of pilots approaching to land on in rough weather – and even worse at night – and having to dash in, trusting that at the critical moment the back end of the flight deck would not either suddenly drop away from them or come up and stop them from 60 or 80 miles an hour to a messy zero, made a great impression on me; that is really arduous flying. I was told that during the war, whereas in the RAF all aircrews had a defined tour of operations before being rested, in the Fleet Air Arm they went on generally until they either died, went 'round the bend' or survived till too old!

Island-hopping

Among the many ills that afflicted service men in various parts of Southeast Asia Command was scrub typhus, and the Supreme Commander (Lord Mountbatten, the 'Supremo') detailed his personal physician, a delightful Surgeon Captain, to lead a mission to study the disease and, presumably, come up with a cure. The mission was to visit, among other places, the island bases in the Maldives and on Diego Garcia, a remote archipelago in the middle of the Indian Ocean about 1000 miles south of Ceylon. I got the job of flying the mission to the islands, to be accompanied also by some official British war photographers and correspondents and a couple of American photographers from Hollywood complete with cine cameras, ten passengers in all.

Our first stop was Addu Atoll at the southern end of the Maldives where our passengers had their initial experience of basic tropical living. Addu was similar to the other Maldives bases except that there was an Officers Mess which boasted, as well as the usual palm-frond accommodation huts, a large dining table in the open on the sand and an anteroom that consisted of a small open-sided hut on the end of a little wooden jetty equipped with wooden boxes on which we relaxed before and after dinner. The photographers recorded everything with great enthusiasm as they did the following day when we did a quick 500 mile dash north to Kelai with some freight and back again to Addu at last light. The long string of islands was a most beautiful sight, most particularly in the evening sunshine, and the photographers went wild with delight; in fact the Americans would have had me circling one tiny coral paradise after another until dark if I had not taken a firm line.

The next day the scrub typhus mission were heavily engaged while I spent a rather irritating time, for the photographers benefit, taxying round with the engines overheating while they asked for this angle and that, ending up with a demonstration takeoff and landing which, together with the other various shots, produced some very effective pictures as I discovered on a visit to the Imperial War Museum photographic library in 1986, over 40 years later!

Swimming in the warm waters of these coral-girt lagoons was wonderful and we spent the spare hours, while our passengers were working, diving off the aircraft and scrambling back on board again through the forward door. In an odd way this sort of activity gave one even more of a feeling that this beautiful aeroplane was indeed our home from home.

The next destination for our passengers was Diego Garcia, 500 miles to the south, all alone in the ocean and 1000 miles from the nearest mainland, Ceylon. We took off early in the afternoon which was a mistake; I was soon to learn that the build-up of clouds later in the day in these parts tended to produce some rough weather with heavy rain and severe turbulence, and so it proved. After a fairly uncomfortable trip we reached the clutch of coral islands, one or two rather bigger than the Maldives, and touched down in the extensive main lagoon.

Early the following morning we got an urgent signal to stand by for an operation later in the day. We had fuel on board only for the return flight to Koggala so we had to arrange immediately to take on an extra 1700 gallons; that sounds simple but in fact the refuelling launch was almost empty and the only aviation fuel on the island was in four gallon tins that had been in store for something like two years and which we would have to decant into the refueller through a chamois leather to trap any dirt and water that might have got in during storage. When we started a human chain to shift the tins from the storage to the jetty we were stunned to find that well over half of them were damaged, some only slightly but the majority so badly that many were only half full. Remembering Aviation Department days I was a bit concerned because the leakage by evaporation would have consisted mainly of the 'light ends', the most volatile elements of the fuel in which the high-octane characteristics were concentrated; this meant that there was a risk of detonation or 'pinking' in the engines under full power, a condition which could cause severe damage in a short time. In the circumstances, though, there was nothing for it but to take a chance.

We rigged a huge funnel, about three feet in diameter, on top of the refueller, fitted a vast chamois leather across it and proceeded to pour tin after tin into the middle, two pouring at a time while the rest opened the tins – those that had not already been open for many months – and heaved them up to the pourers. We all took it in turns but even so the fumes from the fuel were almost overpowering and Danny, the first wireless operator, had to spend twenty-four hours in sick quarters to recover. Soon after the refueller had got out to the aircraft and pumped the fuel on board we got a further signal – "Operation cancelled". We were so worn out that there was no question of de-fuelling that day as we would have to do in order not to be overweight with all our passengers and their masses of gear on board. So we ended the day with a splendid party aboard the Royal Fleet Auxiliary *Shanking* which was sharing the anchorage with us and a Catalina.

Next morning, a little the worse for wear – whether from the 100-octane fuel or the RFA's pink gin who knows? – we off-loaded much of the fuel and I then did an air test to get some idea of whether the grotty fuel would do its job adequately. Happily all seemed to be well. I took the opportunity of the air test to gratify our photographers' and cinephotographers' incessant craving for more shots and gave them not only a takeoff and landing but also a shoot up which they apparently missed because they were all ducking down to miss what they thought was an imminent sticky end.

We took off early the next day to enjoy the better weather on the 1000 mile trip back to Koggala which was combined with an anti-submarine sweep as Japanese submarines as well as the six German U-boats based at Penang were rumoured to be active in our area. That evening we celebrated the end of a most interesting few days with our grateful guests with a party in the mess at

Koggala; it should be explained that drink was so short in that part of the world on RAF operational bases, as opposed to the big headquarters, that beer was allocated entirely to the other ranks while officers, at Koggala at least, generally had enough whisky and gin for one tot of one or the other per night per officer, the remaining treats then being largely Van der Hum or Palestine crême de menthe. My last recollection of that evening is of an intimate conversation with the Surgeon Captain, who had led the scrub typhus mission, while he held a tumbler-full of some obscure concoction and I still had in my hand half a tumbler-full of neat Van der Hum; the last thing I saw of him was next morning, very green, leaning up against the Station Commander's Tiger Moth in which he was due to be given a jolly aerial tour of the surroundings.

The Station Commander, incidentally, who had taken over from Group Captain Mills a month or so earlier, was Group Captain Geoffrey Francis DSO, DFC, whom I had met briefly as a Wing Commander commanding 230 Squadron early in 1941, at a tea party in Alexandria, three and a half years ago – yet another of my wartime coincidences (see page 40).

Four days after the scrub typhus safari I managed to get us a trip, another anti-submarine sweep, that Group wanted carried out to Addu Atoll and the Seychelles. Quite how I talked the CO into giving the job to me I do not know because *S* would be due for a 40-hour minor inspection (a four or five day job) on arrival in the Seychelles and, furthermore, our automatic pilot was not working. However, we set off on the six hour flight to Addu full of anticipation and the following day did the 1200 or so miles to the Seychelles in nine and a half hours; all this, flying the aeroplane manually, was quite testing because absolutely accurate flying was vital for spot-on navigation when aiming for a remote tiny dot over great distances of empty ocean and, in addition, we had three hours of torrential rain and nil visibility on the way so we had practice in bumpy blind-flying on instruments as well. At the Seychelles we landed and took off in an open stretch of sea between the two main islands and, as mentioned earlier, there was always a long, low swell which was very deceptive. On touching down I hit one swell and then another and another, surging off each time which was not my usual standard – in fact in the squadron Line Book (still preserved and read again in 1993 at RAF Aldergrove) there is recorded a remark I apparently made in the mess while talking about the trip afterwards "A three-foot swell at the Seychelles – I bounced and bounced and bounced – I didn't like it – I always make smooth landings!" Just before that in the Line Book was a lovely one by Jack Rand in a broadcast on the Chindit rescue (see pages 138-39): "I don't know whether you're familiar with the Brahmaputra . . . !" For those not familiar with the RAF expression 'shooting a line'; while it sometimes refers in a derogatory manner to plain boastfulness it mostly involves an unintentional or deliberately humorous boast, like the wartime Mosquito pilot flying at nought feet across the Channel "We flew so low that the airspeed indicator was reading in knots!" (in those days all RAF aircraft except those in Coastal Command measured their airspeed in miles per hour).

That evening, Sunday 27 August 1944, there was a huge party at the Seychelles Club. As already mentioned (see page 125), the islands had for long been a French possession and French influence was very strong. News had just come through of the liberation of Paris and naturally the gaiety was unconfined, with emotional speeches in French and much stress on the entente cordiale, only slightly marred by an idiot British army officer who rambled on drunkenly and unstoppably until, mercifully, he suddenly stopped in full flow and slid quietly under the table.

Sunderlands did not operate regularly out of the Seychelles at that time – the only regular aircraft were Catalinas – so we were to be totally responsible, as a crew, for our minor inspection which promised to be a considerable undertaking, particularly as it was to be carried out, of course, on the water. Everyone set to with his own special departmental responsibility plus George who, as navigator, had no bits of machinery to look after but mucked in wherever he could help. The biggest job was changing a cylinder. Duncan Matheson and Joe Eggett, the two flight engineers, had diagnosed lack of compression on one of the nine cylinders on the starboard inner engine and, as luck would have it, it was number nine, the bottom one. Imagine two people balancing on an eight inch wide Duralumin plank slung across under the engine, removing the valve gear and then easing the heavy cylinder off its holding-down bolts, trying to avoid its coming loose suddenly and slipping from oily hands into the sea. They got it off and handed it up to two of us balanced on top of the engine whence it was passed from hand to hand across the mainplane, down into the hull and eventually on to the engineers' bench in the after part of the aircraft. There it was found that about a third of the interior of the cylinder was quite deeply pitted with rust and it was quite obvious that it must have been in that condition when it was fitted at the aforementioned Abu Sueir maintenance unit during the 're-conditioning' of the engine.

After seven days toiling in great heat, interspersed with a great deal of various kinds of hospitality ashore, the job was completed and I did a long air test – an hour and twenty minutes – to make certain that every bit of the boat was working properly – and to give us a final look at those beautiful islands for which we had acquired a considerable affection and, not least, for their people.

A further day was spent clearing up ashore and saying our goodbyes to our numerous hosts and then we were off on a combined transit flight and anti-submarine sweep to Addu Atoll. About an hour out the wireless receiver broke down; every possible test was made and the three wireless operators had the whole set spread out in tiny pieces on the flight deck, all to no avail. There was an absolute ruling in all marine air operations that no aircraft was to take off or continue a flight without fully operative wireless, so I got the three operators to assure me that the set was totally beyond repair in the air and, that given, I announced on the intercom that I was returning to the Seychelles. A great cheer rang through the aircraft which was, very strictly speaking, not quite the sort of reaction there ought to have been, but if you had ever been to the Seychelles you would not have blamed us. Our second attempt, after two days work on the set, was successful and after an anti-submarine sweep of 10¾ hours to Addu and a further five to Koggala we arrived back loaded with beautiful lace – a speciality of the Seychelles – numerous bits of carved wood as well as one of the rather rude wooden outer shells of the coco de mer and many other knick-knacks, irresistible but mostly of little use.

The lighter side

We had quite a lively debating society on the station and I had been cajoled into being its president, a job that I found increasingly onerous. I had asked the committee to find a replacement but when I got back from the Seychelles I found that my request to be relieved of the presidency had been deferred. Now that I was permanently sleeping only three to five hours a night I wanted to drop whatever extraneous burdens I could and I felt I had done my bit for the society over some six months. On such an isolated station various forms of entertainment were very important The lake water was infected and the sea at Koggala was dangerous, so the only swimming possible was eight miles away at Closenburg Bay near the little town of Galle – when one could get transport. There was a cinema in a kadjan (palm-leaf wattle) hut, but the Ceylonese operators frequently got the reels mixed up, which instantly produced a near-riot with chaps invading the projection box and threatening physical harm to the little locals who smiled and wagged their heads and said "No understanding English writing, master."

There was a little Welsh ex-miner, an engine fitter in the station maintenance section, who not only had a wonderful collection of classical records but also possessed an encyclopaedic knowledge of music; he used to put on musical evenings which were surprisingly well attended even though it meant a long walk through the surrounding jungle to reach the abandoned house where he was allowed to hold his shows. At night most of us carried torches because the jungle paths were tricky, with trailing fronds, fallen branches, pools of water and the occasional snake plus, more frequently, an iguana that looked rather like a three foot long lizard – both of these normally slid or scampered away as humans approached but there was one particular snake, called a tic polonga, which was exceedingly dangerous because it was very lazy but also had a bite that was alleged to be fatal within ten minutes. One night I was returning from the cinema with the crowded audience, riding the bicycle I had been issued with, as acting Flight Commander, to help me get around on the vast station more quickly than walking: all of a sudden an airman walking alongside me yelled "Stop, sir!" and as I braked, there, trapped mercifully under the front wheel, was a tic polonga. Fortunately not enough of it was free to strike up at my foot on the pedal but I kept the brake on exceedingly hard while the airman got a stone and bashed the snake to death.

To return to our debating society, I remember particularly two of our debates. The first was on the motion "That sex before marriage is a good thing." As can be imagined, there was a big turnout and I had the job of proposing; among a number of rather random points I remarked that one great advantage was avoiding the situation of 'a round peg in a square hole' – just really on the spur of the moment, but it got a roar of laughter which led on to a total defeat for the unfortunate station padre, a rather earnest fellow, who had the task of opposing the motion.

The second occasion was less happy. At that time – September 1944 – there were a number of strikes in the war industries at home and I suggested that a motion condemning them for letting down those who were doing the fighting would generate a good debate. It was indeed very active but the contribution which literally stunned me and, I think, many others was a fierce and passionate support for the strikers from our music-loving Welsh fitter who praised them for "keeping bright the strike weapon to use against the bosses when we get back home"!

Ding's then navigator was a fairly theatrical English officer who successfully organised two or three amateur shows, one of which was a drama about the French Resistance which captured the whole atmosphere extraordinarily well, even to the point of somehow contriving some very convincing SS uniforms. The tune of *Frère Jacques* was a code and the muted playing of this at moments of tension produced an authentic 'frisson'.

All change

Towards the end of September it became increasingly clear that some changes were in the offing as a number of aircrew, including the CO himself, had been with the squadron for a considerable time. The Flight Commander, Middleton, had already gone and 'Ding' Ingham had taken over from him, so I was at last relieved of the acting position. I very much needed a rest as the squadron had been very active and at the same time I was getting much too little sleep. Both German and Japanese submarines were appearing from time to time, the Germans, who were based at Penang, specially prominent because, as in the Atlantic, they regularly sent long wireless signals to base which allowed direction finding stations to pinpoint their position quite accurately; sadly we were constantly frustrated in hunting them because the search plans were based on obsolete tactical doctrines long since revised in Coastal Command but which, because of the ridiculous protocol restrictions mentioned earlier, we were forced to continue using as the newer instructions could not be requested by India Command from Coastal Command. Less closely targeted operations were the anti-submarine sweeps which were often combined with the mail and personnel transfer flights to and between the remote island bases.

One of these sweeps took us to Addu and then on to Diego Garcia. At the met briefing I had been told that the inter-tropical front was lying across our course, somewhere north of DG. The inter-tropical front is a meeting between two different air masses that moves seasonally north and south over the whole area from the northern Bay of Bengal right down into the empty part of the Southern Ocean, varying in intensity, often over quite short periods. We were flying south of Addu in calm weather with a cloudless sky when there was a slight bump. Jokingly I said on the intercom "That's the inter-tropical front, chaps," immediately after which the engineer reported that the cylinder head temperature gauges of all four engines were suddenly reading zero – all the other instruments were showing normal functioning and the fans continued turning; half a minute later the gauges returned to their normal reading of around 180 degrees C – a complete mystery.

On the return flight in the afternoon, as we approached the position of the front, things had completely changed. There was a huge wall of cloud ahead as far as the eye could see to left and right towering up to probably at least 25,000 feet. We were cruising at 1500 feet as we entered the cloud, at which height turbulence should not be a problem. On the contrary, within half a minute, in spite of flying level, our heavily-loaded aircraft was being whisked aloft at some 1500 feet a minute. I throttled back the engines – still we went on up. I put the machine into a dive at 140 knots – still we stuck in the 1500 feet a minute climb. This was potentially an extremely dangerous situation because in the higher levels of these tropical clouds the turbulence can break an aeroplane in pieces (I once met a man who had watched a Catalina fly into a storm cloud off the west coast of Africa and come out seconds later from high up in several big chunks); while I was still busily cogitating how I was going to get out of this we suddenly emerged, at 7000 feet, into a small hole in the middle of this vast mass of cloud where the air was calm and, looking down I could see the sea. I rapidly converted the dive into a steep spiral and reached cloud base at only 700 feet above the water. Some heavy work on the controls brought us back level not too near the sea and we continued on our way just below cloud base until clear of the front, back in fine weather. That transformation of the front from a clear air bump to a fearsome wall of turbulent cloud had taken no more than a few hours.

After that, we were due for regular leave but once again I had to stay behind because the big changes were beginning to materialise and those due to go were busy preparing for departure. The CO, Wing Commander Bednall, was going and many aircrew also, including, sadly, George my superb navigator, posted to somewhere in India. We had been together for almost two years since meeting at Invergordon at crew formation and I was going to miss his imperturbable nature no less than his totally reliable navigation.

Our new CO, Wing Commander Powell, was fresh out from UK and had last been with the squadron in the Mediterranean two or three years back. One of his first acts was to get me officially confirmed as Flight Commander (Training), though without any promotion. His arrival also enabled us to get hold of a first-class squadron Engineer Officer who was to prove a real tonic in that department. We began to settle down quite well, with a new outlook and a hope of a larger share of work following an improvement in our aircraft serviceability record.

Italy had long since surrendered to the Allies and various units of her forces worked thereafter with ours. One such was a submarine that was based in Ceylon and was used for exercises. One night we spent three hours practising radar approaches and then making simulated attacks using flares to illuminate the surfaced submarine, an exercise that would have been invaluable to us back in the Atlantic days; tremendous concentration and very close co-operation among the whole crew was needed for any sort of success to be achieved. This was followed by a daytime exercise, again using radar approaches followed by attacks, some of them after the submarine had dived, and it was fascinating to be able actually to see her when we were down-sun from her and very close, the water being so clear; such a sighting would be extremely unlikely in the turbid northern waters.

Then tragedy struck the squadron. Group asked for an anti-submarine patrol to cover the whole east coast of Ceylon about 80 miles out. Met reports spoke of a cyclone situated in the east of the Bay of Bengal several hundred miles away; Group considered that this was not a danger to the patrol, but our station met officer, who had spent years before the war as a civilian forecaster in the Malayan Meteorological Service, was deeply perturbed – he knew from great experience how fast and unpredictably these fearsome cyclones could travel and he boldly tackled the Group met people, urging them to recommend scrubbing the operation, but he was overruled. 'Ding' took off and sent his first two regular position signals (wireless silence was not so vital as in the Atlantic) – then silence. As late morning wore on into afternoon concern grew: if his transmitter had gone u/s (unserviceable) his operators would surely have got it going again or, if that had proved impossible, he would have observed the rules and returned to base, abandoning the patrol. By late afternoon the Station Commander, the Ops Room Controller and I were in discussion with Group by telephone (my CO was away presiding at a court of enquiry, so I was acting in his place at this moment) and it was decided that it would be useless mounting a search by night and that plans should be made, in outline, for a big search first thing the following morning.

After a hurried dinner I rejoined Group Captain Francis in the ops room. We checked the aircraft availability of 230 Squadron and the two Catalina squadrons: a total of fourteen aircraft could be available. We reported this to Group and asked whether they should control the operation, working out the area of search, allocation of aircraft to sectors, height to fly for best search and so on, or whether we should. Somewhere towards nine in the evening Group had still not decided. Meanwhile the crews had been alerted (140 aircrew in total), Maintenance had been warned to prepare for the routine daily inspections (without which no aircraft could fly) on 14 machines and the Marine Craft Section had been ordered to have available every possible craft to get the maintenance crews out to the aircraft and back again while the aircraft crews themselves were ferried out; the Officers and the Sergeants Messes had instructions to prepare operational breakfasts for all those who would be flying (in UK the operational breakfast, at any time between midnight and eight o'clock or so, always consisted of bacon and eggs, regardless of rationing, but in Ceylon it was so difficult to get even the measly local eggs that we had baked beans instead. With the reduced atmospheric pressure as the aeroplane climbed the effect can perhaps be imagined!).

With still no sign from Group in more than another hour 'Groupie' Francis took it upon himself to ask them again whether they would control the search – no decision yet. Finally, at midnight they rang to say that Koggala should assume control so the three of us – 'Groupie', Ops Room Controller and I – quickly agreed on the actual area of search and the height to fly. 'Groupie' then said "Well, over to you, Alan" and went off to bed. With the Controller I then set about working out the tracks each aircraft should fly throughout the day to cover the search area thoroughly without overlapping, which aircraft should fly which track (Catalinas were a lot slower than Sunderlands so that had to be taken into account), what time each aircraft should take off based on the smallest interval achievable with the marine craft available and, finally, what time each crew should be called and where the transport should pick them up so as to minimise congestion all down the line.

When all the planning had been completed and every single item re-checked, it was after half past four and the first aircraft were due off at six so I walked back to my quarter, flung myself on my bed, slept for nearly an hour fully dressed and then got up to go down to the jetty to see each aircraft away; if anything had gone wrong at the last moment I should have had to sort it out instantly, there would have been no time to consult the Station Commander and, anyway, it was my show. All went well and we waited throughout the day for some result of the search, while I worked on my share of the squadron's daily administration. In the evening, as each aircraft came back the crew reported having seen absolutely no trace of aircraft or crew.

Meanwhile, in late evening reports were coming through that the cyclone had hit the east coast and roared up through the countryside, cutting a swathe a hundred yards wide in which every single thing, trees, houses, bridges, vehicles had been totally flattened or destroyed, and had then suddenly petered out completely up in the hills. We worked out that 'Ding' would have been precisely where the cyclone passed on its way to the island. Poor Johns, our met man, was in tears, wishing he had insisted more strongly but everyone assured him that he could not have done a thing more in view of Group's decision.

'Groupie' Francis and I went back to the ops room after dinner and put it to Group that we should mount as nearly as possible the same operation again the next day. Group agreed but would not say whether they would prefer to be in control this time as our first try had been unproductive. There then followed an exact rerun of the previous night. Remarkably the squadrons were able, between them, to put up 14 aircraft and crews again and we went through the whole rigmarole – Group deciding at midnight to leave us in control, 'Groupie' Francis saying "Over to you, Alan", me back to bed at five and up again to be at the jetty at six for the first aircraft, work all day in the office, crews returned in the evening with nothing seen, decision taken for a third and final day's search – only ten aircraft this time – Group letting us get on with it this time, me back to bed about 4.30 and back at the jetty at 6.00, a whole day waiting for any news, crews returning in the evening with nothing seen.

Not the smallest trace of either aircraft or 'Ding' and his crew was ever found, so savage had been the impact of that terrible cyclone. We felt that no greater effort could possibly have been made by the exhausted personnel of the squadrons, maintenance, marine craft and ops room staff and, for it all to prove in the end to be in vain was a great sadness for everyone.

New challenges

One day about now one of the Australians, a navigator called Tommy Fawcett, a delightful chap, came up to my office and asked "What's happened, Alan? You never come into the mess in the evenings now." I told him I couldn't sleep and could not face the hilarity in the bar at nights – in which I suppose I had earlier been rather a leading light, and I just had to try to rest. It was a great pity as I had enormously enjoyed those boisterous evenings in which we amused ourselves with sundry ditties and tomfoolery in a way that people today, reading of it or seeing it on films, cannot understand. It was really a way of letting off steam and keeping at bay those thoughts of ever-present danger (even a simple air test could, with bad luck or carelessness, result in a pile-up) which now and again overwhelmed those who flew, at which point the wise commander would put them on rest for a period, otherwise, all too often they bought it on their next trip. It was very much akin to the phenomenon of the soldier in the trenches in the First World War who suddenly became morose and reckoned his 'number was up' – very frequently he was the next one to go. I had just one case in which I had to make a decision and I am sure it was the right one.

Rather surprisingly perhaps, my state of fatigue did not in any way affect my ability to fly until much later, doubtless because I loved flying so much and was totally dedicated to it; which was why, when a couple of staff officers came down from Group to invite me to go on the staff, I told them I had joined the Royal Air Force to fly and that was that, thank you.

A week after Ding's crash I at last got some leave, just two weeks from 8 December. A short while before the squadron had been joined by a Canadian pilot, Harry Sheardown, a very agreeable chap. There was the question of a successor to 'Ding' as Flight Commander and, as Harry had been commissioned three days before me, he was the senior so it was arranged that he would take over as Flight Commander (Operations) while I would continue in the officially recognised post of Flight Commander (Training) in view of various imminent changes that would involve a great deal of retraining of our air crews. Such posts in heavy aircraft squadrons carried substantive Squadron Leader rank but, as Group stated, repeating a memorable Air Ministry instruction ". . . the Royal Air Force has reached global ceiling in Squadron Leaders" (Group headquarters everywhere were stuffed with them, mostly acting), so we would both get only the acting rank which, nevertheless, was more than something – first step into senior rank; the effective date was 10 December 1944.

Two days before that I had travelled by train, close along the seashore, from Galle (near Koggala) to Colombo, a slow journey with long stops which provided ample opportunity for beggars to emerge from the swarming, shouting crowds on the platforms to display, at extremely close quarters, the gamut of deformed limbs, infected eyes, horrible injuries and so on which, I have to admit, turned me off rather than inspiring compassion, so numerous and importunate were they. It was a relief to change trains and start the slow climb through the glorious hill scenery into cooler and cooler air, finally arriving at one of the favourite hill stations, Bandarawela, at an altitude of nearly 5000 feet.

The Bandarawela Hotel was, and maybe still is, a very pleasant old-style colonial hotel with cool, airy spaces and large slowly-revolving ceiling fans and colourful gardens with gentle greens, such a relief after the overwhelming lushness of the coastal jungle. It was ideal for total relaxation and with the aid of quantities of phenobarbitone I began to sleep properly. I walked and read and, on one evening, reluctantly agreed to make a fourth with three rather awful Koggala characters who had invited four Wrens from the nearby naval rest camp at Diyatalawa to dinner and dancing. Having been prised away from the bar I found myself paired off with an enchanting girl from Glasgow who was introduced to me as Margaret Gloag, a good starting point for our conversation as I had bought a copy of *Blackwood's Magazine* to read on the train and in it was a short story which had intrigued me, entitled 'The Cigar' by an author called John Gloag who, it transpired, was the girl's uncle. We had a very enjoyable evening and when we left the Wrens invited the four of us to drop in at Diyatalawa for tea at any time. Whether the others went I do not know but I did not have the energy to turf out from the hotel for an afternoon's jollity so that was that – or so I thought.

Back with the squadron, after my two weeks I found that Charles Potter had arrived back from UK with the first of our new Mk V Sunderlands. This was very exciting as the new aircraft were a great advance on our ageing Mk IIIs. Instead of the 1050 horsepower Bristol Pegasus XVIII engines they had American Pratt and Whitney Twin Wasps of 1250 horsepower, thus giving us a total of 5000 horsepower for takeoff; with the heavier engines the centre of gravity had moved and, to compensate, the setting of the wings was slightly altered as a result of which the handling of the aircraft at takeoff and landing was very slightly different. We also now, at last, had fully-feathering airscrews which meant that in the event of engine failure the blades could be turned so that the leading edge faced the airflow thus eliminating the 'windmilling' that caused such a drag with the older engines and often exacerbated the initial damage inside the engine.

The navigation equipment was also greatly strengthened. The radar now 'painted' a map on the cathode-ray tube with the aircraft in the middle, picking up ships, even lifeboats, as well as submarines, islands and coastlines. A new system called LORAN (long-range air navigation) produced an automatic plot on the navigator's chart which backed up the manual plot that was still maintained for security.

We now had a total of twelve machine guns: the customary four 0.303s in the rear turret and two more in the front turret, while the two in the mid-upper turret had been replaced by a bigger 0.5 inch either side amidships – manually trained which seemed surprising since manually trained guns hardly match turret-mounted guns when following high-speed attacking aircraft. However the greatest advance was the addition of four forward-firing 0.303s, two each side, mounted in the bow compartment and fired by the captain – the first time he moved up from just being a driver while all the others, bar the navigator, did all the banging away. This battery of a total of six guns firing forward was originally developed for Atlantic operations after the Germans had decided that the U-boats often had a better chance of survival by remaining on the surface and fighting it out with the attacking aircraft using a new and formidable battery of anti-aircraft guns, mounted on a 'bandstand' that had been added to the after end of the conning tower The attacking aircraft was thus extremely vulnerable on its necessarily straight run-in at the dropping height of 50 feet but the provision of the six machine guns gave the aircraft crews a chance to incapacitate or, at least, discourage the U-boat's gun crews.

The wireless operators now had a greatly improved set of Morse and voice equipment, which was badly needed, as the earlier gear dated back to prewar. These substantial changes, together with a number of internal alterations within the hull, necessitated a very large programme of training for the ground crews (not my responsibility) and the roughly 120 aircrew, which was my task and I embarked on it as soon as I got back from leave, just before Christmas.

I doubt whether many of us gave thought to the fact that this was the sixth Christmas of the war and few dared speculate that it was to be the last; for me it was the fourth overseas. We had a tremendous party on Christmas Eve in the Sergeants Mess, an occasion on which, traditionally, the sergeants and warrant officers set out to get the officers at least speechless, if not legless. (Warrant Officer is the most senior noncommissioned rank and of my original crew both Jock Moir, wireless operator/mechanic, and Duncan Matheson, flight engineer, had reached that rank while 'Danny' Dandeker, first wireless operator, had been commissioned as Pilot Officer.)

On Christmas morning the runway was given over to racing with the lumbering bullocks that normally pulled all sorts of carts and wallowed in the paddy fields pulling primitive ploughs to prepare for the rice planting. As can be imagined, each race took some time to complete, which was just as well for Harry Sheardown and me as we ran the Tote and, after the previous night, were not at our brightest and best. Before lunch we returned the NCOs hospitality with a pre-lunch party in our mess and then went off, as was, and doubtless still is, the custom, to serve the airmen their dinner. Finally, in the evening we had our own Christmas special followed by a monster party that lasted until midnight at which point four of us took up a challenge and rode furiously up and down the runway on bicycles clad in our underwear.

That was the last occasion on which I rode a bike because as Squadron Leader Flight Commander I was entitled to my own transport which should have been a jeep but with the RAF's chronic shortage had to be a motorbike. When I went to the MT section to collect my machine the corporal in charge brought forward an impressive-looking despatch rider's 500cc Norton. He asked if I had ever ridden a motor bike and I said "No" (my father having bought me a car, for five pounds, at seventeen, his intention being that I should learn how to run a car the hard way which, indeed, I did) so he said "All right, sir, I'll de-tune it a bit and after a fortnight, when you're used to it, bring it back and I'll make it go for you." It was nearing lunch time and I cautiously rode the beast over to the mess which was situated on what might be described as an eminence. The word had evidently got round that 'Dixie' was coming on his new motorbike and when I arrived there was quite a crowd looking down upon me as I dismounted, on the side of the bike opposite to the spectators; I did not know, until a second or two later, that when a motorbike departs from the vertical it is exceedingly difficult to retrieve it, particularly, as in this case, when it is falling away from one. Next moment the Norton hit the ground with a crash with its unfortunate rider sprawled ignominiously on top. I scrambled to my feet, shook my fist in mock anger at the convulsed onlookers and then we all had a hilarious few minutes while they dusted me down and ceremoniously re-mounted me, hoping I would do the same again – which I did not. Subsequently, after it was retuned, that bike was great fun and gave me an experience that I would otherwise, car-bound, have missed.

January 1945 was a very busy month. The training programme was in full swing and we pilots were spending a lot of time getting to know our new Mk Vs. As each one arrived from UK one of the old Mk IIIs was moved out into the jungle to a slow death; there was nothing very much worth salvaging and to move them to some other part of the world would have been totally uneconomic as they, and in particular their engines, were near the end of the line. One such casualty was our faithful *S* for Sugar which was replaced by another Mk III, aircraft *K* (curiously, my very first aircraft, on 246 Squadron had had the letter K and this aircraft *K* was, in the event, to be my last). We took her round the islands and on many convoy escorts; one of the latter was to escort the battleship HMS *Queen Elizabeth* which, accompanied by destroyers, was taking the Duke and Duchess of Gloucester out to Australia where the Duke was to be Governor General. The crew and I were very much hoping to get one of the new Mk Vs as I had completed the demanding training programme by the end of January, but it was not to be as General Slim, commanding 14th Army in Burma, and Lord Mountbatten, Supreme Commander Southeast Asia, had other ideas. Meanwhile any reasonable sleep continued to elude me.

Chindwin Operation

In 1942 the Japanese had forced the British 14th Army, commanded by General Alexander, to retreat from Burma and were only prevented from pressing across the frontier into India by ferocious rearguard actions by exhausted soldiers that finally stopped the enemy near Kohima and Imphal in the jungle-covered hills of northwest Burma. Early in 1944 Bill Slim, a tough but very human man, returned to Burma with a rejuvenated 14th Army that had learned the hard lessons of the retreat two years earlier. At the end of 1944 the Army was poised along the Chindwin River in the area of Kalemyo and Kalewa, ready for the drive south along the Chindwin and the Irrawaddy to capture Mandalay and then, finally, Rangoon, all this before the monsoon broke in May.

Many ideas were produced for speeding up the advance along the river banks as an alternative to fighting a way through the jungle; one was put forward to Slim and Mountbatten by a Lieutenant Commander Penman RNVR who before the war had been an Irrawaddy river pilot. His plan was that a flotilla of heavily-armed motorboats should precede the leading infantry advancing along the banks, shooting up and destroying the Japanese strong points in their way; it was agreed that this should be a naval effort, the motorboats being manned by sailors. Suitable craft existed but were in Bombay, well over 1000 difficult miles from Kalewa. To transport them by road and rail would take many weeks, if not months, and Slim had only some three to four months to get all the way to Rangoon. Air transport was the obvious alternative but no aircraft then available could have carried even one boat so it was decided to take the engines, steering gear, controls, propeller and shaft – every single thing – out of the hull, fly it all to Kalewa and get the Royal Engineers boat yard there to build hulls and fit engines and gear – and guns! – into them. Sunderlands were the only aircraft with the internal capacity to hold the bits and pieces and the powered bomb hoists would be ideal for loading and unloading through a removable panel in the port side of the bomb room which had been originally designed to enable a spare engine to be carried – excellent, except that the new Mk Vs did not have the removable panel. 230 Squadron, detailed to undertake the job, would have to inspect, and refurbish as necessary, its remaining aged Mk IIIs. I knew none of this but was just told to report with my aircraft *K* and Charles Potter in *W* to Trombay, near Bombay, where I should be given the details of a 'special job', which I was to command; Alan Pedley with aircraft *T* would follow shortly. Just before the order came through my crew had been sent on leave so I took Dick Levy-Haarscher's crew instead.

On Friday 2 February, Charles and I arrived at Trombay with a maintenance party of seven complete with spares and tools on the two aircraft. I met Wing Commander Hawkins from 222 Group who explained the purpose of the operation, the location of the landing area on the Chindwin River (which had been chosen by a former Koggala station commander flying over it at 1000 feet!) and the details of the load to be carried. We worked out the weight of fuel we anticipated we would need for the 800 mile flight across India to Calcutta; then we talked to Lieutenant Commander Kedglie RNVR who was responsible for delivering the loads to us at Trombay and together we decided that each load should be of 5100 lbs (approximately 2¼ tons), comprising three marine engines weighing about half a ton each, together with all the control mechanisms and underwater gear for one complete boat. We planned that the whole operation should be completed in six sorties; this would enable us to avoid having to carry out 40-hour minor inspections on any aircraft.

The original plan had been to base the operation at Trombay with Calcutta as a stopping off point for a final inspection and refuelling of the aircraft before the difficult flight into Burma. However we found that Trombay had a large maintenance staff familiar with Sunderlands and, in addition, full stocks of spares, so I decided to transfer our own maintenance crew and spares to Calcutta from where I would control the whole operation – Trombay was too far from the trickiest part to be able to be in immediate touch.

The base at Calcutta was in a suburb called Bally and the moorings were on the Hooghly River, just upstream from the magnificent Willingdon Bridge, named after an earlier Viceroy of India, Lord Willingdon. I learned that we would have to share buoys with a Catalina squadron, No 212, which was understood to be engaged on air-sea rescue work, and BOAC who were by then operating slightly-converted Sunderlands through from the UK.

We loaded the aircraft next day with no trouble: the electrically-operated bomb trolley's chain hoist coped perfectly with the three marine engines, each in a big wooden crate and looking almost exactly like an upright grand piano – the removable panel in the port side of the hull gave ample room to swing them in to rest on the very strong bomb room floor. Then, having arranged an approximate schedule with Kedglie and had the aircraft thoroughly checked I set off on the seven and a half hour flight to Calcutta. We flew at 8000 feet where it was cool and the impression of India that we got was of endless very dry-looking flat country with sparse trees and occasional brown-and-white villages and towns; there were some rivers now and again and a few small lakes but not much in the way of a possible emergency landing place. When the huge hot and dusty-looking sprawl of Calcutta loomed up it was not hard to spot the landing and mooring area at Bally on the muddy-brown Hooghly. Mooring-up was very tricky as the river flowed at 5-6 knots – as we found in time, the wind was often across the tide and the necessary crab-wise approach to the buoy was exceedingly difficult to judge; furthermore the flow was extremely turbulent – a floating boathook dropped into the water was instantly sucked down until only its tip showed – and this was a danger that made me even more anxious to reduce to the minimum the amount of work to be done on the engines, particularly such awkward jobs as cylinder changes and, of course, 40-hour minor inspections.

In the evening I called on our liaison man, Wing Commander Butler, at Eastern Air Command and discovered that no arrangements of any sort had been made for the control of our flights or even for help with the small administration chores involved in an operation of this scale mounted from a detached base. He simply said "We know nothing about 'boats here – you're on your own!" As far as administration was concerned they had arranged that, although no office accommodation could be provided, the adjutant of the Catalina squadron would get my signals sent and received – just that and nothing more. As I was obviously going to be in and out of Calcutta myself and mostly at different times from the other captains, I had expected that 212 would act as a contact point for us but, on the contrary, it was made plain that handling of signals – as a sort of post office – was the limit of what I would get. I felt bitter about this at the time – surely a little help would not be hard to provide – but I learned later that the squadron's main activity was the transport of agents into and out of the Japanese-occupied territories to the east and clearly they would not want any outsiders nosing around; the air-sea rescue duties they performed were obviously a convenient cover for the clandestine side of their operations on which, incidentally, an old friend from GR School at George, Rolf Luck, was killed.

So it seemed that I was going to have to be a sort of mobile detachment office myself; I did at one stage attempt some delegation by leaving instructions for one crew with another one who should have crossed, either at Trombay or Bally, but on two occasions a change in the schedule prevented their crossing and the resulting muddle took some sorting out. The urgent need for the earliest possible completion of the operation was always uppermost in my mind as the word from General Slim and the Supreme Allied Commander had made it clear that it should be; my eyes had, in fact, been very fully opened to this by Butler showing me the file of signals, at top level, setting up the operation of which I had been put in charge.

Very early on the morning following my arrival I set off, with Butler – and my enormously heavy camp kit – by DC3 Dakota for Burma. The aircraft was filled with tank spares and I spent a couple of uncomfortable hours perched on a rolled-up tank track. After passing over the huge Ganges delta, with its innumerable meandering arms leading to the sea, we started to climb up over the Chin Hills; these are a succession of ridges running north-south and becoming steadily higher until at around 9000 feet the last two or three ridges led to a sheer cliff dropping straight down to the valley floor of the Chindwin River where Kalemyo lay. The hills were entirely covered with thick jungle, huge trees tightly packed together with no roads, tracks or clearings as far as one could see – anything that fell into that would never be spotted, let alone reached. The prevailing westerly wind rolled over these ridges and, above a certain strength, produced considerable bumps and then at the cliff edge curled over to an absolutely monumental bump just as one was looking down the 9000 foot drop – it made even our huge wings waggle up and down.

At Kalemyo it was the real war – aircraft of every sort coming and going – fighters, transports, little L5 casualty evacuation aircraft, light bombers. It was the dry season and every inch of ground was covered with six or eight inches of yellowy-brown dust which was thrown up in dense clouds every few minutes as an aircraft took off and covered the army of sweating troops and airmen dressed just in boots, shorts and bush hats. Butler and I clambered aboard a jeep that was then driven at hectic speed along a road, equally deep in dust (which would turn into a similar depth of liquid mud in the monsoon), which led to a 400 yard long Bailey bridge that the Royal Engineers had built to span the Chindwin over which we rattled in order to reach Kalewa, a little distance away on the other side of the river. All around was a mixture of small bits of parched open land and jungle-covered hills with everywhere those enormous trees, most of them teak, I imagine. Military vehicles were on the move constantly and aircraft swept in and out of the Kalemyo airstrip.

At Kalewa we met the commanding officer of No 5 Inland Water Transport Group of the Royal Engineers, Major Corbett, and saw the impressive boat yard on the banks of the river where 'our' motorboats would be built. We discussed the sort of craft most suited to carrying our cargo and I explained how it should approach and come alongside. The actual landing area was six miles downstream at a place called Shwegyin (pronounced Shwejeen) and a motor launch took us a winding trip between high jungle-covered banks to a point where the banks suddenly opened out and the river was straight for a distance

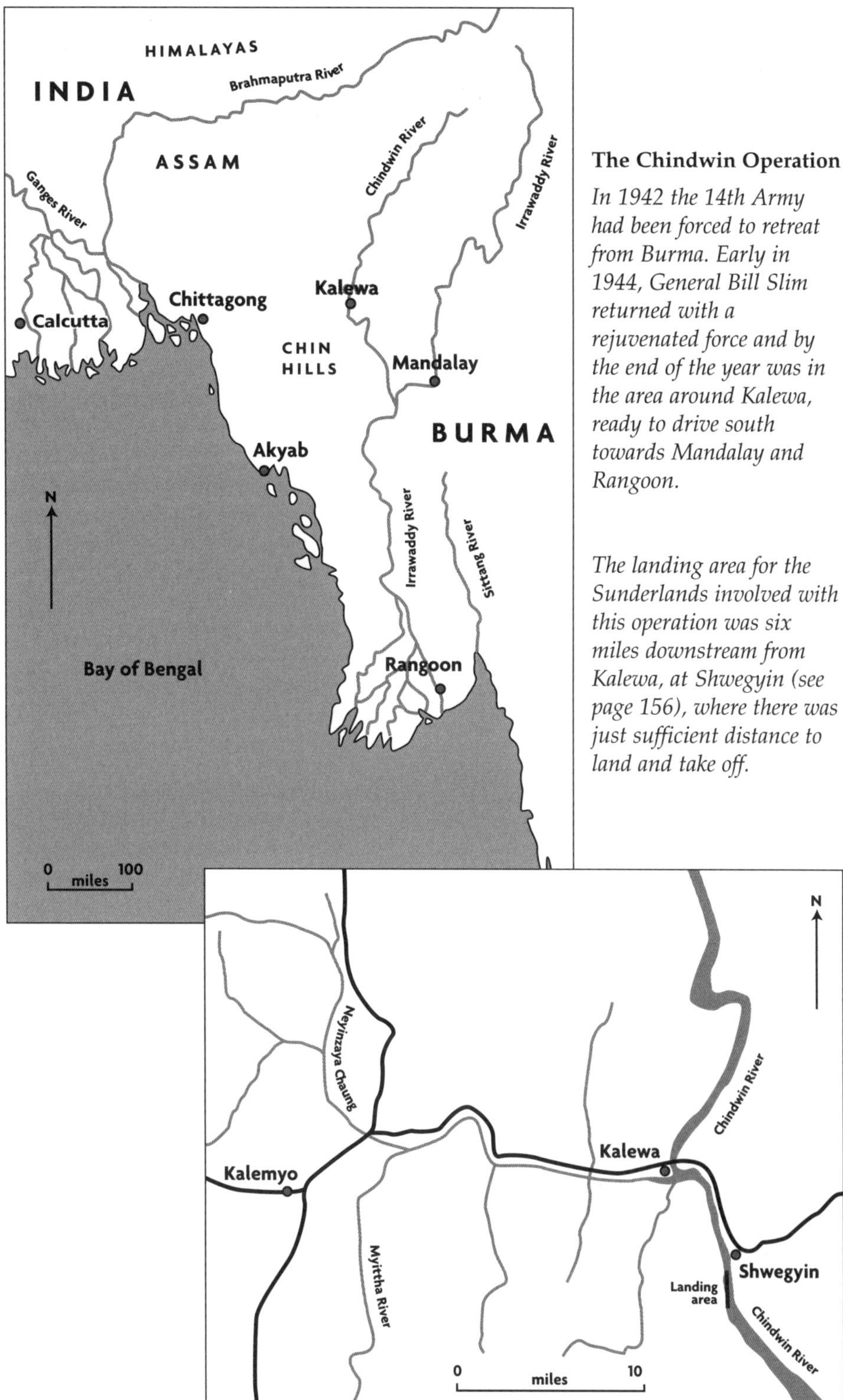

The Chindwin Operation

In 1942 the 14th Army had been forced to retreat from Burma. Early in 1944, General Bill Slim returned with a rejuvenated force and by the end of the year was in the area around Kalewa, ready to drive south towards Mandalay and Rangoon.

The landing area for the Sunderlands involved with this operation was six miles downstream from Kalewa, at Shwegyin (see page 156), where there was just sufficient distance to land and take off.

of about three-quarters of a mile: this would be just sufficient for us to get down and off again but along the left side was a hill forming a vertical escarpment about 200 feet high, in places less than 100 yards back from the river bank, uncomfortably close for me; at the end of the straight stretch the river made a sharp right-angled turn to the left through a gap in the escarpment, which at the same point continued on to the right for a mile or more, forming a high barrier at the end of our landing run. At the approach end of the area the river swept round in a curve from the right so that we would have to come in over the high trees on the left bank and drop quickly down to the water so as to come to rest well before the barrier escarpment at the far end. The effect of all this was that we would have to come in with a steep full-flap, full-glide approach over the trees and be absolutely certain of making a correct landing because any attempt to open up and go round again after a bad landing would mean colliding with the escarpment – trying to escape to the open right side would necessitate such a steep turn at very low altitude that the starboard wing tip would hit the water or the bank. At takeoff, in the reverse direction of course, the aeroplane would naturally be very much lighter and in the event we had no difficulty in just clearing the trees. The engineers had installed a satisfactory mooring buoy but it needed to be re-sited and they undertook to see to this, so all in all the operation looked to be a feasible proposition.

Once back at Kalemyo Butler and I got fixed up in the huge tented headquarters of RAF 221 Group, commanded by Air Vice-Marshal the Earl of Bandon (an amusing character who called himself the Abandoned Earl!), and was situated alongside another huge tented encampment that was the headquarters of General Slim's 14th Army. In the mess in the evening I was telling one of the headquarters people about our job and mentioned that I needed someone to check the re-siting of the mooring buoy; they said the only person who knew about flying boats was the Group Navigation Officer – "He's over there by the bar" – and I needed only one look at the back of that head I had seen bent for so many hours over his chart table during two years to recognise George Allen, my former navigator! We were both absolutely amazed to meet casually like that in the middle of the Burma jungle. He said he would go to Shwegyin next day and ensure that the buoy was in the right position.

I spent the night in my tent on my camp bed, having sat out for a while under the stars in my canvas camp chair, soaking up the impressions and sounds of the deep purple jungle night. I washed in my canvas camp washbasin and in the dewy morning, next day, had a quite reasonable splash-about in my canvas camp bath – the only time in my entire service in the Far East that I actually used that immensely heavy and cumbersome camp kit, originally developed, no doubt, for the officer-sahib with his train of bearers in the 'piping days of peace'.

I hitched a lift back to Calcutta with an American colonel in his personal Lockheed fourteen-seater; having climbed to over 10,000 feet out of Kalemyo we approached that sheer wall of a cliff and, caught in the downwash of the westerly wind curling over the cliff edge, we hit such a huge bump that we all hit our heads hard on the cabin roof. I filed that one away for future reference!

Back in Calcutta I collected my navigator and wireless operator and proceeded, as instructed in Trombay, to the headquarters of Strategic Air Force for briefing and to arrange control of our first flight to Kalewa/Shwegyin next day. I was sent a message from the Senior Air Staff Officer (SASO) that Strategic Air Force had no instructions to control me and could give no assistance of any kind. Our little band of three went off in the heat of the afternoon to the other side of Calcutta to get help from Eastern Air Command who concluded, after discussion, that the Photographic Reconnaissance Force, who operated in the same area, would be able to help; various sections of the PRF were in different parts of Calcutta and our patient jeep driver ferried us from one to the other where we got the same answer every time – the very idea of flying boats seemed to produce a sort of nervous bafflement in everybody. By late evening it was obvious that only Strategic Air Force were in a position to help so I went back there, only to get the same answer. Only too conscious of the urgency of my job I got on my Squadron Leader's high horse, telephoned Eastern Air Command and insisted that they give a directive to Strategic Air Force which they immediately did whereupon, without further ado, we got a full signals briefing, met forecast (reasonably favourable) and complete arrangements for the control of our flight. That done I settled down to work out a complete schedule for all the six sorties, planning each aircraft's number of hours so as to avoid minor inspections and taking into account our restriction to a maximum of two buoys at Bally, time taken to load at Trombay and so forth – all put in a lengthy signal to Koggala, Trombay, Strategic Air Force, Eastern Air Command et al which went off nearly at midnight after which I went to bed full of anticipation for the next day.

Into Burma

Having checked that none of the numerous country boats and other craft using the busy river would get in our way I took off very early in the morning for Kalewa with Charles Potter on board also so that he could get an advance look at the route and the water at Shwegyin. As soon as we got off I started to climb so as to give us a head start before reaching the Chin Hills proper. As I mentioned earlier (see page 129) our engines were supercharged only sufficiently to maintain full climbing power up to around 5000 feet and as we passed that level the power began to fall off with the thinner air so I had to increase the engine speed to the full 2300 revolutions per minute allowed for climbing supposedly for a maximum of 30 minutes; we were clearly going to need that rate of operation for one and a half hours or even more and with our ancient engines having to be flogged to that extent I had more than a few qualms, but there was nothing for it but to push on in hope and I did manage to get the heavily-loaded aircraft to about 10,700 feet at which height she was literally just hanging in the air so much reduced was the engines power.

The met forecast had been reasonably good but as we approached the highest ridges of the hills we entered very turbulent towering cloud in a solid wall up to at least 13,000 feet and rising. The aeroplane was being flung about, up and down and then surging 30 or 40 degrees off course and back again; we only had about 1500 feet clearance above the highest hills, flying completely blind in thick cloud and rain, and, when a sudden violent downdraught plunged us down about 800 feet in about five seconds to under 10,000 feet, I decided that the risk – not least to the aircraft's structure itself – was too great and I turned back to Bally from within about 100 miles of Kalewa.

As I came ashore at Bally, I was told that Burmah-Shell, whose refuelling launch was supplying not only BOAC under contract but also 212's Catalinas while the RAF refueller was being repaired, had refused to take on the extra commitment of our Sunderlands. This meant that I could not be refuelled for another attempt next day – and in any case the met forecast was bad and I had come out in spots.

The following day I went into Calcutta to the Burmah-Shell offices where I wheeled out the old boy thing and persuaded them to continue to look after us for the rest of our stay. Back from hot and dusty and unbelievably crowded Calcutta I was greeted with a refusal by BOAC to continue ferrying our crews and those of 212 with their launch to supplement the partially-unserviceable RAF dinghy – they were understandably worried by the extra strain on their craft at a time when spares were almost impossible to obtain anywhere East of Suez. After a hasty lunch I went off to the BOAC office and succeeded in persuading them to carry on helping us with the promise that I would push hard to get the RAF dinghy properly repaired – and quickly.

Meanwhile the doctor and specialist said my spots were just due to overwork. The aircraft had been inspected and refuelled and we had hope of getting out to the aircraft without having to swim, so all was set for next day. As usual I had got Strategic Air Force to send the routine signal to Kalewa that evening, giving our ETA (estimated time of arrival) for the next day and had been given a satisfactory met forecast.

Early in the morning of Saturday 10 February, after sorting out some confusion on shore, I took off, thundering over the brown Hooghly waters in thick mist. Over the hills the cloud was still solid – 'ten-tenths' as we used to say – but the base was at about 11,000 feet so we had reasonable clearance above the hills although the bumps were tremendous – every crew member on duty had to be strapped in – and in the clear air the sight of our great wings waggling up and down with each sudden uplift and alternating crashing down-shock was impressive. The landing area at Shwegyin was easy to find and the full-flap, full-glide approach and landing went very well with the aircraft finishing its landing run comfortably short of the escarpment barrier at the end. It must have been the first time a big flying boat had landed on any part of the Chindwin River.

We moored up to the improvised buoy and shortly afterwards a big barge towed by a launch was spotted rounding the bend of the river. The barge was expertly manoeuvred alongside and Major Corbett and his officers and Indian Other Ranks (IORs) had obviously taken all their instructions to heart; they were immensely impressed with the aircraft and the way the bomb-hoist coped with all the heavy items in the load. With unloading completed the barges departed upstream and we settled down for a quick lunch on the water and a brief look at our surroundings. Shwegyin was actually the place where the 14th Army had crossed the Chindwin on the retreat in 1942 and it gave quite an eerie feeling to look at the remains of the abandoned vehicles on the river bank and think of those exhausted soldiers scrambling across with the Japs close behind them; General Slim, in his book *Defeat into Victory*, describes how his force took a brief rest in the area between the river and the escarpment just to the left of our landing area, before making the crossing to the west bank.

On taking off we cleared the trees on the high bank at the end of the run by a good 30 feet and then circled round and round over Kalewa for half an hour, putting on more and more clothes as we got into the colder air, while we struggled to gain height to 10,000 feet to clear the highest part of the hills starting with the sheer cliff at Kalemyo. Flying straight towards an obstacle like that one has an optical illusion that there is not sufficient altitude to clear it and only repeated checks of the altimeter set one's mind more or less at rest. On the way out we reached 12,700 feet but even at that height the turbulence was very severe and it was slightly comforting to be wearing parachutes, as we did throughout this part of the operation, which must be the first time most, if not all, of us had ever done so in a flying boat.

From this point on the story is best told day by day, largely as I recorded it in my diary:

11 February – Reported on the first trip to Butler at Eastern Air Command who handed me a signal from on high increasing the total lift from the original 30,000 lbs (5100 lbs on each of six sorties) to 50,000 lbs; this would necessitate an additional four sorties and I worked out a plan to do this with only one minor inspection but requiring a number of special arrangements that I put in hand and then reported the revised schedule to all concerned in a long signal. Charles Potter had a successful trip to Shwegyin in *W*.

12 February – Back to EAC: Complications over new arrangements but got little help from there. This prevented me from going to Trombay for my second load; as we only had the two buoys at Bally and I had signalled Trombay to send Alan Pedley over in *T*, Charles Potter was sent off to Trombay in *W*. When Alan arrived in *T*, he told me that Trombay and 222 Group in Colombo had made completely different arrangements for dealing with the extra four loads that would have been complex, time-wasting and impracticable and had sent me not a single copy of their signals. The movements they had arranged had to be stopped immediately to prevent chaos, so I wrote a peremptory signal to 222 Group, Koggala, Trombay, EAC etc, saying "proposed plan unworkable, schedule in my signal stands" and, as signals traffic was chaotic, I gave it the priority "Emergency"; when I handed it to 212's adjutant for despatch, he went white and said "But, sir, this priority is for the use of commanders-in-chief and cabinet ministers only!" I had nothing to lose but a great deal to gain and I said "Send it off, please." It went, none of the offending arrangements happened and I never heard another word!

13 February – Sent off signals detailing next flights for *K* to Trombay, *T* to Kalewa and *W* to Bally tomorrow.

14 February – Poor met forecast for Alan in *T*, so postponed to 15th. Had a good trip across to Trombay in *K*, arriving to find that *W* was having an engine change: Charles had taken off early in the morning with a full load and just after crossing a 5000 foot range of hills not far from Trombay a cylinder had cracked, jamming the piston and smashing all nine connecting rods. With considerable skill he had got the aircraft back over the hills to Trombay, the windmilling engine sounding like ten thousand tin cans rattling, and landed it safely.

15 February – Learned from Lieutenant Commander Kedglie that 10,000 lbs of the extra lift had already been sent off by rail to go by surface transport to Kalewa, so total lift now reduced to 40,000 lbs. Flying the seventh and eighth loads all the way, instead of going by rail, would be much quicker and could be done if the aircraft promised by Koggala to replace *W* temporarily, could do two sorties and *W* do a second after the engine change. Signal sent to all, outlining this plan.

16 February – Took off from Trombay with the third load at 8am and had a calm flight in just under seven hours, landing at Bally to find that Alan Pedley had successfully flown in to Shwegyin but at the start of the return trip, over the highest hills, both his inner engines had failed; fortunately he had already reached 14,000 feet but he had some 300 miles of hostile country to cover before reaching the first good water which was Bally; the safest course would have been to turn back and fly the short distance to Shwegyin, but to make a double engine change on the water, or even just a prolonged overhaul, 1200 miles from the main servicing base at Trombay, would have been a disaster for the whole operation. With great determination he carried on and, after a while, a way was found to get a small amount of power from both engines and they went on losing altitude only quite slowly, more or less at the same rate as the height of the hills diminished as they staggered on westwards to Calcutta.

It took me three hours from the time of arriving over Bally to get back to the mess; this was exceptional but it was always a difficult trip and it meant a very early start in the morning to get a takeoff in the cooler air, followed by a late return to the mess after the trip into Burma and then, for me, a quick visit to 212 to get any signals and finally a return to the mess to sort out the latest tangle and send appropriate signals.

17-19 February – Examination of *T*'s inner engines showed that nothing could be done except to patch them up for a safe return to Koggala. My *K* at Bally was having a difficult cylinder change, *W* was at Trombay having an engine changed and the expected replacement aircraft from Koggala had yet to arrive, so I used the period of relative inactivity to try to sort out our difficulties over marine craft that had been precipitated by BOAC's ultimatum refusing to provide any more trips for us. I phoned Butler and told him that unless high-level pressure could be put on BOAC or on the RAF to get us some suitable marine craft the whole operation would be held up by our simple inability to get out to the aircraft and back again to shore; his only reaction was to suggest that I should talk to the Navy and yet another RAF headquarters – RAF Bengal-Burma. This meant shuttling back and forth across Calcutta; the Navy had nothing and no ideas of where I could get anything, but the RAF agreed to send a smaller craft than a 70 ton river boat, the *Birkie*, that they had obtained for us a day or so earlier and which we had floated down towards the aircraft from the mooring buoy so that we could scramble from its stern into the aircraft's bow compartment, a difficult and potentially dangerous performance; Bengal-Burma had misunderstood what we needed, their small craft having a high wheelhouse that made it impossible to get it alongside without fouling the wing, so that was sent back. In the middle of all this I spent a whole afternoon and evening taxi-testing *K* after its cylinder change and trying to trace an elusive misfiring which was cured in time for me to beg just one more trip from BOAC to get us aboard for tomorrow's flight to Shwegyin – number four.

20 February – Had a marvellously smooth and cloudless trip to Shwegyin carrying with us Lieutenant Commander Penman RNVR who, it may be remembered, was responsible for the whole idea of our project. On the return we brought out seven British officers, men and IORs on leave or repatriation – they were thrilled to be able to get a quick and reasonably comfortable passage instead of a rough journey of some hundreds of miles by lorry and train. We sponged yet again on BOAC, while the RAF here appeared to have done nothing – flying boats were very definitely lodger-units and nobody's baby.

21 February – Koggala sent Dick Levy-Haarscher with old *N* as replacement aircraft and they arrived in the afternoon, with a load from Trombay, Dick having brought my crew who had returned from leave – it was really good to see them again. Dick brought a message from Koggala saying they wanted *W* to go back there direct from Trombay when she was ready; this was lunacy but he confirmed what I had suspected – due to signals incompetence, Koggala had not had copies of any of my signals and so knew nothing of all that had been going on up here! I promptly wrote the CO a long letter to put him in the picture, to go with Alan when he took *T* back to Koggala. Meanwhile, as *K*'s engines were showing signs of deterioration, *T* was out of the show, old *N* was known to be in shaky condition and *W*, apart from the one engine failure, had performed better than any. I signalled Koggala direct, asking to be able to retain *W*.

22 February – Early down to Bally to see Alan off to Koggala in *T*, via Madras – fingers crossed! Then got the maintenance party doing a thorough check on *N* prior to her flight in to Burma; her engines looked very shaky and the general view was that it would be unwise to make her do a second round trip. Phoned Butler to tell him how things looked and learned, to my amazement, that he too had seen none of my recent signals even though he, like Koggala, 222 Group, Strategic Air Force etc, had been on the list of "Repeated to . . ." on every signal. We were also having trouble with Kalewa because Strategic Air Force seemed unable to get our ETA signals through to them quickly so that, although sent the previous evening, they mostly arrived in the afternoon after we had taken off on the return flight. To get over this, I arranged to telephone Kalewa direct even though it was an open line and conversation had to be very guarded. The call had to be relayed to Kalewa (codeword 'Oxford'), via an intermediate exchange (codeword 'Moscow') and the first time I called up the Calcutta military exchange and said "I want Oxford via Moscow", the operator was evidently new and thought I was either barmy or just having a joke; in fact it worked well until the line was broken just before our last sortie – hardly surprising as it went for several hundred miles through open country, hills and jungle, miracle work by the signals people.

23 February – Dick Levy-Haarscher, having taken back his own crew from me, took off in *N* early for Shwegyin – a really hairy moment; I was on board the *Birkie* to keep the takeoff area clear and at the last moment, just as Dick was at full throttle half a mile away, a big country boat, under a minute sail but virtually out of control, was drifting down on the racing current and suddenly started to move in the path of Dick's aircraft then approaching at some 80 knots. We yelled at the lone skipper of the country boat – a peasant of peasants, and tried to get the slow-moving *Birkie* alongside to tow it clear – much too late of course and the two craft were virtually motionless right in the path of the aircraft which was a truly terrifying sight from head-on with its huge hull riding on an immense bow wave and the four engines bellowing at full power; it actually passed by us just on the point of leaving the water but the port wing tip went directly over us and we could almost have touched it. The aircraft performed reasonably well and brought out four British officers and men for leave, but on her return the exhaust collector rings round the front of all engines were found to have burned right through on part of their circumference and Dick agreed, though very disappointed, that there was only one possibility – fly *N* back to Koggala for scrapping. Koggala signalled that I could keep *W* after all and, with the fifth sortie completed by *N* and *W* restored to health at Trombay, I decided that *W* would fly the sixth, I would take the seventh in *K*, leaving *W* to do the eighth and final trip. Late into the night I arranged that tomorrow *W* would come over to Bally, while I would take *K* over to Trombay and *N* would return to Koggala, all this signalled as usual with brief explanations of state of aircraft, etc.

24 February – As Dick Levy-Haarscher was taking over his crew, whom I had had to borrow at the start of the operation, and he was thus handing over my crew to me, we had a great scramble on this morning to get marine craft to enable the two crews to ferry their gear back and forth for the changeover and then for me to get off with *K* to Trombay – the crew and I were extremely pleased to be operating together again; I also had a new second pilot, Flight Sergeant Boorman, who was an agreeable and very competent addition to the crew. The aircraft seemed to respond and we had a very good trip to Trombay where I found that *W* had just completed a successful air test and her engines were considered to be in very good condition. The Trombay base people offered to do the minor inspection that *W* would need on returning from her next sortie so only *K*'s minor would remain, to be done at Bally, therefore I signalled *N* to take surplus maintenance people and spares back with her to Koggala next day.

25 February – *W* loaded the sixth consignment ready to depart the following day. A new Mk V arrived from UK on its way to the squadron at Koggala, flown by Ken Nicholson, our (white) Fijian and Ted Garside, and we had a fine party in Bombay to celebrate; they were fascinated to hear about our operation. Ted was sporting the DFC that he (and Middleton) had been awarded for last year's Chindit rescue (see page 138) – very gratifying.

26 February – Saw *W* and the new Mk V off to Bally and Koggala respectively. Koggala sent a signal wondering what was happening with *N* and urging me to speed up the operation; I replied that *N* was about to leave for Koggala via Madras and that in the prevailing circumstances they could not expect miracles. However this seemed to confirm rumours that had filtered through to us about an imminent squadron move; no one knew to where. *K* was checked and loaded ready for tomorrow.

27 February – I took off early for Bally and had a good flight except for one moment when, just halfway across India at 8000 feet, the port outer engine suddenly stopped, followed immediately by the port inner and then the starboard inner: with only the starboard outer working the port wing dropped and we went into an uncontrollable slow spiral to port while I hastily sought – in vain – for some patch of water or even some open ground where we could put down, one hoped, without running into a boat or a tree. Fortunately Matt, the first engineer who had just left the engineer's panel, realised what had happened, leapt up the companionway and banged open the two master cocks which restored fuel to the engines and I was able to resume a straight course and regain the 3000 feet of altitude we had lost in those 15 or 20 seconds. On the panel there were ten small levers, each operating the shut-off cock on one tank, together with two in the middle, just the same shape as the others but each controlling the entire flow from the five tanks on one side; when changing over from an empty tank to a full one the cocks had to be operated in a fixed sequence to avoid airlocks but Joe Eggett, who had just taken over on the panel and was due to change tanks, had a momentary aberration, closed the master cocks and gave us all a fraught few moments – the crew never ceased jokingly reminding him of it.

Arriving at Bally, I found *N* had left and *W* had been thoroughly checked and found to be in good condition for tomorrow's effort. Even better news was that the RAF's dinghy had at last returned in a serviceable state and we were able to return *Birkie* and eliminate the difficult and rather risky procedures we had been forced to adopt – fortunately with no damage resulting.

29 February-1 March – *W* flew into Shwegyin with an additional load in the form of various foodstuffs to enliven the diet of the chaps at Kalewa; she got back early in the afternoon with three lucky fellows to go on leave and with a request for eggs, which I arranged to get for us to take in on the 1st. As *W* was early I arranged for her to be checked immediately so that she could leave on 1 March for Trombay for the eighth and last load.

On 1 March *W* got off as programmed and I left for Shwegyin in *K* shortly afterwards, the crew delighted to have even one trip as part of this rather special operation. On the way in we heard Japanese radio followed by the voice of an Australian pilot being vectored to a rendezvous saying "Will be at the opera in two minutes" – we missed the performance. I went up to Kalewa on the barge that had taken on our cargo and was tremendously impressed with the scale and variety of their boat building work – they should do a really good job with 'our' motor boats. That was load number seven and, with my constant unrelieved sleeplessness, I was beginning to worry that I might collapse before the operation was completed. *K* was now due for a minor inspection which was to start tomorrow: at the start I had been very anxious to avoid any heavy maintenance work, such as cylinder changes and minors, because I was afraid someone might fall into the turbulent Hooghly which would swallow them instantly, but they were all understandably extremely careful and we got away with it – otherwise, with one aircraft after another failing, the operation would have dragged on and probably have been a partial failure.

2-5 March – *K*'s 'minor' progressing well and should be ready for us to return to Koggala when *W* has taken in the final load. In the afternoon a signal from Trombay reported that another of *W*'s engines had failed completely (main bearing failure) on the way over and Charles had flown the last three hours back into Trombay on three engines, landing safely – after all, he had had some previous practice! It was almost too much to bear, just on the last lap. I was in a dilemma since it seemed like too much of a chance to flog *K* over the whole performance for a fourth time; on the other hand to wait for a replacement aircraft to come up from Koggala – even if any serviceable Mk IIIs were still available there, now that nearly all the new Mk V's had arrived – would drag out the remainder of the operation to an unacceptable degree as all the authorities were now pressing me for its completion. Nevertheless I felt I had to give Koggala the chance to do something and signalled asking for a replacement. Corporal Rand of the maintenance party went into hospital with suspected appendicitis.

In the afternoon of the 3 March, I did an air test on *K*, Sergeant Clarke having said that they had found the engines to be in a better condition than anticipated before the inspection. As several cylinders had been changed, I flew another short air test on the afternoon of Sunday 4 March, to confirm Clarke's judgment together with Matt, my first engineer's own confidence. It was a lovely Sunday afternoon and the unpressured stooging round the delta area was really quite refreshing; the aircraft felt fine and in a moderately buoyant mood I decided to use it for the final trip and signalled Koggala for their agreement to my setting off on the 6th – in two days time.

On the afternoon of 5 March there was still no signal from Koggala so I decided to go ahead and signalled Trombay to be ready with the last load next day.

6-9 March – Just in bed on 5 March I was handed a signal from Koggala at a quarter past midnight giving their approval for *K*'s sortie. As I had already made the administrative arrangements, signalling Trombay to be ready to load as soon as we arrived, thus saving a day, and had obtained the met forecast, we were able to get off to Trombay earlier on the morning of 6 March for a very bumpy trip. On arrival I found that *W* was still awaiting an engine and, much worse, our load was not ready; I had some sharp words with Lieutenant Commander Kedglie on the telephone and eventually the load arrived at the jetty at 7.30 in the evening. We set about loading straight away and finished at 11pm after which I joined the crew for a short party in the Sergeants Mess, when they heard some of the horror tales of the past five weeks. Next morning we made an early departure, saying goodbye to Trombay for the last time, and had a remarkably smooth flight across in seven and a half hours. When I finally got into the mess I felt completely exhausted so I asked the fellows near me in our accommodation if they would be quiet after dinner and I got into bed at six, full of phenobarbitone, and did not wake until seven the next morning, feeling much fresher.

I went into Calcutta to do some shopping, mostly provisions to take into Kalewa. Sergeant Clarke confirmed that *K* was fit for the trip so I laid on the organisation for tomorrow; the telephone line had been broken so I gave a message to the Royal Engineers colonel in Calcutta to pass on to Kalewa through his link – in the event it did not get through, so Kalewa were very surprised to see us but delighted with all the food. So on Friday 9 March, we did the last trip, with the eighth load. The flight in was very smooth – so unlike the first two or three – and we got back to Bally to find a strong wind blowing across the tide; mooring-up was a nightmare and when at last the aircraft was made fast, I crossed my arms on the wheel and put my head on them, dead to the world – this was it, I could scarcely believe it, the whole thing finished; the next thing I knew was Jock Moir shaking me and saying "Skipper, the dinghy's alongside" – the crew had got everything shipshape and all I had to do was stumble over the side. By the afternoon I had collected the energy to signal to all those concerned "Operation completed" – an enormous relief.

10-13 March – I telephoned Butler in the morning and he sounded as relieved as I was, not that he had ever seemed to be losing sleep over the affair. *K* was having to have another cylinder changed. Meanwhile I was dragged off in the afternoon to preside at a court of inquiry into a Catalina crash which I was able to wrap up the following morning, 11 March. A great many loose ends needed to be tied up, not least getting Corporal Rand out of hospital – all requiring numerous journeys into and out of Calcutta. Next day I flew a satisfactory air test on *K* and we got all the spares and tools on board and refuelled – for the last time – ready for departure. Thus it was that on Tuesday 13 March, after every carefully made arrangement had, typically, gone wrong, we got off at 7.30 in the morning and had what was almost a strange experience for us – flying over the sea. A hasty refuelling stop at Madras, during which I had a brief chat with Larry Laws, who had been our CO on 246 Squadron at Bowmore, and was now a Group Captain, and then finally off to Koggala, where we arrived to find preparations already under way, albeit at an early stage, for the squadron's move.

The Chindwin Operation had undoubtedly been a success. We had flown a total of 220 hours over some 29,000 miles and carried in to Kalewa a total weight of 17.9 tons in eight sorties of which we in *K* had done half (even a little more than half if the first, abortive, sortie is added in), a total of exactly 100 hours. For me that amount of flying, together with the increasing administrative complications over six weeks and bad sleeping, proved extremely exhausting; I was given four days' leave which turned into two because the government rest-house where I went gave me violent food-poisoning on the second night so I had to return to Koggala. A major share of the credit for the success of the operation undoubtedly goes to Sergeant Clarke and his maintenance team who had such formidable difficulties throughout in keeping the worn-out engines turning, so that we aircrew all survived.

The sequels

Almost three weeks after the end, the local papers printed a somewhat highly-coloured item on the operation and this caused great hilarity in the mess – I think, in fact, that it found its way into the Line Book. I learned later that the items had been repeated in our local papers at home also. At the same time the BBC did a broadcast in which they called it "one of the world's most perilous flights"! Later still, in mid-June, I did a broadcast on Colombo radio.

On 29 January 1946, the *London Gazette* promulgated the award of the Distinguished Flying Cross (DFC) to Alan Pedley, Charles Potter and me – they arrived by registered post, as the backlog of gongs was so great that only a proportion were presented by the King at investitures – rather disappointing in a way.

I heard not a word of whether the motorboats had done the job until many years later. I was having breakfast in the dining car on the way from Brockenhurst to Waterloo, sitting opposite to a man from the Foreign Office; we got talking and in some way arrived at the subject of Burma from which it transpired that we had both served there in the war: I told him about my operation and he was most interested because he had been an infantry officer and had advanced along the banks of the Chindwin and the Irrawaddy after the way had been very effectively cleared by 'our' motorboats.

A while after this, in a television documentary on the life of Lord Louis Mountbatten, there was a short sequence showing him and General Slim christening two of the boats at Kalewa – Lord Louis calling his HMS *Pamela* after his daughter while Bill Slim named his HMS *Una* after his daughter. In his book *Defeat into Victory* (pages 399-400) Field Marshal Viscount Slim, as he became, wrote about the 'Chindwin Flotilla' – sadly not mentioning how the bits and pieces got to Kalewa – and revealed that Their Lordships of the Admiralty had delivered a 'distinguished rebuke', pointing out that "only Their Lordships themselves were authorized to suggest names for His Majesty's ships of war". He went on "The little ships and their Navy crews maintained the real Nelsonian tradition of steering closer to the enemy. They were often in action and both suffered damage from enemy shot. In their day they swept the seas, or at least the rivers."

The start of the last lap

When I got back to Koggala I learned that the squadron would shortly be moving to Akyab, about halfway down the west coast of Burma and that we were to have a new role, anti-shipping. We were to become a Fully Mobile Squadron, ie we should be based aboard the squadron's old friend, the troopship SS *Manela* and we should incorporate all the features of a station as well – a full maintenance section, marine craft section, operations room, intelligence, sick quarters and motor transport section. At this time the squadron was building up towards the consequent expansion which eventually took it to a total strength of 510 by the time the move came.

The aim of our new anti-shipping role was 'interdiction' – low-level gun and bomb attacks on the numerous small ships, mostly wooden and propelled by sail and in some cases motor, which plied up and down the east coast of Siam (Thailand) and Malaya supplying the Japanese forces, cut off since the railway had been put out of action. It was not known to what extent these craft might be armed so, as soon as I had completed my lengthy report on the Chindwin Operation, I started a training programme which essentially involved the pilots practising the 'undulating approach' to the target originally adopted in attacks on U-boats in the Atlantic. The standard form of attack on a U-boat was to approach from about a half to three-quarters of a mile at 50 feet above the water and in a dead-straight line, thus offering a perfect target for the U-boat's gunners; if on the way in the aircraft was eased up some ten feet and then down again – undulating – this slight movement would not be noticed by the enemy gunners but would greatly reduce the chances of hits on the aircraft. We got the Navy to provide a motorlaunch to act as target and spent many days with each crew practising attacks from all directions. In one case undulating got a bit out of hand; one of the captains was a Canadian of continental extraction, known as 'The Baron' (though whether by right I know not), who was phenomenally strong; I went out with him on his first practice and when he started undulating he wrenched the aircraft up and down so violently that, flying at some 180 knots, the G-forces were enormous – when pulling up, those of us standing on the flight deck were forced almost to our knees and then going over the top the negative G almost lifted us off the deck – my microphone which was dangling on its lead down around my stomach shot straight upwards and literally stood for a split second just in front of my face. 'The Baron' stood a good chance of pulling the wings off, or at least straining them, and I told him smartly to moderate his enthusiasm.

The squadron move was to be made in two halves: the CO and Harry Sheardown would take the first five or six aircraft that were serviceable and I would stay on at Koggala in command of the rear half of the squadron to get the remaining aircraft serviceable and then follow to Akyab. At the beginning of April the CO decided that I should no longer have the responsibilities of running an aircraft and crew, as well as my new command, so the sad day came when I had to hand my faithful crew over to Ken Nicholson, actually known as 'Nick', a really good skipper; we had a little ceremony, very informal, when I thanked them all – particularly Matt (first engineer), Jock Moir (wireless operator/mechanic) and Danny (first wireless operator), as already mentioned the first two now Warrant Officers and Danny now Pilot Officer, who had been with me since the very beginning at Invergordon in September 1942 – and commended Nick to them. Quite an emotional moment really.

At this time, early April, it was becoming clear that the war in Europe was nearly over. The Canadian and Australian governments, in particular, were anxious to start repatriating their overseas forces, the Australians because they were fearful of an attack by the Japanese. As a result the squadron was losing a number of its aircrew, especially pilots and navigators; Harry Sheardown stayed on for a while until the squadron move was completed. We started to receive an influx of new pilots and navigators, nearly all of whom were young and fairly inexperienced, the logic for this being the Age and Service Release Plan. Under this scheme, every serviceman in the British (ie non-Commonwealth) forces was allocated a group number worked out on a combination of his or her age and length of time they had served in the forces and they would be progressively released back to civilian life as the reduction in hostilities allowed. Clearly it would be ridiculous to use scarce transport to bring out to the southeast Asia theatre experienced replacements who, ipso facto, would have a low (ie early) release number, and then very shortly have to ship them back to the UK for release. Hence the arrival of predominantly green crews, resulting in my spending a good deal of time giving dual instruction to the pilots and crews in their new environment and with a quite new role.

Towards the middle of the month, the order to move came; a huge squadron photograph (reproduced on page 95) was taken in front of one of the aircraft – chaps on the mainplane as well as every other possible place, 510 – and then a monster removing job was undertaken to shift everything and everybody in the advance party, except, of course, the aircraft and crews, to Colombo for embarkation in the old *Manela*. On 17 April the CO, and the advance aircraft and crews, took off for Akyab, leaving me, as officer commanding the detachment, with a considerable job to do, not only getting the remaining aircraft serviceable and ready to move but also administering what was still half the squadron, for which purpose I was granted the powers of a subordinate commander, with Ted Garside as my very efficient and, mercifully, relaxed adjutant. I was by this time showing signs of fairly advanced nervous fatigue with the incessant sleeplessness that nothing seemed able to cure.

Ted had a girlfriend who was a Wren working at the naval rest camp at Diyatalawa (see page 151) and she had arranged to come down to Galle at the beginning of May to spend a leave together with another Wren. We were both looking forward to this greatly – I assuming that I should partner the other Wren – because in our wretched jungle hole we virtually never saw any women and certainly no white women. Then suddenly the blow fell. I was given the order to move to Burma on a date just before the girls were due to arrive. Our despondency was only partially submerged in the hectic preparations for the move, which was to be accomplished by taking those of the remaining ground personnel who were not due for release in the near future with us in the aircraft. The bureaucracy involved in getting a body of men and a number of aircraft cleared from a station, with numerous equipment clearances and so forth, was monumental. However all was at last ready for the following day when, just as Ted and I were leaving the office for the last time, the phone rang and a voice at the other end said "Squadron Leader Deller? SASO 222 Group here: your move is off for the time being" – end of message! So we should be able to meet the girls on their leave after all!

While we worked on towards our own departure for Burma, the news from

Europe was more and more of an approaching end, with the Allied troops actually in Germany itself at last. And then, suddenly, on 8 May it was all over. It was really quite hard to realise except by thinking back to that September Friday in St Helen's Court, listening to somebody's radio out of the office window reporting the German invasion of Poland, the instant realisation – unspoken and spoken – on everybody's part that this was *it*. Where would it all lead? When, if ever, would we see each other again – and how many? And as we now listened to those cheering crowds in London and elsewhere at home, we all felt a pang – all right for them but here we were, thousands of miles from the homes they were all lighting up after the blackout, still sweating it out with an implacable and cunning enemy who showed no sign of crumbling to defeat, even though the 14th Army had won the race and occupied Rangoon on 3 May, actually just after the monsoon had broken.

On 9 May the whole station at Koggala was given a holiday to celebrate the victory in Europe. On that day also, Ted Garside's Wren girlfriend, Pat, had arrived in Galle accompanied by her Wren friend who was apparently prepared to 'play gooseberry'. They were staying in the New Oriental Hotel which had been the headquarters of 230 Squadron when they operated from Koggala in 1942 after evacuating from Singapore; they had christened it 'The No Hotel', with good reason. As soon as we could get away, Ted and I jumped on my motorbike, he on the pillion, and roared off to Galle where we met the girls in the Galle Club. The other girl was none other than Margaret Gloag with whom I had enjoyed a dinner and dance at the Bandarawela Hotel in the previous December (see page 151). We had an enjoyable time together whenever our work gave us the opportunity to slip away into Galle for a swim and a meal.

Meanwhile, the three squadrons on the station had been preparing for a formal celebration on 13 May of the victory in Europe. There would be a full parade on the waterfront in Galle and, at the same time, three Catalinas followed by three Sunderlands would fly over the parade, each three in a close V formation. I had always dreamt of leading my squadron on a formal parade but during the rehearsals on the station runway I found, to my acute embarrassment and great sadness, that I was unable to coordinate my thoughts so as to give the required orders. I was by then in such a condition of nervous exhaustion through lack of sleep that, while I could cope perfectly normally with all the habitual activities, including having absolutely no trouble flying, anything outside the normal tended to flummox me quite seriously; I had no alternative but to order my most senior Flight Lieutenant to take over command of 230 Squadron on the parade.

As I would not be on parade, I decided I would take charge of our fly-past with Ted in his aircraft and a not-too-reliable New Zealander in the third: he would lead as number 1, Ted would be to starboard as number 2 and I would be to port as number 3 and controlling the flight by radio; we would make a shallow dive approach so as to fly over the parade at 100 feet and 180 knots and would then pull up sharply, number 1 continuing straight ahead while Ted and I broke to starboard and port respectively – the classic 'bomb-burst' We practised formation flying for a total of an hour and three-quarters on two days and got quite good at it, with Ted's and my wing tips actually overlapping those of the New Zealander's machine; it was no easy task making constant minute adjustments to the four engines while allowing for the inertia in the response of a big aircraft and keeping the thing straight and level with the left hand. On the day, we roared in over the parade in our closest formation and very fast. As we went over we pulled up and I called over the radio "Break!" and, to my consternation, the New Zealander, instead of going straight ahead, turned hard to starboard right into Ted's path. With great presence of mind Ted pulled up very sharply to pass over the top of the New Zealander's machine and got away with it – at that speed the G-force on the pull-up was such that all the ground staff who were his passengers (we had all agreed to take some for the ride) were forced to the floor. When we got down I tore an imperial strip off that idiotic captain but, fortunately, we had been so fast and in such close formation compared with the Catalinas before us, and thus made such an impression, that no one on the ground noticed our near miss which, but for Ted's split-second manoeuvre, would have turned into a hideous pile-up.

I felt I really desperately needed some leave (in 11 months when, according to regulation, I should have had a total of nine weeks leave, I had had just two) and, the CO being at Koggala on a short visit from Rangoon where the squadron had just moved from Akyab, I prevailed on him to give me a week's leave which I planned to spend at Diyatalawa to be with Margaret, and I arranged that Ted would come up on the last evening with transport to take me back.

One of the most difficult things for operational aircrew going on leave in Ceylon or India was to get transport – in Colombo or Delhi or anywhere else nobody wanted to know. For my week in Diyatalawa, I eventually managed to scramble aboard an ambulance returning to Colombo and then talk Movement Control into, grudgingly, booking me a berth on the train. The week passed very agreeably and really cemented our relationship. The air at some 4000 feet altitude was wonderfully refreshing after the heat and overwhelming humidity of the coast. There was plenty of entertainment, including the weekly 'Bandarawela Ball' which was where Margaret and I had first met the previous December. The day before the end of my leave, Ted came up with a vehicle he had apparently, as a good adjutant, been able to extract from the MT section as 'detachment transport'. It was exactly four-square with a wheel right at each corner so we named it 'The Biscuit Box'. The wheelbase being perfectly square made it somewhat unstable directionally and on our way back next day I was taking it down a steep hill that was covered in wet leaves. Inevitably the back end tried to get to the bottom before the front end and we proceeded the whole way down the hill on a corkscrew course, each skid in turn, on being corrected, leading straight into one in the opposite direction. Ted said he was preparing to bail out but control was not lost and we reached the bottom facing the same direction as that in which we had started at the top.

With aircraft being sent north as soon as they were serviceable, we did very little flying in June apart from dual instruction, which included two sessions of 'circuits and bumps' to give a demonstration and dual instruction on the Sunderland Mk V to the Catalina squadron's COs and Flight Commanders as they were about to convert to Sunderlands – they seemed favourably impressed with the aircraft, as indeed they should be after lugging their lumbering Cats over goodness knows how many thousands of miles.

On 1 June the CO produced the aircrew annual assessments and to my astonishment and great joy mine read: "As captain and first pilot of Sunderland flying boats: Exceptional" – the top grade. Just for a moment I thought back in time to December 1941 when, at the end of flying training in Rhodesia I had got an 'Above average' and wondered then whether I should ever get 'the big one' (see page 57). That was after 178 hours 30 minutes flying. Now after a further three years and five months the total was 1358 hours and 20 minutes, of which 626 hours and 5 minutes were on war operations.

On 13 June I caught a flight from Koggala to Ratmalana, the airport of Colombo, and took a rickshaw to the Ceylon Broadcasting Corporation studios where, in a somewhat dingy room, with an announcer sitting at a battered table, I did a broadcast on the Chindwin Operation which seemed, from reports, to have gone quite well; Margaret was twiddling her handkerchief all through it!

Our move to Rangoon was finally fixed for 19 June and on 15 June Ted and I flew with his crew to Addu Atoll, where the base was to be closed down, in order to evacuate the 15 remaining ground personnel. So no more island trips – it really did begin to feel as if the end of our war was beginning to loom a little nearer. My optimism was such that I wrote off to the Lagonda people to ask for an estimate for putting my beautiful 1932 2-litre back in running order after its six years storage.

The home straight – almost

On 19 June I finally shook off the dust of Koggala – no tears shed – and took passage with Ted on the nine hour flight to Rangoon. The aircraft moorings were in fact at Syriam Point, some miles east of Rangoon, at the mouth of the Sittang River, the jetty being part of an oil refinery belonging to the Burma Oil Co that had been extensively damaged and was now abandoned to the jungle; the wrecked plant, almost hidden in a huge dark creeping canopy of trailing foliage, gave an eerie feeling as one drove through it, as indeed we had to do very frequently since our base was in the *Manela* moored by the river bank nine miles away in the Rangoon River. The squadron had been allocated as transport only two clapped-out jeeps and with these every movement of ground crews, spares, tools and aircrews between the ship and the aircraft at moorings had to be made, day and night, along a single rough road which in part was just a track in fields and which became a sea of mud when the frequent heavy rains hit us; halfway along its length this 'road' went right along the edge – unfenced – of a small lake.

On arrival on board *Manela,* I was introduced to the captain and his officers and then taken to my cabin, which was also to be my office. At least it was an outside cabin, but it was only about eight feet by six with, on one side, a small bunk and a tiny desk (lashed up by the ship's carpenter) fitted up at the foot of the bunk, and on the other side a minuscule washbasin and a small wardrobe. A field telephone communicated with the jetty as long as nothing interfered with the tenuous nine mile long line winding through the jungle. The ship's dining saloon, in which the entire squadron and the ship's crew ate – quite well in fact – was kept bearably cool by big fans but everywhere else, inside and out, the heat and humidity were so great that the regulation day uniform was shorts only, with insignia of rank worn on khaki-drill wrist straps.

Shortly after my arrival, Harry Sheardown left for repatriation to Canada, so I took over as Flight Commander (Operations) on 28 June and really got down to running the squadron's interdiction operations. The craft we were attacking were in fact mainly quite small sailing ships, wooden, some with motors. They nearly all flew the flag of our Chinese allies but we were instructed to disregard these as they were merely a ruse to try to put us off. There was little opposition except from the occasional Japanese machine guns when our aircraft flew close inshore: one of these kept on firing as the aeroplane flew right over him and he drilled several holes in the planing bottom which had to be stopped with leak-stoppers and special putty before the aircraft could land. On the other hand, we regularly flew at two or three hundred feet over two or three airfields on the way across the Kra Isthmus to the east coast, on which were parked a number of the renowned Zero fighters, but not one ever came up to challenge us; we did hear later that they were found to have been flown until they were due for a minor inspection and no one had bothered to get them airworthy again; if true that spoke volumes for the deterioration of at least some Japanese morale in this area, so remote from their main centres of authority. I hardly think, though, that they were disheartened by any of the tens of thousands of leaflets we dropped to encourage the locals to make things awkward for them and thus hasten the liberation.

The complications of running our operations, with communications between the base in the ship and the aircraft moored nine difficult miles away at Syriam Point, proved to be very great. The second-hand jeeps were worked to death carrying ground crews, spares and so on back and forth. When an aircraft was due to take off on an operation first thing in the morning – all ops were in daylight – the daily inspection party had to be taken to Syriam in the dark, which on occasion caused whoever was driving the jeep to lose his way in the often muddy fields and one night, returning empty, to drive off the 'road' into the lake; if there was some snag that would delay the takeoff, a decision had to be made on whether the operation should be cancelled or whether there was time to get another aeroplane and crew ready to take the duff machine's place. All these problems came to my door and, as many of them arose during the night, my already sparse hours of sleep (in spite of phenobarbitone) were interrupted, often two or three times in the night – knock on my cabin door (4am) "Sorry, sir, but so and so . . . what do you wish me to do, sir?" – exhausted brain cranked into action, then shortly afterwards off to attend the crew's briefing and then away in a packed jeep – often me driving – to Syriam to be on hand for a decision in the event of some last-minute hitch, then back for breakfast and a busy day with usually little or no respite even after dinner.

Indeed, I often finished my last bit of paperwork at midnight or after. The point was that we were in effect running a station as well as a squadron and, although most of the responsibility ended up with the CO, I was most often the first port of call and it was obviously up to me to field as many of the problems as possible myself.

I did one bit of local flying in mid-July trying to improve the New Zealander's fairly ineffectual low-level bombing as revealed by the pictures of his attacks taken by the automatic rear-facing camera. But I was clearly getting near the edge: one evening, as I was talking to the CO in the ops room that was part of the ship's bridge, with the intelligence officer and one or two others present including the ship's captain, I realised I had forgotten to organise some detail connected with the next day's operation and I suddenly started to get hysterical – fortunately the captain spotted what was happening and barked at me "Shut up! The second officer's in there trying to sleep before going on watch at midnight!" The shock brought me up short and the whole thing was over in not many seconds.

I did feel a little uncomfortable that the others were all flying busily down across the Kra Isthmus and roaming the far side of Siam and the Malay peninsula while I was sitting, not comfortably but at least securely, trotting out the equivalent of "Take off I say", the mythical staff officer's mythical invocation to yet more endeavour by tired aircrew. I was determined to get a look at what was going on and with the CO's permission I joined Nick and my old crew on an armed reconnaissance of the Kra Isthmus, the Bay of Bandon and south to Singora, returning by the same route.

We took off soon after daylight, the marine craft having carefully checked the river for any of the huge teak logs that were floated down the river to the sawmills; an aircraft hitting one of those, waterlogged and almost submerged, at speed would have been instantly wrecked. We flew low, at about four or five hundred feet down the west coast of Burma and I took over the controls from Nick to cross over into Siam at somewhere near Chumphon and continue on down the east coast. Flying between the mainland and Ko Samui, one of two small islands just offshore, we found a ship of the type used to supply the Japanese and decided to attack it with bombs of which we had four plus four depth charges. I dropped to 50 feet and without opposition let go the four bombs to straddle the target; the second bomb of the stick made a direct hit on the wooden vessel but did not explode, obviously, as we reasoned later, because the fuse fitted was of a type to be detonated by hitting the target vertically whereas, dropped at only fifty feet, the bomb was still travelling horizontally when it hit. We left the ship stopped in the water and went on, Nick taking over; we alternated in that way and each had a share in making machine gun attacks using the two guns in the front turret as well as – for the first time in our careers – the very effective four fixed guns fired by the pilot. There was undoubtedly a certain thrill in swooping down and opening fire with six guns simultaneously, each firing at 1200 rounds a minute, and seeing sails, masts and chunks of ship flying through the air as a result. By that time, the ships crews had become crafty and rigged lines over both sides so that they could jump over the side opposite to that from which the attack was coming, shelter behind the hull while holding on to a line and then clamber back on board when the attack was over!

After having a go at several ships in and around Singora, we started on the return trip, dropping altogether 40,000 leaflets on the way. When we got to Ko Samui, we found our ship still just afloat but clearly heavily damaged and completely waterlogged, with no sign of life. Nick was flying at the time so he did a low-level run and dropped the four depth charges, also right on the line, and they all exploded, one of them very close to the ship which disintegrated into matchwood. When we arrived back at Syriam in the evening, I realised that that was almost certainly my very last operational trip of the war and that indeed was the case, bringing my final total ops hours to 605 hours 20 minutes day, and 71 hours 35 minutes night, ie 676 hours 55 minutes in all.

The very last lap

Meanwhile I had heard that Margaret was in hospital in Diyatalawa with amoebic and bacillary dysentery together – a very dangerous combination; I wanted to be able somehow to get back to Ceylon, but our war was still on and I had to stay. However, a little over a week later, the powers-that-be decided that our interdiction activities were no longer needed and the squadron was ordered to move to Red Hills Lake, a few miles outside Madras. On 26 July the CO and I left the *Manela* and took passage with Nick to our new base – a turbulent trip of nine and a half hours through skies darkened by numerous tremendous thunderstorms with spectacular lightning almost blinding against the towering black clouds. We all felt that this was some sort of fanfare of farewell.

Four days later, having installed ourselves in the comfortable mess overlooking the lake, the CO and I took Nick's crew and made a transit flight to Koggala. On arrival I was summoned to an interview at 222 Group in Colombo where I was offered the chance of a permanent commission in the RAF post-war; it was flattering but, just as when 'Groupie' Francis suggested some while back that I should apply for one, I really felt I should find the peacetime Air Force a bit of a let down, even with the flying, and I should do better to stick with 'Joe' Shell.

On Thursday 2 August, I managed to get to Diyatalawa; Margaret and I went to the Bandarawela Hotel and there, in a little gazebo in the garden, we talked serious matters and finally got engaged. We decided against getting married straight away, firstly because I had seen and heard so much of the anguish of fellows being killed and leaving behind a wife and, even worse, children and I was determined I would not marry while I was still flying operationally; secondly, we both felt that after such a long separation from our families they deserved to be able to share the jollifications of the wedding.

Next day the CO and I flew back to Red Hills Lake, again in Nick's aeroplane with his (my old) crew and at the end of that trip I had flown a total of one thousand hours and twenty minutes on Sunderlands – some sort of a milestone,

I felt. Change was in the air and in the early part of the month a rather pompous Squadron Leader fellow I had met, and disliked, somewhere before, turned up and made it clear he was for taking over as Flight Commander; I had not yet been removed from that post and the result was a rather messy standoff. However, as a new experience, we had the time to sit quietly in the next few evenings on the verandah of the mess, looking over the silent lake in the setting sun and, the CO having tracked down some excellent gin that came in handsome stone jars holding a gallon at a time, several of us rapidly developed a custom of adding Rose's lime juice and enjoying a civilised preliminary to our dinner. After a few days of this, however, the CO, Wing Commander Lionel Powell, was posted away, his place being taken by Wing Commander Hawkins, an agreeable man.

As things were quiet, the squadron not having been given any new role following our withdrawal from Burma, I hitched a ride with one of our aircraft that was to have a minor inspection at Koggala. The date was 15 August and while in the air, on our way south, we picked up on our wireless the voice of the Prime Minister, Clement Attlee, announcing that Japan had surrendered and the war was over; somehow it seemed particularly dramatic to hear it in those circumstances and the excitement throughout the aeroplane was tremendous. It would take time for it all really to sink in.

Final months in the Far East

When we touched down at Koggala from that last trip of wartime we had some difficulty getting transport to shore because the whole station was in a state of jubilant chaos. As it was obvious that there was no chance that the aircraft's 'minor' would be done in the next forty-eight hours, I telephoned Diyatalawa and found that Margaret was at the Mount Lavinia Hotel, a pleasant spot right by the sea, not far from Colombo. I had luck in getting transport and we had a very cheerful VJ Day dinner and dance together.

We conceived the wild idea of my flying her to Madras for a few days when Nick's aircraft had completed its minor inspection. 'Groupie' Francis gave his blessing and I was thrilled to be able to fly my fiancée in my great big aeroplane! On the appointed day, Margaret came down from Mount Lavinia and we went out to the aircraft in the dinghy at high speed, she nearly losing her Wren's hat – the second most important thing for a Wren to lose – on the way.

Having parked my ladylove between the pilots seats, so that she could see how it was all done, I got the aircraft under way towards the takeoff area where I swung the aircraft round, opened the throttles fully and eased her forward on to the step at about 35 knots. At 70 knots, not far from takeoff, the second pilot pointed urgently to the port inner rev indicator which was showing 1200 revs instead of 2700. I throttled back immediately, pretty mad and disappointed. The engineer said the fault could be quickly corrected so we sat on the buoy for a quarter of an hour or so and then the engineer emerged from the engine nacelle (the engine housing) and pronounced the job completed. Off we went again: all was well on the run-up checks and, taking a deep breath, I opened up all four throttles again, feeling those 5000 horses urging us forward, then suddenly my eye – partly focussed on that rev indicator – spotted the hands as they swung back to 1200 rpm. There was nothing for it – the trip was off and I had, somewhat crestfallen, to scrub the whole idea.

Meanwhile it was becoming daily more obvious that, for reasons both of health and circumstances, my ability to be of much further use to the squadron was diminishing day by day; my position was becoming increasingly humiliating, with my successor – not yet appointed but acting more and more on his own – constantly in evidence. The new CO was totally sympathetic and moves for a posting were set in train. At the same time, however, the squadron Medical Officer had said I must have a month's sick leave; this heartened me considerably as I was actually getting rather desperate for a rest. But simultaneously there was disappointment – an announcement that by 20 January next year only up to release group 23 would be out – my 27 looked to be far into the future. Fellows everywhere instantly set about writing to their MPs, as I did myself. I also submitted an application for accelerated release under Class B – "urgently required to assist in post-war reconstruction" – together with a letter to the head of Shell's aviation department in London asking him to back my application.

At the same time as this was going on, a personnel officer from Group arrived with the offer of a posting as Squadron Leader (Administrative) at Koggala of all places! I demurred emphatically and we compromised on the possibility of Senior Operations Officer at Naval/Air Operations Room with the chance of getting to Singapore in a little while. With that I set off to get myself organised for a recuperative stay in Srinagar, the capital of Kashmir.

My leave in Kashmir was a complete change from the dusty heat of Madras. I joined a naval surgeon on a trek in the foothills of the Himalayas; with five ponies and three servants we walked and climbed among immense towering mountains and in great valleys where we camped at night, often by rivers in which we took an early morning bathe – quickly, because they had left their mother glaciers not more than an hour or two before. To augment the food stocks we carried with us, the servants occasionally bargained with a shepherd for a sheep which they then slaughtered and turned into surprisingly good meals, which tasted all the better for the wonderfully stimulating air at the fairly high altitudes we inhabited for most of the ten days of the trek. Back in Srinagar, footsore but exhilarated, I did some shopping for some of the beautiful craft products and finally hitched a lift in an Indian Air Force Dakota to Rawalpindi where I got settled into a far-from-express train for Madras.

Back at Red Hills Lake after a four and a half day journey I learned that the first campaign medals had just been promulgated and we all avidly studied the qualifications for each one and then dashed off to Madras to get the ribbons and have them sewn on – I collected the 1939-45 Star, the Atlantic Star, the Africa Star (for the SOE/naval job), the Burma Star and clasp for southwest Pacific (the Singora trip) and the Defence Medal which was the ridiculously inappropriate award for operations in the Indian Ocean theatre – as remote as it could be from blacked-out Britain and all the bombs and fires.

All this time I had been anxiously waiting for news of my posting which I hoped would be rather better than the earlier offer of admin at Koggala, in fact something involving flying of a less stressful kind. Just after I got back Wing Commander Hawkins told me I was to be Senior Flying Control Officer at Ratmalana, a big RAF airfield that was at the same time the airport of Colombo. I demurred at the idea of a ground job but the CO told me that he considered I was no longer fit to fly and that after a lot of effort he and the personnel people had got me this job, a Squadron Leader post, as the nearest thing to actually flying. Fortunately I was quick enough to see that this was indeed the best I could expect and that they had done their best for me.

However, before settling down in a wingless calling, I was given one last job – to go with the CO to Singapore with much-needed food and medicines and to bring back some of the unfortunate ex-prisoners and civilian internees. I was pleased at the prospect even though I was only too conscious of almost overwhelming exhaustion that the Kashmir trip had done little to mitigate. The takeoff, very heavily loaded, was at night with a strong crosswind; I coped all right with the necessary differential throttle handling but it was untidy as I was doing the right things – by instinct, I suppose – but always a fraction of a second too late. We were to call at Penang for the night so that we could get to Singapore and leave the same day in order to help in a small way to reduce calls on the scarce accommodation and even more scarce food. At Penang the landing area was parallel with the waterfront in a broad channel; there were numerous small boats moored in the roads and such craft were normally the best indication of the wind direction – these were all pointing directly to the north so I approached from the south to land upwind. As we touched down there was a thunderous rumble from the planing bottom and the aircraft was trying to turn a somersault – the CO yelled "We're downwind!" and it was all both of us could do, heaving back on our control columns, to prevent the aeroplane turning over. We were both extremely shocked and puzzled until, as we were taxying in to the moorings we saw a very inconspicuous orange windsock – pointing exactly to the south! Evidently there was a very strong current from north to south in the roads, strong enough – most unusually – to keep the moored craft facing downwind instead of swinging into wind. We had touched down at something like 115 knots instead of 95! The CO was not impressed, even though he agreed that the circumstances had been a bit unusual. He was even less impressed next day when I approached to land at Seletar, Singpore, flying too close to the landing area so that, instead of doing a wide, controlled circuit to get on to the final approach, I almost hurled the aircraft into a tight turn and dived down to the water, fortunately making a smooth touchdown, but then taxying too close to a couple of buoys on my way to our mooring. I think he was being very kind when, a few days later, after I had left for Ratmalana, he wrote my final assessment as 'Above average', but I was pretty crestfallen to have slipped from 'Exceptional' back in June.

After a brief look at Singapore town at night I got down to the aircraft – the

CO remaining behind to prepare for the squadron to move over to Seletar – and waited for our passengers to be brought alongside. When they came aboard – 15 ex-prisoners of war and one civilian ex-internee – we were all profoundly shocked: clothing they had been issued with hung on their emaciated bodies but worse than that was the vacant look in their eyes and their utter listlessness; the crew were kindness itself and shepherded them into the wardroom where they then sat throughout the twelve hour flight back to Red Hills Lake, not responding to any attempt at conversation, not eating or drinking, just staring blankly into infinity. It was one more red-letter entry in our individual books of hate for the Japanese.

With that in mind it seems almost indecent to record that for me the trip back was a true joy. We flew via the Andaman Islands – now quite harmless – and throughout the twelve hours I just savoured the joy of flying the magnificent Sunderland, being able to gaze at the beauty of the wide ocean without having to give a thought to a lurking U-boat – it was wonderful and, to cap it all I came in to the broad expanse of the calm lake at Red Hills and brought the aircraft down to an absolutely perfect landing – for the first three or four seconds only I knew that we had touched – my last ever Sunderland landing after 1042 hours and 5 minutes!

Two days later I left Red Hills Lake and the squadron where things were already much changed, nearly all the captains and crews very recent, the fairly relaxed wartime procedures and relationships beginning to give place to the rather different peace-time regime of a professional Air Force. I had been extraordinarily lucky in so many ways in my flying war and had enjoyed it greatly in spite of some frustrating intervals, overwhelmingly because I had had the enormous good fortune to be able to do what I had set my heart on doing which was to fly – *real* flying!

Last of the Royal Air Force

I arrived on 16 October and RAF Station Ratmalana was quite a change – no water, no big boats – but it was obviously a very busy place and, as the Station Commander told me, was set to become even busier as the huge rush that was developing to expand the links between UK and the Far Eastern and Australasian countries was putting Colombo at the crossroads, though mainly military and naval flying was involved as yet, apart from BOAC.

My predecessor in the job was a former Shell man, whom I had known by sight before the war. He had always been a good supporter of the bar and the mess at Ratmalana probably did particularly well. On making my first inspection of the big control tower and its administrative section I discovered an extensive and chaotic filing system, amendments to Air Ministry Orders, going back months, not incorporated and, worst of all, a large amount of excellent American flying control equipment lying around with no effort having been made to get it installed. I was having to get quickly used to the much more regulated ways of land aircraft, in contrast to our very independent way of making our own decisions concerning when to taxi out, which way to take off and similarly with landing. There having been no handover, I was 'the one who' from the word 'Go'. At the same time I had to set about getting the admin mess cleared up, not to mention a little bit more discipline in the control tower where the general slackness clearly arose from their having been left largely to their own devices. In the event my little staff reacted well to the call for more efficiency and pride.

Soon after I had settled in, Margaret and Pat arrived in Colombo ready to sail for home. We were able to have a couple of dinners and dances but at the one or two other times we arranged to meet, Margaret, being an 'Other Rank', could not go into the hotels where I could and I could not go into the canteens where she had to go; the pursuit of romance was of almost insuperable difficulty – we did once finish up on one end of a concrete bench on Galle Face Green while a couple of Ceylonese nattered away on the other end. The next morning Margaret telephoned to say that she and Pat were about to go aboard their ship for what proved to be a fast passage home.

With the heavy traffic through Ratmalana there were the classic air traffic control problems of competing requirements by users, ensuring safety of operation whatever the pressures to make short cuts and, above all, maintaining an atmosphere of calm, firm control. As Senior Flying Control Officer I was in the firing line day and night, having the ultimate authority – under the Station Commander – to run the 'signal box', as it were. On the whole the system, well proved, worked remarkably satisfactorily and showed itself able to cope with the occasional special challenge.

One such was the case of a York, a four-engined airliner developed from the Lancaster bomber and used widely by the RAF for VIP and other passenger transport. As this aircraft was preparing to land the pilot discovered that one of the two undercarriage legs would not lock down and would thus inevitably fold during the landing run, leaving only one main landing wheel and the tail wheel, with results that can be imagined. I was called to the control tower and arranged for the whole surrounding airspace to be cleared of aircraft to allow the York to fly round and round to burn up as much as possible of its fuel load prior to attempting a landing. I told the pilot that the runway and surrounding areas would be cleared, fire engine and ambulance lined up and everything set up to allow him, in his sole discretion, to decide when to come in. I alerted the Station Commander and the CO of the squadron to which the York belonged; the latter came in hotfoot and started to advise the pilot what to do and what arrangements had been made for his reception – which the pilot already knew from me. Then the squadron's engineer officer came in and checked over with the pilot what had been and what might be done to get the offending leg to lock – his was 'good gen'. Then another York pilot, who claimed to have a lot of experience, arrived and started *his* stream of advice. By this time the York pilot was getting pretty fed up and made it plain that *he* was the pilot and knew perfectly well what he had to do; I diplomatically marshalled all these and other would-be advisers out of the tower and told the pilot he was on his own and there would be no more nattering; for this he was duly grateful.

Meanwhile I checked our own arrangements and got confirmation that the emergency services, including sick quarters, were on the top line. The faulty undercarriage leg, the port one, had resisted all attempts to get it to lock so when the aeroplane started to slow down and lost lift from the wings the leg would collapse, allowing the port wing tip to hit the ground and causing the aircraft to swing smartly round to port, at some 55 or 60 knots; fortunately there was a grassy area about 40 yards wide all along to the left of the runway and the hope was that the soft ground would slow the aircraft to a stop before it hit the perimeter fence. So the whole place settled to an uncanny silence, broken only by the hum of the York going round and round burning up fuel. After some five hours of anxious waiting everything and everyone was suddenly galvanised into action by the pilot's voice "I'm coming in now" to which I replied "We're all ready for you. Good luck!" What seemed to be the entire station personnel strained their eyes to pick the aircraft up at the start of its approach as I went rapidly over in my mind all that we had done in preparation, not that there was time by then to do anything that might have been missed – but my responsibility was obviously very great. Down he came, very gently, with lots of engine, touched down smoothly and started his landing run while we all watched, hardly breathing. It was going beautifully and then, about halfway along the runway, the leg folded, the port wing hit the concrete, the machine swung to port at speed while we all stood transfixed; the fire engine and ambulance were already tearing up the runway as the York plunged into the grass, stopped abruptly about ten feet from the fence and was instantly doused with a huge sheet of water thrown up from the marshy ground by the impact – this of course, fortuitously, eliminated any danger of fire. Crew and passengers had all been strapped in and no one was hurt – so we all went off to lunch. I had a strong whisky.

After I had been at Ratmalana for about three weeks my Release Group (27) was promulgated – much earlier than had been stated while I was back at Red Hills Lake (see page 178). This should have been cheering news but I was more and more feeling the strain of making the unremitting effort to keep my mind working in spite of constant sleeplessness and, when I found myself occasionally muddling up the controls on my car, once nearly driving straight into a fence, the station Medical Officer sent me to a psychiatrist who said it was just overwork but that I was so nearly "round the bend" that I should go home – all of which told me little I did not already know and got me little farther ahead. When the MO had given me the usual test by bashing my knee with a wee hammer I very nearly leapt off the table – my nerves were as taut as piano wire.

So it was a matter of 'pressing on regardless' as staff officers were allegedly in the habit of saying to the surviving bomber crews. As a diversion from the usual round, I was called in to a conference with the Station Commander, some intelligence high-guys and the CO of a naval flight that was flying a courier service between Ceylon and China. It was suspected that a pilot, or pilots, was, or were, smuggling gold out of China and I was required to arrange for a particular incoming flight, in a few days time, to be given special handling, in such a way as to appear anything but special, to enable the intelligence people to swoop. As far as I was concerned it went well but whether the swoop was a scoop I never did find out.

A big new airport at Negombo, north of Colombo, was nearing completion and I had to start organising for the whole flying control setup, equipment and everything, to move there – a monster job in my twitchy state, but the gloom was lightened slightly by the arrival of my clearance papers – the first stage towards repatriation by ship. However I thought it might be worth seeing whether I could wangle the trip home by air in exchange for staying on a week or two to settle the flying control in at Negombo instead of packing in as the Ratmalana control closed as the medical people had recommended; the Station Commander was delighted and told me that I had done more in my first four weeks than any other SFCO he had ever had.

In the event the plan fell through, because a week later I had a medical board at which I was told I could not be flown home but that I should sail from Colombo instead of going through the huge transit camp at Worli, near Karachi, which was apparently jammed with people due for release and waiting with diminishing hope for a boat. Meanwhile I had handed over my job as SFCO on the day the outfit moved to Negombo and was prepared to sail, as I had been told, in six days time, on Sunday 2 December.

I was by now feeling desperately ill and when on the Friday, 30 November, I learned I should not be sailing until 17 December I went straight to the Group MO in Colombo and, regrettably, got so worked up in my tense state that I shouted at him. He was very understanding and said I was suffering from acute tropical fatigue and must be shipped home urgently. At that stage I was stumbling about the place hardly knowing whether it was Tuesday or breakfast time, but a week later there was still no news and on 8 December I finally left Ratmalana for a comfortable NAAFI Club in Colombo. After another week the final move to transit camp was at last ordained and four days later, after the army had been defeated in an attempt to commandeer the RAF accommodation, I joined five other Squadron Leaders in a cabin for four aboard the SS *Nea Hellas*. We sailed at 5pm the following day, Friday 21 December and I watched, with as much glee as I could muster, as Colombo and Ceylon's 'golden strand' thankfully disappeared in the darkening eastern sky. I arrived home to Margaret and my family on 11 January 1946 and, after some perfunctory treatment, was finally ditched, not even half cured, by the Royal Air Force on 19 February 1946. But that is another story.

So ended my War in Four Movements, having held commissions as Second Lieutenant in the army (Romania), Sub Lieutenant in the Royal Navy (SOE Mediterranean) and Squadron Leader in the Royal Air Force – and I suppose having a code designation as D/H5 in the Special Operations Executive could also be called holding a form of commission, so four in all.

Coda

Looking back to that night in April 1940 in the train thundering through the Carpathian mountains (see page 13), I had indeed jumped into the big lake, and through many varied experiences and by the grace of God, had – unlike more than twenty of my good friends including the closest, Duggie Lumsden especially, and Frank Haddon – got to the other side, not quite whole (the elastic once overstretched does not go all the way back) but on firm ground, ready for a future with Margaret my wife, my mother and sister, and in due course two sons, a daughter-in-law and two grandchildren. With that – and much more – I can say with the Psalmist, in my eighty-nineth year, truly "my cup runneth over".

Glossary

Aerofoil A structure shaped so as to cause air passing over it and, by the resulting venturi effect (qv), to produce an area of reduced pressure which generates the lift which keeps the aircraft airborne.

Aldis Lamp A powerful electric lamp with a reflector that can be made to oscillate by pressure on a trigger, the resulting flickering of the beam being used to flash messages in Morse Code.

Asdic (from Anti-Submarine Detection Investigative Committee) An apparatus mounted in a dome on the underside of a warship which sends out repeated ultrasonic beams through the water. The beams reflect off any solid object in the water, the time delay between transmitting and receiving the reflected beam enabling the operator to estimate the distance of the object.

Backstay A rope aboard a sailing ship, leading from the head of the mast to a fixture on the deck, that helps the mast to resist the forward pressure of the sails.

Belay Making fast a rope aboard a ship by taking one or more turns round a belaying pin or cleat.

Boost pressure The degree of supercharge at which the engine is operating and is indicated by a gauge. By regulating the boost pressure in conjunction with the controllable-pitch airscrew (qv) the actual power output of the engine is controlled to suit the circumstances of the flight at a given moment.

Circuit A standard pilot's flying exercise involving four equal 'legs' involving take off, a climb to a set altitude, a 90° turn to port (the crosswind leg), another 90° turn to port (the downwind leg) bringing the aircraft onto the reverse of the heading at take off and two further 90° turns which will bring the aircraft on to the approach heading. The aircraft should, in theory at least, reach the ground or water roughly at the point from which it took off. This drill is traditionally called 'circuits and bumps' by pilots and is normally carried out in a left-hand direction unless, for example, it would interfere with a neighbouring airfield's circuit.

Controllable-pitch airscrew The pitch of an airscrew (or propeller) is the angle at which the blade engages with the airflow to drive the air backwards and, by reaction, propel the aircraft forwards. In very small aircraft the pitch is fixed, but in all other aircraft the airscrew incorporates a mechanism for turning the blades so that they present a coarse angle to the airflow (coarse pitch) or a fine angle (fine pitch). This varies the effort required by the engine to turn the airscrew. In most cases, in the event of an engine failure, the blades can be turned end-on to the airflow, called 'feathering', thus stopping the engine and preventing 'windmilling' that produces heavy drag and can increase the internal damage to the engine.

Dakota The name given by the RAF to the Douglas DC-3, a rugged 'workhorse', famously reliable, used worldwide in war and peace for innumerable different applications in a huge variety of environments.

Deck head A ceiling on board ship.

ENSA Entertainments National Service Agency – the organisation that enabled thousands of actors, actresses, singers and bands to travel over the world during the Second World War to give shows to British service men and women, often in the most rudimentary conditions.

Fully feathering airscrew A controllable-pitch airscrew (qv) that can have its blades set end-on to the airflow

Flaps Auxiliary aerofoils (qv) that are mounted on the rear of the aircraft's wings. They remain withdrawn to form part of the wing in normal flight but are moved out into the airflow to provide additional lift at low speeds, particularly on the approach to landing. They can also be lowered at a more acute angle to act as an airbrake to help to reduce the aircraft's speed as required, especially on the approach and at touchdown.

Full-flap, full-glide landing A method of landing Sunderland flying boats by starting the approach unusually close to the desired alighting point. The engines are throttled right back to idling; the flaps are run out to their full extent; and the aircraft is set on a steep descent at an angle approaching 45° and an airspeed slightly above normal approach speed. The descent is continued in this configuration until within some 250/300 feet of the water, when the aircraft is gently eased out of the dive so that the attitude gradually becomes level at the same time as the keel is about six inches above the water and the airspeed is just about at stalling. An almost imperceptible backward pressure is maintained for ten seconds or so for the remaining small margin of airspeed to be dissipated and the aircraft settles gently on the water. This method requires great skill and sensitivity to the degree of lift throughout the approach, bearing in mind that the engines are not used at any stage – to do so would reduce the prime advantage of the method which is the very short horizontal distance from the point of throttling back at altitude to the point of touch-down followed by a considerably shorter landing run. This method can enable a pilot to make an approach and land where nearby obstructions and shortness of the alighting area would rule out the conventional method. However it should never be attempted if the water is flat calm as this makes the judgment of height above the water uncertain.

Gaff A spar laced to the head of a four-sided fore-and-aft sail to keep it spread to the wind.

G-Force The force of the earth's gravitational field acting on the human body. When pulling out of a high-speed dive, the natural force is multiplied by as much as six times, forcing the blood to leave the brain and causing blacking-out. When sharply going over the top of a fast climb the opposite force, known as negative G, occurs but with less disruptive consequences.

Heat-exchange vessels In an oil refinery and many similar installations, such vessels are used to help economise on heat. A cylindrical vessel contains a number of tubes running from one end to the other. A liquid, which is at low temperature but which needs to be heated in the next stage of a process is passed round the outside of the tubes while a high-temperature liquid from a later stage in the process is passed down inside the tubes, 'exchanging' heat with the liquid outside. The same principle can also be used in reverse to cool down liquids.

JU-88 A very fast German twin-engined two-seater fighter-bomber, armed with 20mm cannon. Large numbers of them were based on the northwest and west coasts of France from where they had a short flight to attack Sunderlands and other aircraft that were attacking German U-boats on their way to and from French bases. They arrived very rapidly, often in groups of four, and when a crew were surprised by them they were said, very aptly, to have 'been jumped'.

Limpet mine A steel ordnance, generally hemispherical, in form, with powerful magnets on the flat side by which it could be attached to the hull of a ship by swimmers or canoeists. It was filled with high-explosive and detonated by a time-delay fuse known as a 'pencil' (qv).

Nacelle The metal covering designed to streamline an aircraft engine. It is normally removable in sections to enable engineers in ground crews to reach all parts of the engine.

'Pencil' A time-delay fuse, looking exactly like a pencil, that is attached to a detonator which in turn sets off the explosive charge. This may be in a limpet mine or in a lump of plastic explosive used for a variety of destructive applications. At the bottom end is the striker that sets off the detonator and is restrained against a spring which, in turn, is restrained by a wire. At the top end is a very small container that holds very strong acid. When the container is pinched the acid flows on to the wire and after a predetermined interval eats it away, thus releasing the spring and, with it, the striker. At sea, sugar is used instead of acid – with the pencil set facing the direction of the ship water is forced into it and this dissolves the sugar, thus releasing the spring and the striker.

'Phoney War' In the early months of the Second World War neither the Germans nor the British and French undertook any war-like activity on land apart from small patrol actions and, in the air, mostly reconnaissance flights. The RAF also bombarded Germany with millions of leaflets threatening the population with dire consequences if they did not surrender. Only the ruthless U-boat campaign was waged from day one. As far as most people were concerned, there appeared to be no proper war going on, so what little was happening was called 'phoney'.

Planing bottom The bottom of the hull of a high-speed motor boat or a flying boat is shaped to enable the craft, once a certain speed has been reached, to 'plane' or skim over the water instead of ploughing through it. This means the hull meets greatly reduced resistance and reaches the desired speed in a much shorter time – an object that is greatly assisted by having a 'step' part-way along the bottom and mounted across it. This step is generally not more than a few inches in depth but enables the rear portion of the bottom to be lifted clear of the water well before the forward portion, thus significantly reducing the overall water-drag of the craft. The planing bottom needs great strength in order to withstand the battering from the fast-moving water, specially if the water is at all rough.

Reduction Gear An arrangement of gear-wheels fitted between the engine and the airscrew to enable the airscrew to turn at its most efficient speed while the engine driving it can turn at a higher speed where it, in its turn, is most efficient.

'Scrambled eggs' Colloquial description of the single or double rows of gold wire oak leaves embroidering the peaks of the caps of Group Captains (one row) and Air Commodores and above (two rows).

Shoot up To fly very low and very fast to impress, amuse or intimidate earthlings.

'Shufti-kite' Middle-East RAF jargon for a reconnaissance aircraft – 'kite' is an aeroplane and 'shufti' is derived from the Arabic 'shouf' – to look!

Slipstream The air-mass passing over an aircraft in motion.

Slipway A sloping surface projecting into the water up or down which a vessel or flying boat can be hauled or run out.

Stalling The point at which the speed of the slipstream over an aerofoil becomes insufficient to maintain lift.

Supercharge/boost As an aircraft climbs, the air becomes thinner and, while the natural flow of air to the aircraft's engine at low altitude (say up to 5000 feet) is sufficient to deliver normal power, as altitude increases so the thinner air causes progressively less and less power to be developed. This power loss is wholly or mainly overcome by fitting the engine with a rotary air-pump called a supercharger. This turns much faster than the engine (being driven through gears that multiply the engine speed) and forces air into the carburettor exactly as in a supercharged car.

U-Boat A German submarine (Unterseeboot – literally under sea boat) a name full of menace to millions of seafarers and all others concerned with the safe arrival of all sorts of supplies on which Great Britain's survival depended in 1939-1945.

Venturi Basically a device through which air passes and is compressed by a special from of restricting orifice, then instantly allowed to expand thus creating an area of reduced pressure. Nature abhors a vacuum so the force created by the rush of air (or equally liquid in a liquid system) to eliminate the reduced pressure can be harnessed to perform useful work.

Very Light Pistol A pistol invented by an American naval officer, Edward Wilson Very (1847-1910) and designed to fire a variety of coloured balls in succession. The variety of colours in an individual discharge and the order in which they appear constitutes a code. Aircraft operating with Royal Navy and other vessels, particularly escorting convoys, identified themselves as friendly by firing the Very light code in daylight and, at night, by signalling, with a shaded Aldis lamp, the letter applicable to a particular time period as Very lights would reveal the position of the convoy.

Warping buoy 'Warping' a vessel is the act of moving short distances by tow and the same applies to flying boats. When an aircraft is to be taken up the slipway (qv) it is manoeuvred very slowly to pick up a buoy that is situated some 80-90 feet off the end of the slipway. On top of the buoy is a large pulley through which a rope, the 'warp', is rove to enable the stern of the aircraft to be hauled round so that the machine lies stern on to the slipway. After that men in waders float out the beaching gear – double wheels each side secured under the mainplane and a small steerable trolley secured to the extreme aft end of the keel. After the gear is in place a large gang of men or a vehicle such as a Coles crane hauls the aircraft, stern first, up the slipway while the warp is paid out via the warping buoy to keep the aircraft steady until the wheels of the beaching gear are firmly on the slipway.

'Wimpy' The RAF nickname, basically affectionate, for the Wellington bomber – designed by Barnes Wallis who also designed the 'bouncing bomb' for the Dambuster raid.

Appendix 1

Extract from Spanish newspaper ABC, Tuesday 24 April 1934, morning edition. (Translated from the original Spanish by the author)

. . . shots which the police fired into the air while being attacked with stones and knives from the calle del Arenal the police were attacked by shots from a large group, shooting then becoming general and lasting some minutes. The panic among the public was really extraordinary as hundreds of people rushed for doorways, which were promptly closed.

After the first moments of nervousness, calm began to descend on the scene and groups of people began to appear carrying in their arms people wounded in the disturbance. From the door of a house on the corner of the calle del Carmen, they brought out a boy of about twenty, poorly clothed, who had a bullet wound in the head and who, when he was taken into the police surgery, had hardly been put on the operating table when he died without recovering consciousness.

The police judge, D Felìpe Arín, arrived at the "beneficent establishment" (ie the surgery!) and ordered the removal of the corpse to the Judicial Mortuary, without having been able to establish his identity as the dead man had no form of document in his clothing.

Meanwhile, the medical team of the police surgery, D Cosme Valdovinos and D Antonio Cabellero and their assistant nurses Cargia Lagunal, Mateos and González Duarte attended the following injured:

Teodoro Somolinos, 19 years old, of calle de Maria de Guzmán 26, bullet wound in the right side of the face, condition uncertain.

Alan Deller, 18 years old, English subject, born in London, living in Madrid, calle de Padilla 80, who had a bullet wound in the face and another in the left lower jaw with exit in the shoulder on the same side. His condition was described as very serious.

Florencio de Gracia Garrido, seriously wounded in the left side of the vertebral column.

Other details of the tragic occurrence:

At the start of the bloody disorder in the Puerta del Sol, seconds before the first shots rang out, some eight or ten individuals who were standing at the corner of the calle del Correo, took out their pistols, at the same time shouting "No need to run, we're going for that lot." Hardly had the first shot been heard than these people started firing at the police while the people who were running, in confusion tried to seek refuge in the calle del Correo itself and actually ran into the line of fire.

At the same time, some individuals who had managed to get to the top of the Manzanedo building, were firing from the rooftops at the police. This building, situated in the calle Mayor on the corner of the Puerta del Sol, also gives onto the aforementioned calle del Correo, calle de Esparteros and the plaza de Pontejos, all of which contain many doorways, some of them giving direct access to the rooftop. It is thought, therefore, that the gunmen, taking advantage of the inattention of one of the door-keepers, were able to get upstairs and position themselves along the parapets facing the Puerta del Sol from which they opened fire.

Moments after the incident happened, we had the opportunity to speak to one of the occupants of the building who lives in the calle de Esparteros, No. 3. This gentleman confirmed to us in detail the occurrences in the building and at the same time told us of his belief that none of the occupants had been involved in the dangerous game.

When the police who came out of the Pontejos police station saw the attack to which their colleagues were being subjected from the top of the Manzanedo building, they started firing at the criminals until they succeeded in dislodging them from the parapets.

The police, as we said earlier, fired the first shots into the air so as to give time for the passers-by, who included a large number of women and children, to seek shelter. The public, seized by an indescribable panic, fled as fast as they could into the adjoining streets and invaded the café Oriental, the bar Flor, the bar de la Montaña, the café de Lisboa and the La Tropical beer-hall which were open at the time. In one of these establishments, as a result of the crowds of people and the various commentaries on the incident, several rows broke out.

In the upper part of the façade of the building where the Radical Circle has its offices as well as in the neighbouring building, number 9 Puerta del Sol, there could be seen numerous bullet marks, doubtless caused by the first shots that were fired into the air.

Appendix 2

Extracts from the special article "Secret orders - destroy the oil wells - English conspirators on the Black Sea" by Alfred Gerigk, in the *Berliner Illustrierte Zeitung*, July 1940.

'Pencils' from the Nile

Through the streets of Ploeşti the noise of the gay life led by the English trainees sounds. They arrived a few days ago, youngsters from the Sudan, from Syria, from England, youngsters who have been placed in the English oil wells as trainees. The strange part about it is that not one of them is a technical man. It is also strange that these young men, who rush about and enjoy themselves in a boisterous manner without worrying about anything, are scarcely ever to be seen in the office or the refineries of the oil companies. That means that they have even more time for parties at night, Taylor and Tigg and Stanger and Riley and all the others. These young men have a lot of money and also smart motor cars. They shake up the pleasure haunts of Ploeşti and they are quickly taken up by the well-known beauties of the town of Ploeşti, but also by families who otherwise have a good reputation. Their nightly parties often take place in female company in Doina, that haunt of pleasure seekers with red painted walls and discreetly lighted corners. But the nightly journeys which the young men make round the town in their cars are not only taken for pleasure, and the strange letters in which they order a few hundred fountain pens and pencils or other utensils from Egypt likewise seem to have little to do with the work which they should be doing as trainees.

Noise and much pushing at the entrance to the hidden back room. Flushed, with ties torn off and pop eyes, a few trainees rush in. One shouts out "Whisky, 3 large Whiskies!" "What's up, Riley? Where have you left your tie, Deller? Who has been boxing with you, Stranger?" "Row in Doina. The Germans threw us out. An awful fuss with the women."

Doina is one of the few good places which exist in Ploeşti. It is a popular theatre showing dialect plays, and next door is a bar with music and dancing within red painted walls and discreet red lighting. The Doina bar is broken up. The circumstances were a few German engineers dancing with Roumanian girls, a few Englishmen who interfered, and also a few Roumanian officers, and finally a mix up with glasses, chairs, table legs, torn clothes and bleeding noses.

Green shakes his head in a worried fashion. "You must behave more quietly, chaps. Masterson will give you an awful row. You can't carry on like that. Things are already going wrong, and if you do this sort of thing the Roumanians will eventually throw you out. You are not here solely for the amusement of the women."

The mood in the back room of Berbec is subdued.

Shots in the Night

The first blows against England's organisation of agents in Roumania fell in June. The merchant Kahn from Turnu Severin, who was the helper of Mr Blackley, is arrested in Sulina and sent to prison in Bucharest. The maps of Astra Românã were seized when they were in the act of being sent away on an English ship, and above all the first steps were taken by the Roumanian police to extradite various people.

Taylor and Tigg and Stranger and Riley, all those English students who had been brought with so much trouble from Egypt, Syria and Palestine to Ploeşti, were expelled from the oil zone. They spent their time sitting in the Astra Românã club on the Snagov Lake close to the border of the oil zone, meditating on their plans for revenge.

"Louba is to blame", says one of them, " he had us watched. He knows what is happening in the railways and what we did there. Also what we did not do. We ought not to let him carry on like that. Military surveillance of the oil zone sounds fine. Oil zone closed by the military might almost be taken seriously, but I know how we might get away with it. Mr Louba will be very much surprised.

In a joyous and drunken atmosphere in the club on the Snagov Lake a plan is thought out. Major Louba, of the Roumanian General Staff, has been some time in Ploeşti. One of his duties is the prevention of sabotage, and he has been energetically intervening by investigation and measures for watching important places.

In the darkness of a cool June night a boat is rowed across the Snagov Lake. On the banks of the Snagov Lake are the limits of the military zone or the oil region. On both banks all roads and openings are well watched. The question is, how can the Snagov Lake itself be watched since part of it lies outside the closed zone. The military authorities have overlooked that point. The boat glides over the dark surface of the lake, past the watching posts. The boat lands on the far side of the closed zone. A few unrecognisable figures creep through the residential suburbs of Ploeşti.

A noise from one of the villas. Sounds of stones being thrown. Broken windows, a suppressed cry. "There is the bed!" a few shots ring out through the night. Excited voices. People running up, and the dark figures disappear in the shadows of the houses.

Attack on Major Louba! Three shots fired into his bed as he was by chance in the bath. That is the news which surprised and terrified Ploeşti. Mrs Louba saw the attackers as they were running away. The police showed her the pictures of all the Englishmen who were living in Ploeşti. As soon as she saw them she recognised the trainees Henderson and Deller, but the English trainees took good care to have sound alibis. Expulsion from Roumania was finally the only method the police could use against the suspected men.

From Banishment into the Legation

In the British Legation more and more conferences and talks are held. We must be more severe. We must handle the Roumanians more energetically. That is the gist of all these talks. And English hopes rise as in the last days of June Russian troops march into Bessarabia and Bessarabia is ceded by Roumania. Joyous celebrations are held in the English circles of Bucharest. A cheerful and drunken celebration is held in the Astra Românã club on the Snagov Lake. "Now Russia and Germany will start something. New opportunities for England."

England's retreat from Roumania

Then the next blow falls. Expulsion orders are issued against Ted Masterson and his assistant Elias. Expulsion orders also against Blackley, against the trainees from Ploeşti and a whole crowd of agents. They are forced to leave the country via Konstanza, Sulina and Giurgiu.

Has Sir Reginald already sent the last of those many thousands of ciphered telegrams which have passed, since the outbreak of the war, between London and the Legation in the Strada Jules Michelet, the last telegram which is destined to draw the final line under a diplomatic career: " Secret orders impossible to carry out. Destruction of the oil wells impossible."

Appendix 3

See instructions for use of this form in K.R. and A.C.I., para. 2349, and War Manual, Pt. II., chapter XX., and notes in R.A.F. Pocket Book.

OPERATIONS RECORD BOOK

R.A.F. Form 540

of (Unit or Formation) 230 Squadron.

No. of pages used for day..................

Place.	Date.	Time.	Summary of Events.	References to Appendices.
	1940. NOV.			
SUDA BAY.	9th	a.m.	Two Sunderlands detached at Suda Bay carried out patrols in the South Eastern Ionian Sea in connection with C-in-C's M.B.8. Nothing was sighted. Visibility nil at times.	
ALEXANDRIA.		1415	An unidentified submarine was reported by 202 Group in position 31°12'N: 27°57'E. One Sunderland took off to locate and destroy the submarine. No sign of submarine was seen and the aircraft returned.	
SUDA BAY.	10th	a.m.	One Sunderland carried out a search for enemy submarines off the West Coast of Crete and the Anti-Kithera Channel for two hours, but sighted nothing. This aircraft later returned from Suda Bay to Alexandria.	
ALEXANDRIA.		0530	Sunderland L.2159 flew from Athens to Alexandria. This aircraft had been interned in Greece since 27.8.40.	
SUDA BAY.		1200	Sunderland L.2161 flew on three engines from Athens to Suda to change an engine.	
	12th	0254 1332	One Sunderland carried out a patrol in the S.E. Ionian Sea for enemy surface forces (C-in-C's Operation M.B.8). No enemy forces were sighted. Our own battle fleet and cruiser force was sighted and signals exchanged.	
ALEXANDRIA.	13th	0712	One Sunderland left conveying General Sir Archibald Wavell and Staff to Suda Bay. Two War Correspondents and various R.A.F. passages were also taken. One small sailing ketch, looking suspiciously smart, was sighted in position 3234N 2841E.	
"		0957	One Sunderland returned from Suda Bay.	
"	14th	0516	Four French Merchant Vessels were reported to have been seen by the Sunderland on route to Suda Bay on 13th Nov. in position 34 40'N 25 25'E steering 1000.	
"		1230	One of the bombs in the raid on 12th November did not explode and is in the vicinity of certain aircraft moorings. These will not be occupied for some days, in case it is a delayed action bomb.	

The 'small sailing ketch', the sighting of which on 13 November 1940 by a Sunderland of No 230 Squadron RAF based at Alexandria is reported above, was HMS *Dolphin* in which the author was then serving as a Sub Lieutenant RNVR and as an agent of the Special Operations

Appendix 4

Captain Jim Pertwee

Captain Jim Pertwee played a prominent part in the operations in Burma of the Chindwin Flotilla, one of the most unusual naval units of the Second World War.

The Flotilla was originally intended to have 16 gunboats, but delays and difficulties reduced the final number to two, named *Pamela*, after the daughter of Lord Mountbatten, the Supreme Allied Commander in South East Asia, and *Una*, after the daughter of General 'Bill' Slim, the 14th Army commander.

Slim himself named them on April 9 1945 at Kalewa shipyard on the Chindwin River, breaking a bottle of what he called "wine of doubtful quality" across *Pamela*'s bows and then, with a swing of a Gurkha Khukri, severed a rope allowing *Pamela* to slide into the water. He then did the same for *Una*.

Pamela and *Una* were built of local teak, 51ft 6in long overall, with a beam of 13ft and a designed draught of 2ft 9in (although they leaked so much their actual draught was always well over 3ft). They were intended to provide anti-aircraft protection for Inland Water Transport convoys along the river of Burma, to operate as gunboats in support of forward troops and to carry 40 soldiers.

In practice, none of these objectives was fully achieved. Pertwee arrived in Calcutta in February 1945 with what everyone called 'the hopeless task' of trying to expedite the delivery of stores. Everything from spare engines to relief crews from the Burma RNVR failed to arrive. But despite the frustration and difficulties, Pertwee did well enough to be able to come to the Chindwin himself and take command of *Pamela* on April 10. Both boats moved down river on April 29 to operate with 100 Brigade at Prome on the east bank of the Irrawaddy.

Pamela and *Una* patrolled the rivers, ferried troops and destroyed country boats which might be used by the Japanese. On May 5 *Pamela* was straddled but not damaged by fire from a Japanese 75mm gun and replied with her Bofors. At one Japanese crossing point where the river narrowed, both boats came under machine gun and rifle fire at about 50 yards range and *Pamela* was hit several times.

Living conditions on board were appalling. The sailors lived for weeks in hot, damp, cramped and petrol-fume ridden spaces, with poor food and a shortage of clean drinking water. Most had septic sores and chronic diarrhoea. Pertwee bore the scars of jungle sores on his ankles to the end of his life.

By mid-June 1945, the gunboats' war was over. On June 16, they took part in the Naval Review held by Mountbatten to celebrate victory in Burma.

Pamela and *Una* were certainly no oil paintings. 'Chunky' best describes them. Slim called them 'punt-like'; but they had, he said, "brought the White Ensign, and all it meant to us soldiers, back to the Chindwin and the Irrawaddy".

Pertwee was highly praised for his part and always thought the Chindwin Flotilla the most exciting episode in his career.

From an obituary in The Daily Telegraph, *Tuesday 15 August 2000*

Appendix 5

Notes on the handling of large flying boats

(Note: the formal word for a flying boat landing is alighting.)

A Differences between flying boats and land aircraft

Flying boats have:

1 No wheels (except some Catalinas and small aircraft): They taxi, takeoff and land on the very strong bottom of the hull (not fuselage) which is formed so as to pass easily through the water and, when a certain speed is attained, to plane or glide over the water thus greatly reducing water-drag on takeoff.

Water-drag is also reduced by shortening the length of the hull in the water. This is achieved by having a 'step', varying between four inches and, in the later marks of Sunderland, one inch, facing aft across the planing bottom at about halfway, the after portion of the bottom then being faired in smoothly to the end of the keel so that at a fairly early stage in the takeoff (depending on the aircraft load) the boat-shaped forward planing area lifts the after portion clear of the water while the step ensures a clean break-away of the water-flow.

2 No brakes: Once the mooring is cast off the flying boat has to keep moving ahead, unless there is a stiff breeze from ahead and the flaps are lowered fully when a stop or even (very cautious) sailing astern may be achieved in what is a totally unstable situation requiring unceasing attention.

3 No runways: In principle it is the pilot's responsibility to choose the area of water where he will do his preflight engine checks and then take off or land, taking into account local obstructions near the area and on the water and (vitally important) any other vessels that will, or may move into his area of operation; surface vessels rarely have any understanding of the flying boat's limitations or requirements, in particular its lack of an astern gear, and anticipation must be the pilot's watchword, especially when under way, ie from the moment of leaving the mooring.

4 Normally to be accessed and departed from by means of a suitable powered craft that can approach from the port quarter and move carefully ahead below the mainplane to the forward door, having no high structure that would collide with the underside of the mainplane or the airscrews. Bringing a craft alongside from ahead of the aircraft is difficult because powered craft often do not handle easily when going astern and if the wind is at all strong the craft's bow can be blown off to leeward before the painter can be belayed to the aircraft's bollard.

5 In general to have all except major maintenance carried out on the water where ground crews are often exposed to severe weather, except in the tropics, and a spanner dropped is a spanner definitely lost.

6 In most circumstances to live attached to their mooring buoy which is not difficult to leave but can demand delicate handling of the aircraft and engine controls to bring the aircraft's bow near enough and slowly enough for the crew to have a chance to pick up the mooring to secure the aircraft, a particularly difficult operation in high wind and rough water with the aircraft pitching and yawing.

B Characteristics of a typical flying boat

A prime example of a large flying boat, exhibiting all the basic features of the class, and many additional refinements, is Short Sunderland, a high-wing monoplane with four engines, a wingspan of 112 feet 9 inches, a length of some 87 feet and a single tail-fin and rudder rising 27 feet from light-load water level. It is fully equipped with anchor, 120 feet of chain and anchor winch and carries, in special stowage, cradles – duralumin planks and an A-frame – to enable all maintenance, including an engine change, to be done independently; a boathook and a "fog-bell for use when manoeuvring on the water" also included. Gun-turrets, armament and bomb gear do not concern this note.

The following notes refer to the Short Sunderland which proved highly versatile, manoeuvrable in spite of its tendency to 'weathercock' because of its high sides, and splendidly seaworthy. Once airborne it behaved exactly like a land aircraft, as indeed does any flying boat.

C Handling the flying boat

1 Leaving the mooring buoy and taxying

a The first, vital activity is to assess the wind and water conditions and to identify any physical obstacles and other actual or potential users of the water space – in essence to get a 'feel' of the environment within which the pilot is about to move his aircraft with no brakes, with the help only of the rudder and engines, with no place to stop and think.

b The state of the aircraft must be checked: ground crews will have completed the technical checks and the aircraft crew their own areas of responsibility while two vital matters remain – the bilges must have been pumped dry using the pump operated by the auxiliary power unit (water from small leakages in even the soundest bottom plus water from rain when collected in the bilges can add up to a significant weight affecting the length of the takeoff run); and the Pitot head cover must have been removed (the Pitot head receives air pressure from the forward movement of the aircraft, thus enabling the airspeed to be registered. Instances where aircraft have taken off with the cover on were almost always fatal).

c While still on the mooring buoy both outer engines will be started so as to ensure adequate control of the aircraft immediately the moorings have been cast off. The aircraft then heads off to an area of water with sufficient room for the preflight engine checks to be performed. These consist of running up the engines to near full power, first the outers together, then the inners together while each of the two magnetos on each engine is briefly switched off and on again – if there is a drop in revolutions per minute (rpm) of more than 100 a return to the buoy and an examination of the engine is mandatory – full power is not used so as to avoid possible damage to the engine in case one magneto is faulty. Simultaneously with this check, the airscrew pitch controls on the two engines are moved through their full range to prove correct functioning. Lastly both engines are opened up briefly to full takeoff power to see that full boost (+6 lbs/in) and full revs (2650 rpm) are available. The same procedure is followed with the inner engines together. The procedure is performed as quickly as prudently possible so as to minimise stress on the engines but also because quite high water speeds can develop very quickly, thus a sharp lookout is essential throughout the procedure; as far as possible it is worth trying to plan the procedures so that they lead the aircraft close to the takeoff point, thus avoiding long periods of slow taxying leading to overheating of the engines and possible oiling up of the spark-plugs – the latter could cause a fatal weakening of the performance of the engine, particularly on a full-load takeoff when the stress on the engine is high.

d. Before, during and after the foregoing procedures taxying demands unceasing vigilance and anticipation, taking into account the aircraft's lack of brakes and the often unpredictable movements of other vessels in or approaching the area. Engine temperatures must be watched while the rule-of-the-road at sea must be observed – a flying boat while water-borne is a vessel – and navigational lights and buoys conformed with. If taxying on a very large expanse of water it is sometimes difficult to judge one's exact position and the – informal – use of transits can be helpful, the navigator and pilot noting the relative positions of known local features and their progressive change – there are no roadways on the water.

2 Taking off

a Check with the crew that both entrance doors (hatches) and water-tight halfdoors are closed. The vital cockpit check is performed; engines set to rich mixture, airscrew pitch fully fine, rudder and elevator trimming tabs set, flaps out, fuel master cocks fully open and, at night (except in war), navigation lights switched on.

b The aircraft is turned to face the wind and the giro direction indicator is set to the actual heading; this latter precaution is particularly helpful at night when usual visual references are few or even absent and when takeoff in difficult conditions is prolonged beyond the flare path.

c All four engines are given full throttle immediately so as to get the aircraft well up in the water as soon as possible in order to bring the airscrews clear of the bow-wave – the outer portions of the airscrew blades are moving through the air at supersonic speed and when hit by water their edges can in time become roughened or even split. As soon as the aircraft comes up on the step it will be levelled until it 'feels right', with the nose not too low which causes the aircraft to 'dig in', with fatal results if it somersaults, and not too high which will slow the takeoff due to the coarser angle at which the mainplane and planing bottom meet the air and water respectively but, above all because the aircraft may leave the water prematurely, stall and fall back heavily on to the water with likely damage to the planing bottom as it is hit at speed. Torque reaction from the four airscrews revolving in the same direction causes the aircraft to swing powerfully to port as soon as the throttles are opened; this must be corrected instantly by full starboard rudder and, in extremis, by momentarily throttling back the starboard outer engine slightly. An exactly similar situation, with the same remedy, arises in a crosswind takeoff. In very rough water particular care must be taken, early in the takeoff before the airflows are fully effective, to keep the aircraft level to protect the wing tip floats from head-on shock.

d If the takeoff is aborted in severe weather, and another attempt is to be made, it will be very difficult to turn the aircraft through 180° to return to the starting point; this is due to the very pronounced tendency of the Sunderland, with its high sides, to 'weathercock' back to facing into wind. To make the turn high power from the windward outer engine, or even the inner engine as well, will be needed as a result of which speed is rapidly built up while the wind is lifting up the windward wing, forcing the downwind wing tip float deep into the water at some speed; very great care is essential since, if the float goes, the wing will instantly fill with water, before men and weights can be got out on the opposite wing and the aircraft will capsize and sink. The turn can often be helped initially by making the aircraft swing a small amount in the opposite direction to that which is desired, thus providing a longer arc for the desired swing as the throttles are opened.

e In some circumstances, for example where there is a dog-leg in the takeoff path, it is possible to turn the aircraft while on the step, at say 75 knots, while keeping it perfectly level to protect the wing tip floats and taking care not to reach a speed at which there is a risk of premature takeoff.

f Normally the aircraft will virtually fly itself off the water but in flat calm conditions, and even more at higher altitude (eg Kisumu on Lake Victoria), the water is reluctant to leave the portion of the planing bottom that is still in the water and the breakaway needs to be helped by getting a launch to roughen the water surface by crisscrossing the takeoff path and/or, in the worst case, by rocking the aircraft very slightly backwards and forwards with the most extreme care to avoid 'porpoising' which can develop a rapid harmonic increase with fatal results unless instantly checked by throttling back to reduce speed.

3 Landing (or alighting)

a On approaching the landing area, assess the water conditions and check on obstructions near or on the area of water chosen for the landing together with the nature of other traffic in the area.

b Safe/Night landing procedure

Perform cockpit check: trimming tabs set appropriately, flaps out, airspeed reduced to 115 knots, at 700 feet turn on to final approach heading, level the aircraft, put airscrews in fine pitch, set outer engine throttles to give engine speed of 2000 rpm, using inner engine throttles settle the aircraft on a rate of descent of 250 feet/minute at 100 knots airspeed, thereafter use engines to control rate of descent and use the aircraft's attitude to control airspeed until the keel touches the water, then on landing run, work ailerons vigorously to keep the aircraft level so as to protect the wing floats and pull the control column hard back to raise the elevators out of the rush of water at the moment that the aircraft comes off the step and settles in the water. Then stop the inner engines and run the flaps in unless they might help the taxying in light airs; while in flat calm they are useless.

c Short-distance landing procedure ('full-flap, full-glide')

This procedure allows a landing to be made, at a distance horizontally, from the point of throttling back at 1000 feet altitude, of only some 600/800 feet with, in addition, a slightly shorter landing run; it can be extremely useful where a difficult approach has to be made to a restricted safe landing area; but it demands a skilful and experienced pilot and is potentially dangerous – it can be impossible to clear from a bungled landing.

After careful assessment of wind and water conditions and the risk of obstructions and any other users of the water; set airscrews of all four engines in fine pitch, reduce speed to 115 knots on the crosswind leg at 1000 feet; run flaps fully out; simultaneously, close all four throttles to idling and set the aircraft on a steep approach to maintain airspeed of 5-10 knots above normal approach speed; continue steep approach until 300-250 feet above the water then ease the control column back quite gently so that stalling speed is reached just as the aircraft is 6-8 inches off the water and level; then, with the control column, hold the aircraft off extremely lightly until the point of the keel touches and the aircraft settles quickly in the water with rather less forward speed than in the normal landing procedure; then continue as in the 'safe landing' procedure ('b' above). The essential for success in this form of landing is fine judgement and great sensitivity to the 'feel' of the aircraft at all stages.

4 Anchoring

a In circumstances where there is no mooring buoy or access to some mooring facility ashore the aircraft can be secured by its own anchor, provided good holding ground can be found, probably by trial and error; a sand or mud bottom is best while a rocky bottom represents a risk of fouling the anchor which may then have to be abandoned.

b The anchor needs to be shackled to the chain, with the shackle moused with copper wire. It is then laid on the coaming while an initial length of chain is paid out and stowed clear on the deck. On arrival at the chosen location, under the outer engines, the anchor is carefully lowered over one side until the flukes are clear of the aircraft's hull. On the captain's order "Let go" the anchor and chain are run out until bottom is reached when further chain is paid out through the anchor winch to allow the anchor to get a grip; as soon as the anchor appears to be holding – feeling the chain helps to give a guide to this – more chain is run out under control of the brake on the winch as the aircraft pulls against the anchor thus helping it to dig in. As long as the chain is 'live', ie vibration indicates that the anchor is dragging, chain is paid out until the weight of the chain lying horizontal on the bottom takes the strain and the vibration in the chain is no longer felt, ie the chain is no longer 'live'. This condition must be monitored frequently by an anchor guard which must include at least one crew member capable of taking charge of the aircraft in gale conditions if the anchor should drag out of control. The chain stopper must be fixed when the anchoring is complete.

c To weigh anchor the outer engines are started and run slowly and the chain is winched in steadily until it is 'up and down'; at this point the engines should be opened up prudently to cause the anchor to 'break out'; as soon as the anchor is free it must be winched up until it is just below the aircraft's bows and then carefully lifted inboard ensuring that the flukes do not damage the hull.

Index

If you enjoyed reading this book, then these Colourpoint publications may also be of interest.

Landfall Ireland

The story of Allied and German aircraft which came down in Éire in World War Two

Donal MacCarron
1 904242 03 0 £13.99
152pp, pbk,
260 x 210mm,
168 b/w photos.

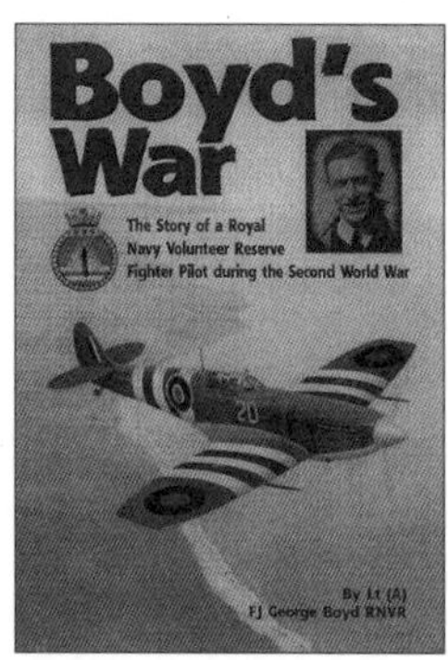

Boyd's War

The story of a Royal Navy Volunteer Reserve Fighter Pilot during the Second World War

FJ George Boyd
1 898392 06 4 £7.99
128pp, pbk,
210 x 148mm,
82 b/w photos.

Army Aviation in Ulster — Summer 2004

Guy Warner and Ken Boyd 1 904242 27 8 c£16 pbk
c208pp, 260 x 210mm, 120 b/w and colour photos.

The story of army aviation in Ulster dates back to September 1913 when Captain George Dawes of the Royal Flying Corps landed on the beach at Newcastle, Co Down. This book gives a brief history of army aviation before looking in more detail at the connection between Northern Ireland and the post-World War II Army Air Corps, covering the period from 1957 to 2004. The authors have received tremendous co-operation from the Army Air Corps and this can clearly be seen in the depth of the text and the selection of accompanying photographs.

No 230 Squadron Royal Air Force — Autumn 2004

Kita chari jauh – We search far

Guy Warner 1 904242 33 2 £18 hbk
192pp, 260 x 210mm, 150 b/w and colour photos.

No 230 Squadron was formed on 20 August 1918 at Felixstowe, Suffolk and from where it was tasked with patrolling the North Sea. In 1938 the majestic Short Sunderland flying boat arrived and No 230 Squadron became its first operational squadron, seeing service across the globe in places as diverse as Alexandria and the Arctic. The association with 'boats' continued until 1957 when the squadron was disbanded. On re-formation, No 230 Squadron moved to fixed-wing aircraft and in 1963 made a further change to rotary-wing flying. In 2004 No 230 Squadron is based at Aldergrove, Northern Ireland, its home for the last eleven years, flying the Puma HC1 helicopter in support of the security forces.

View the full range of Colourpoint titles at our web site:
www.colourpoint.co.uk